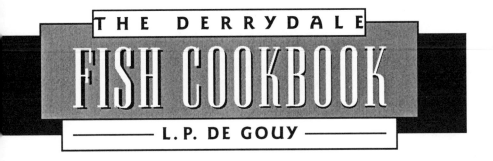

THE DERRYDALE

FISH COOKBOOK

L. P. DE GOUY

THE DERRYDALE
FISH COOKBOOK
L. P. DE GOUY

THE DERRYDALE PRESS

LANHAM AND NEW YORK

THE DERRYDALE PRESS

Published in the United States of America
by The Derrydale Press
4720 Boston Way, Lanham, Maryland 20706

Distributed by NATIONAL BOOK NETWORK, INC.

First paperback printing 2000

British Library Cataloguing in Publication Information Available

Library of Congress Cataloging-in-Publication Data

De Gouy, Louis Pullig, 1869-1947.
The Derrydale fish cookbook / L. P. De Gouy.
    p.   cm.
Originally published as vol. 2 of: The Derrydale cook book of fish and
game. New York : Derrydale Press, c1937.
    ISBN 1-58667-009-3 (pbk. : alk. paper)
    1. Cookery (Fish). I. De Gouy, Louis Pullig, 1869-1947. Derrydale cook
book of fish and game. II. Title

TX751 D347   2000
641.6'92—dc21   00-043111

CONTENTS

CONTENTS

CONTENTS

CONTENTS

· xiii ·

CONTENTS

· xv ·

CONTENTS

CONTENTS

CONTENTS

CONTENTS

· xxiii ·

CONTENTS

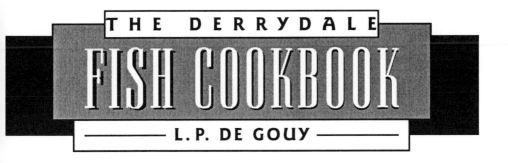

THE DERRYDALE

FISH COOKBOOK

L. P. DE GOUY

FISH AS FOOD

Fish is almost universally recognized as one of the most important of foods and enters into the diet of the majority of American families.

From recent data published by the Bureau of Statistics, United States Department of Commerce and Labor, it appears that the approximate total weight of the fish marketed yearly in the United States is two billion pounds, with a value in the neighborhood of seventy-five million dollars.

The preference for fresh-water or salt-water fish is a matter of individual taste. Both are, so far as known, equally wholesome.

The market value of fish is affected by various conditions. Among these are the locality from which they come, the season in which they are taken, and the food on which they have been grown.

Fish are sold either dressed or "round," *i.e.,* whole. Sometimes only the entrails are removed. Often, however, especially when dressed for cooking, the head, fins, and less frequently the bones (fillets) are removed. This entails a considerable loss in weight as well as of nutritive material, which should be taken into consideration by the buyer when marketing.

In dressing fish the following percentages are commonly lost:

Fish	*Percentage of Loss*
Shad	11
Butterfish	12
Small-mouthed Black Bass, Eel, Spanish Mackerel, Porgy, Turbot	13
Pike (grass), Black Bass (medium-mouthed), White Bass, Yellow Perch, Salmon	15
Brook Trout	16
Large-mouthed Black Bass, Sea Bass, Kingfish, Mullet,	

HOW TO BOIL FISH

This method of preparation is considered to be the most delicate of all, but because of the slippery skin and gelatinous consistency, it is hard to boil fish so that its appearance will gratify the eye. To attain the best results, it is imperative to observe several rules.

1. The fish must be weighed.
2. It must be carefully bound up in thin muslin; coarse cheesecloth is excellent for this purpose.
3. The fish kettle must be large enough to accommodate the fish easily and the cold water must be well salted before the fish is placed in it, or the flakes will have a tendency to separate.
4. For sliced fish, the water must be at the boiling point when the fish is put in, and should be in sufficient quantity to cover it fully, but not in excess, or the flavor will be washed away.
5. Keep the water boiling very slowly, extremely slowly, "smiling," after first coming to the boil, in order to "poach" the fish, as it were.

DIFFERENT WAYS OF BOILING FISH

There are several recognized ways of boiling fish, each suited to the texture, size, and nature of the fish to be boiled. These various methods are included in COURT BOUILLON OR SHORT BROTH.

If the fish is to be cooked whole, it is laid down on the crate of the fish kettle, usually of an elongated shape, after being scraped, cleaned, pared, and washed, and disgorged if it is a turbot; then it is covered with plain Court Bouillon or plain salted water, according to directions, and brought rapidly to ebullition, skimmed thoroughly, and the cooking process continued by allowing to simmer, slowly, "to smile," without any appearance of ebullition, until cooked to the required degree.

If the fish is divided in slices, these slices, which must never be too thin, lest they disintegrate, are always thrown into the boiling water or Court Bouillon, and the fish kettle is immediately set aside to simmer gently as indicated for whole fish.

The reason for plunging the sliced fish into boiling broth is to sear the exterior as rapidly as possible, which being less strong than in the whole fish might fall to pieces; and also to concentrate all the juice and essence as well as nourishing parts which the fish may contain and which escape in considerable degree when the fish is placed in cold water. This process is not applied to the whole fish or to a large piece because shrinkage and breakage are less likely than when sliced.

PARBOILING or "POACHING" FISH

Besides the several court-bouillon or short-broth methods indicated, there is another one called in culinary art "poaching"—as you would poach an egg—which is applied to small fish, or slices of fish, or fillets.

The fish, or slices of fish, or fillets, after being cleaned, washed, sponged, and slightly salted, are arranged in a shallow pan previously well buttered, then covered with a liquid which may be salt water—salt water to which has been added a little strained lemon juice or simply lemon slices, seeded—or vinegar, or either one of the previously mentioned court bouillons, or a fish broth, made of the heads and trimmings as well as the bones, or it may be a mushroom liquor, or it may be plain milk. These liquids may be single or compounded. The pan is covered with another so as to permit the heat to rise to the top of the enclosure, then fall back on the fish, and set into a moderately hot oven and the fish basted often, especially if it be large.

The cooking time varies according to the size. When done, the fish is lifted carefully, dressed on a hot platter and garnished according to directions of the recipe, lightly covered with the indicated sauce, the remainder being served separately.

Usually the fish sauce is made with part of the cooking liquor from the pan, reduced to the desired point and mixed with another sauce. This is what is called "poaching."

COURT BOUILLON CALLED "AU BLEU"

Besides the court bouillon or short broth described below, another special one, called "Au Bleu," is employed for certain fish, as trout, carp, pike, and a few others of the same classification.

For this special court bouillon, the fish should be alive, if possible, cleaned carefully, never scaled, washed inside but not outside, as the slime adhering gives its particular flavor to the fish cooked this way. The fish is then placed on the crate of the fish pan, boiling vinegar poured over, then the chosen lukewarm court bouillon, or that indicated in the recipe, is poured over the fish slowly and carefully so as to prevent the skin bursting and the cooking process follows as indicated previously, that is, rapid boiling first, then slow simmering until the fish is at the required point. The fish is then skinned and the inside flavor is entirely preserved, plus the particular flavor of the slime mixed with that of the vinegar and court bouillon.

Fish thus prepared may be served hot or cold with the appropriate garnishing and sauce as indicated in the recipe.

HOW TO PREPARE COURT BOUILLON
or SHORT BROTH

Let us turn our attention to the different court bouillons or short broths adapted to various kinds of fish.

VINEGAR COURT BOUILLON

(Suitable for Large Pieces Such as Salmon, Large Trout)

2 quarts of cold water	A few thyme leaves
⅔ cup of vinegar	A small bouquet garni
2 tablespoons salt	12 peppercorns, slightly bruised
2 small carrots, sliced	and added only 15 min-
2 small onions, sliced	utes before fish is done

All these ingredients are then placed together in a fish kettle, the fish added, and cooked until done as indicated at the beginning of this section.

WHITE WINE COURT BOUILLON

(Suitable for Trout, Eel, Pike, Etc.)

Use the same ingredients, proportions, and directions as indicated for VINEGAR COURT BOUILLON, omitting the vinegar and substituting for it the amount of white wine as indicated for recipe and a quart of water.

RED WINE COURT BOUILLON

(For Trout, Carp, and Fish Stew in General)

Same ingredients and directions as indicated for WHITE WINE COURT BOUILLON, substituting red wine for white, and adding one-third more of carrots and onions.

MILK OR CREAM COURT BOUILLON

(For Large Pieces of Turbot, Salmon, and the Like)

Cover the fish with salted cold water and add ⅔ of a cup of milk or cream for each quart of water and a peeled, seeded slice of a medium-sized lemon (no vegetables at all).

When fish are cooked with white or red wine court bouillon, they are usually served with a little of the broth containing some of the vegetables used, as a sauce. These vegetables should be always well done, the quantity of broth necessary reduced to a third of its original volume, and a little fresh butter added just before serving.

The cook should remember that fish must never be stabbed with a fork or skewer to ascertain if it is done, but it must be seen to that the water simmers steadily and does not stop an instant. The average time required to boil a fish is from six to eight minutes per pound, after the first boil. Fish should always be well done, otherwise it will be indigestible.

The vegetables which accompany boiled fish are usually plain boiled small potato balls, and cucumber salad with French dressing, served on a separate plate.

When the fish represents the main course, a vegetable such as string beans or Brussels sprouts may be passed around, but never served on the same plate as the fish.

If the fish is served for the evening dinner, do not have a creamy dessert, but a tart dessert, followed by fruit if desired.

IMPORTANT POINTS ABOUT BOILING, STEWING, ROASTING—GRILLING or BROILING—FRYING, BRAISING, and BAKING

BOILING

The primitive method of boiling water consisted in filling up a hole dug in the ground with water and throwing in hot stones taken out of the fire. Later, as the arts of pottery making and metal working became known, utensils were employed.

On the subject of so-called boiled food, the expression "boiled" does not imply that the food has been boiled in the same sense in which the water has been boiled. The food in such case is merely heated, not boiled, and even such water as is contained—and fish does contain a lot—is not itself boiled in the process, for owing to the salts held in solution its boiling point is higher than that of the surrounding water.

A scientific fact not appreciated by many cooks is that when water has once reached the boiling point its temperature cannot be further elevated until it is all converted into steam; for all the additional heat which is required above that needed to warm the water and drive off the air bubbles in the process of ebullition is expended in vaporizing the water into steam.

Consequently, however hot the fire or prolonged the cooking, the temperature of the food suspended in boiling water cannot be increased above that of the water itself; and, in fact, the temperature of the interior of a large mass of food, such as a large piece of fish, is by no means as great as that of the surrounding water. For this reason raising the fire when water has once reached the boiling point will have *no further effect* than that of accelerating the rate of ebullition, *without* actually raising the temperature of the water or any food immersed in it. Five and a half times as much heat is required to convert water at the boiling point into steam as that which is needed to raise water from the freezing to the boiling point.

The operation of boiling, if continued for an hour or more, gradually converts the connective tissue of meat or fish fiber into gelatin, which is partially dissolved in water, and the heat of the boiling water usually melts a little of the fat, which, being unable to mix with water, forms a scum upon the surface.

STEWING

Stewing differs from boiling in the fact that the juices of the fish, meat, or vegetables are dissolved in the heated water, whereas in boiling, the juices are kept from passing out into the water by the coagulation of the external surface of the food mass produced by immersing it suddenly into boiling water.

The proper temperature for stewing is between 135 and 160°. In thick stews, the juices dissolved in the water are eaten together with the cooked food, but in some substances, as in the making of beef tea and some kinds of soups, the aqueous solution only is used. Obviously, the more the food is subdivided the greater the surface exposed to the solvent action of the water and hence the object of mincing meat thoroughly which is to be used in the preparation of beef tea. If such minced meat has been soaked for a long time in cold water, a part of the albumen and the extractive materials are obtained in solution, but the meat or fish which is left, is colorless, tasteless, and unpalatable.

As both the solid substance of the fish, meat, and vegetables and the fluid materials which have been extracted from them are eaten together in the stew, this is an economical form of preparing fish. Nothing is lost by evaporation, and nothing is thrown away.

Roasting—Grilling or Broiling

The processes of roasting and grilling or broiling when performed over a very hot fire, result in cooking the fish in a manner which is in some respects analogous to stewing; in fact, the interior portions of the fish are stewed in their own juices instead of in water.

A coating of coagulated albumen forms upon the outer surface of the fish, while the albuminous material or myosin of the interior is gradually warmed and more slowly coagulated.

The outer coating prevents the evaporation of the juices of the fish which, together with the extractive materials, are retained, and add flavor to it. Roasted and broiled or grilled fish therefore have a decided advantage in flavor as well as in nutritive value over fish which has been boiled for a long time, although the latter may be tender and more easily digested. Roasting and broiling or grilling are universal methods of cooking. For them the savage or the hunter or fisherman requires no cooking utensils.

In roasting, the high temperature which is applied to the fish produces a firmer coagulation of its outer layers than occurs with boiling. Owing to this fact, the natural juices of the fish are almost completely retained and, as in boiling, the heat should be strong when *First Applied,* but it may subsequently be reduced to prevent charring of the surface. This may be accomplished by removing the fish farther away from the fire.

The process of roasting and grilling or broiling is conducted mainly by radiant heat, although there is slight convection through the air. The main object of an oven is to prevent burning by uneven cooking.

Broiling or grilling is a means of quick cooking which requires very much less time than roasting or boiling, because intense heat is applied to comparatively small pieces of fish. It is really roasting on a smaller scale.

The object of broiling as well as quick roasting should be to raise the interior of the mass promptly to the point of coagulation or about 180°, so that the water formed shall not have time wholly to evaporate. It is consequently advisable for the fish to be cooked as near the glowing surface as possible to increase the radiation and diminish the convection of air currents. It is for this reason that steaks and chops are often better cooked in restaurants, where specially adapted grills are used which bring the meat in closer relation to a radiant surface of glowing coals or gas flames than it is usually possible in home cookery.

FRYING

In this process of cooking the heat is transmitted through contact of the food with melted fat, butter, or oil, and not by radiation, as in the case of broiling, roasting, or grilling.

The fat does not necessarily boil, for the food, as well as the fatty material itself may contain a considerable proportion of water which, by being suddenly vaporized, produces the familiar spluttering which accompanies the process of frying.

The boiling point of fats is very much above that of water, the vaporization of the latter being complete at 212°. Between 300 and 500° may be required to vaporize the so-called volatile oils, but fats and oils used in cooking do not apply to this class, and when heated above 400°, they turn dark brown or black and emit a disagreeable odor and smoke, leaving a nonvolatile carbon residue.

The process of frying bears somewhat the same relation to boiling that the broiling of fish or meat does, in that the heat employed is considerably greater. It is suddenly applied and as a result the external surface of the food mass is coagulated and hardened before the juices in the interior have time to escape. For this reason, delicate fish, like trout, are much more highly flavored and palatable when fried than boiled.

The popular idea in regard to frying is that the fat used, whether butter, lard, oil, or drippings, is simply for the purpose of preventing food from adhering to the frying pan, but, from the explanation of the process quoted above, it may be seen that this is not the case, and the best frying is done by immersing the food *completely* in a bath of fat or oil. The fish or other food is lowered in an open wire basket or netting into a deep pan which contains the fat, in which it is completely submerged. There is no danger of the fat soaking into the food if it is sufficiently hot and if the process is not too long continued, for the water amid the fibers of the fish is boiling and driving out steam so rapidly that no fat can enter if the heat is maintained to the last moment.

Fritters cooked in this way are light and puffy from the sudden expansion of the water which they contain into large bubbles of steam, and are consequently *decidedly more digestible*. Bacon fries in its own fat, and not otherwise.

Frying is less perfectly understood by housewives than almost any other method of preparing fish, and the process as usually carried out results in very unwholesome products. The pans used are too shallow, and the food and fat are apt to become scorched.

When the fish is dipped into hot melted oil or fat, more or less clings to the surface of the fish, and for this reason the food may be rendered unfit for persons with feeble digestive powers.

In some countries, as in France, certain fish are cooked in this manner with their scales on, red gurnet, for example; the fat adhering to them may be easily removed before eating, and the meat within will be found to be quite digestible; but meat, such as steak, cooked by frying is notoriously indigestible.

Braising

Braising is a method of cooking fish or meat through immersion in a covered vessel containing a solution of vegetable and animal juices called "braise," hence its name, in which the fish is exposed to a strong but not boiling temperature. This method is of value especially in the cooking of meat that is tough, whether from age, or being too fresh or young. The cover of the kettle is so arranged as to prevent evaporation to any appreciable extent; the meat or fish in the long cooking process becomes permeated with the juices of fresh vegetables and herbs which prevent its drying up.

At the beginning or toward the end of the process any kind of wine or flavoring or spices may be added. The amount of fluid should be barely sufficient to cover the fish, thus maintaining concentration of the surrounding broth. Sometimes the fish which is braised is previously partially roasted or boiled.

Baking

The baking of fish or meat is accomplished through cooking in a confined space, thus preventing the volatile products, which are driven off in roasting, from escaping, and consequently the fish or meat has a somewhat stronger and less delicate flavor than when roasted; it is also richer, and disagrees with dyspeptics. It becomes saturated with empyreumatic oils unless its surface is protected by a piecrust, but even this does not add to its digestibility.

MEANING OF THE WORD "FILLET" IN COOKERY

The word "fillet," as applied to fish, poultry, game, or butcher's meat, refers to the flesh or any part of it which has been raised skilfully clear from the bones, and divided or not, as the manner in which it is to be served may require.

It is the elegant French mode of dressing various kinds of fish, and even those which are not valued very highly afford an excellent dish when thus prepared.

The fish, to be filleted with advantage, should be large; the flesh may then be divided down the middle of the back, next separated from the fins, and with a very sharp knife raised clean from the bones. When thus prepared, the fillets may be cut into attractive portions, dipped in yolk of egg, rolled in fine bread crumbs, fried in the usual way, and served with the same sauce as the whole fish or any other sauce which may be indicated; or the entire fillet, if quite small, may be rolled up, or, if large, divided and rolled up, and fastened with a little twine or a short, thin skewer, then dipped in egg yolk, crumbed, and fried, or steamed, or sautéed, or grilled; or it may be well flavored, floured, and fried in butter or any other fat a few minutes.

When the fish are not very large, they may be boned, without being divided down the middle, spread with butter or oil, discreetly seasoned, and then each is rolled from tail to head in a small quantity of bread crumbs; or the fish are rolled in pounded lobster mixed with a large portion of the coral, the same seasoning used and proportion of butter, laid in a dish, well covered with bread crumbs and clarified butter, and baked from ten to fifteen minutes in a moderate oven, or until the crumbs are colored to a fine brown.

The fillets may likewise be cut into small strips or squares according to requirements, of uniform size, lightly dredged in mixed pepper, salt, and flour and fried in butter over a brisk fire; then well drained, and the indicated sauce applied, which may be a cream, a compounded butter, or a fancy sauce, or it may be a plain butter flavored with a teaspoon of minced parsley, or chervil, or chives, or any other kind of aromatic herbs.

Such is the secret of the fancy fish dishes which have attracted your attention in various restaurants, while you longed to know how such were prepared.

MODES OF FRYING

How To Deep Fry Fish

We have given in a preceding section the whys and wherefores of frying food. Now let us consider how to prepare fish for frying and the procedure.

As a standard rule, large fish should never be fried, due to the fact that it is essential to bring the frying fat to a high temperature. This would cause the exterior of the fish to dry up before the inside could be cooked sufficiently.

As a general rule, with the exception of very small fish such as anchovy, whitebait, sardines, and the like, fish to be fried should first be soaked in salted milk, then rolled in flour or bread crumbs, before being plunged into the hot deep fat.

The proper method is entirely to immerse the article of food in boiling fat, but finding this inconvenient, most cooks use the half-frying method, that is, frying in a small amount of fat in a frying pan. The fat should half fill the kettle or there should be an amount sufficient to float whatever is to be fried; the heat of the fat should reach such a degree that, when a piece of bread is dropped in it, the bread will turn brown almost instantly. Yet the temperature must not be so high that the fat will burn. Some amateur cooks advise that the fat should be smoking, but this advice is erroneous, as the fat under this condition would soon be ruined. When the fat begins to smoke, it should be moved slightly to one side, though still kept at the boiling point. If fish are dropped into fat that is too hot, the exterior becomes crusted before the inside has fully risen, resulting in heaviness, and imparting to the fat a burnt flavor.

Many French cooks prefer beef fat or suet to lard for frying purposes, considering it more wholesome and digestible; it imparts less flavor and does not adhere or soak into the food as does pork fat.

In families of any size, where there is considerable cooking required, there are enough drippings and fat remnants from roasts of beef and skimmings from the soup kettle, with the addition of occasionally a pound of suet from the market amply to supply the need. All such remnants and skimmings should be clarified about twice a week, by boiling them altogether in water. When the fat is all melted, it should be strained with the water and set aside to cool. After the fat on the top has hardened, lift the cake from the water on which it lies, scrape off all the dark particles from the bottom, then melt the fat over again; while hot, strain into a small clean stone jar or bright tin pail, and then it is ready for use.

Always after frying, the fat should stand until it settles and has cooled somewhat, then be turned off carefully so as to leave it free of the sediment that settles at the bottom.

How To Short Fat Fry Fish

The second excellent mode of frying fish, using a frying pan with a small quantity of fat, applies either to small fish or to slices of large fish. However, this method may also be used, if great care be taken, with fish weighing not over one pound, and if butter is used it must be clarified to prevent scorching and to guard against the flavor of the milky part of the butter impairing that of the fish.

To ensure the best result, this method of frying demands that the frying pan should first be heated and the fat in it actually boiling before the fish is placed in it, under which condition the intense heat quickly sears up the pores of the article and forms a brown crust on the lower side. The fish then is turned and the other side browned similarly. Of course the fish should be seasoned with salt and pepper before placing into the fat.

HOW TO BROIL FISH

This method may be applied to small fish, fillet of fish, or slices of large fish.

For the white or dry-fleshed and flaked fish, it is advisable to roll first in flour after seasoning and sprinkling with butter, oil, or bacon drippings before placing on the wire broiler or broiler rack. From the coat of flour, under action of the heat, a tempting golden-brown crust will form which otherwise could not be had and which will prevent drying.

Strong fish, such as bluefish, eel, herring, mackerel, pompano, Spanish mackerel, red snapper, salmon, shad, swordfish, tuna, and turbot, need not be floured. For certain small fish, on account of their fragility, it is advisable to use the double-wire broiler, well greased, which in turn may be placed on the rack of the broiler oven. This will permit turning them easily without breaking.

Fish weighing not more than one pound are split down the back and head and tail removed. Small fish, such as smelts, sardines, or anchovies, are usually broiled whole, without splitting.

The fish should be turned often while broiling. Whole fish should be first broiled on the fleshy side, then turned on skin side, just long enough to make the skin crisp and brown.

When the fish is done, it is dressed on a hot platter, and copiously buttered, the only garnishing consisting of fresh parsley and sliced or quartered lemon.

BATTER FOR FRYING FISH

BATTER I

Mix a cup of flour with ⅔ cup of cold milk and season with a few grains of Cayenne pepper and ½ teaspoon of salt.

BATTER II

Mix 1 cup of sifted flour with 1 tablespoon of sugar and ¼ teaspoon of salt. Add ⅔ cup of cold water and beat well; then add ½ tablespoon of good olive oil and finish with 1 egg white beaten to a froth.

BATTER III

Mix 1⅓ cups of flour sifted with 2 teaspoons of baking powder and ¼ teaspoon of salt and add, beating all the while, ⅔ cup of cold milk.

BATTER IV

Same as BATTER No. III, adding an extra well-beaten egg white and 1 tablespoon of olive oil.

BATTER V

Mix through a sifter 1 cup of flour, ¼ teaspoon of salt, pour over gradually ¾ cup of water or cold milk into which 2 egg yolks have been beaten, 1 tablespoon of olive oil and fold in 2 well-beaten egg whites.

FISH FORCEMEAT AND FISH STUFFING

Fish Forcemeat plays an important and frequent part in cookery; it is used for stuffing and also for garnishing. It should always be in harmony with the fish in the preparation of which it is employed.

There exist many complicated methods of preparing Fish Forcemeat and Fish Stuffing, but as this book is specifically intended for home use, the author has confined himself to the simplest, most popular, practical, and economical methods.

In addition to its employment in stuffing and garnishing, Fish Forcemeat may also, according to its composition, be advantageously served as a course with accompaniment of vegetables, such as spinach, greens paste, and the like, in which case the Fish Forcemeat is shaped in croquettes, cutlets, balls, etc., according to fancy; and their size should never be above the size of a large egg, shaped, rolled in flour or bread crumbs or cracker crumbs, browned in butter or in deep frying fat, and a sauce served aside or poured over.

Fish Forcemeat may also be rolled the size of a small walnut and dropped just before serving into rapidly boiling fish stock or in plain salted water.

Fish Forcemeat may be prepared in advance and kept on ice until wanted.

FISH FORCEMEAT I

(Suitable for Garnishing, Stuffing, or Fish Course)

Clean, bone thoroughly, then cut in small pieces or flake enough small white-fleshed fish to obtain a cupful, and pass through the meat chopper. Combine with 1 cup of soft bread crumbs soaked in milk, then squeezed through a cloth and tossed lightly to loosen, and 1 cup of creamed butter (beef suet may be substituted but the results will not be the same, the fineness will be missing), season with salt, pepper, and a little nutmeg. Pass through the meat chopper and work a while with a wooden spoon and pass again through the meat chopper adding 1 egg white, slightly beaten. Keep on ice until wanted.

FISH FORCEMEAT II

(Suitable for Garnishing, Stuffing, or Fish Course)

Combine 1 cup of soft bread soaked in milk then squeezed through a cloth and tossed a little to loosen with ½ cup of butter, well creamed, 1 teaspoon of finely chopped onion, ½ teaspoon of finely chopped shallot, both onion and shallot cooked in butter 2 or 3 minutes, 2 generous tablespoons of finely chopped raw mushrooms, 1 teaspoon of finely chopped parsley, a very tiny bit of garlic (may be omitted), 3 or 4 thyme leaves, salt and pepper and a little nutmeg to taste, and a slightly beaten egg white. Pass twice through a meat chopper and work with a wooden spoon to ensure smoothness. Keep on ice until wanted.

FISH FORCEMEAT III

(Suitable for Garnishing, Stuffing, Fish Course, Filling Fish Loaf and Fish Patties)

Skin and bone thoroughly enough raw whiting or pickerel, or the like, to obtain 1 generous cup of flesh and pass through the meat chopper, adding alternately a generous ½ cup of soft bread crumbs moistened with milk, then squeezed through a cloth and tossed a little to loosen. To this add ½ cup of butter well creamed with a large pea size of anchovy paste, ½ teaspoon each of very finely chopped shallot and parsley and 1 whole egg. Mix thoroughly, seasoning to taste with salt, pepper, a little nutmeg, and 3 or 4 thyme leaves and pass twice through the meat chopper to ensure homogeneity and smoothness, adding little by little a teaspoon of thick fresh cream. Keep on ice until wanted.

FISH STUFFING I

(Suitable for Stuffing Small Fish)

Melt 2 tablespoons of butter and cook in it a tablespoon of finely chopped parsley with a teaspoon of finely chopped shallot and equal part of minced chives. When beginning to brown, sprinkle over 2 tablespoons of flour and blend well while stirring constantly; moisten with enough scalded milk to make a thick cream to which add a walnut-sized portion of anchovy paste. Boil once and incorporate gradually as much soft bread crumbs as the mixture will hold (about ½ cup). Keep on ice until wanted.

FISH STUFFING II

(Suitable for Large and Medium-sized Fish)

Mix ingredients in order given: 1 cup dried bread crumbs, ½ cup melted butter, ¼ teaspoon salt, ⅛ teaspoon pepper, a few drops of onion juice, 1 teaspoon of finely chopped parsley, 1 teaspoon of finely chopped capers, 1 teaspoon of finely chopped sweet gherkins. Fill the fish and sew up.

FISH STUFFING III

(Suitable for Large and Medium-sized Fish)

Mix ingredients in order given: 1 cup of bread crumbs, 4 tablespoons melted butter (bacon drippings may be substituted), 1 tablespoon of finely chopped parsley, 2 tablespoons of grated onion, the juice of a medium-sized lemon and the grated rind, 2 tablespoons of finely chopped bacon (raw), salt, pepper, a little nutmeg or a few grains of Cayenne pepper to taste and 4 or 5 thyme leaves. Fill the fish. Sew up.

FISH STUFFING IV

(Suitable for Large and Medium-sized Fish)

Same ingredients as above, substituting ham for finely chopped bacon and adding a teaspoon of finely chopped chives. Fill the fish. Sew up.

FISH STUFFING V

(Suitable for Large and Medium-sized Fish)

Mix ingredients in order given: ¼ cup of cracker crumbs (4 crackers), ½ cup stale bread crumbs, ½ cup melted butter or bacon drippings, salt and pepper to taste and a few grains of Cayenne pepper, a few thyme leaves, ½ teaspoon onion juice, 1 tablespoon of finely chopped green pepper, 2 tablespoons of finely chopped mushrooms, 1 tablespoon of finely chopped olives, 1 tablespoon of flaked crab meat, 1 teaspoon of finely chopped parsley, and enough water or fish stock to moisten solid. Fill the fish. Sew up.

FISH STUFFING VI

(Suitable for Large and Medium-sized Fish)

Combine 1 cup of cracker crumbs (8 crackers) with a generous ½ cup melted butter or bacon drippings and add salt and pepper and a few grains of nutmeg to taste, 1½ teaspoons strained lemon juice, 1 teaspoon finely chopped parsley, a few drops of anchovy essence, the whites of 2 hard-boiled eggs (chopped fine), a cupful of oysters (cleaned and the tough muscles removed); add the soft part to the mixture with 2 or 3 generous tablespoons of oyster liquor to moisten solid. Fill the fish. Sew up.

Fish Stuffing VII
(*Suitable for Large, Medium-sized and Small Fish*)

Mix ½ cup bread crumbs with 3 tablespoons of butter or bacon drippings (butter melted), and a generous ⅓ cup of fresh mushrooms (coarsely chopped); add a teaspoon of finely chopped parsley, 1 teaspoon of finely chopped shallots, salt and pepper to taste, and ½ cup of flaked crab meat or coarsely chopped cooked shrimps. Fill the fish. Sew up.

Fish Stuffing VIII
(*Suitable for Small Fish*)

Cook 1 tablespoon of finely chopped shallot with 1 tablespoon of butter 3 minutes. Add ¼ cup of very finely chopped raw mushrooms, ¼ cup of soft part of oysters (first parboiled, drained, and finely chopped), ½ teaspoon of chopped parsley, 3 tablespoons of cream sauce, and ½ cup of Fish Forcemeat III, page 17. Mix well, season with salt and pepper to taste; fill the fish. Sew up or keep on ice until wanted.

TABLES OF MEASUREMENTS
Table of Equivalents
Level measurements are used in all recipes.

Terms Used and Their Equivalents

A few grains equal less than ⅛ of a teaspoon
3 teaspoons equal 1 tablespoon
2 tablespoons equal 1 fluid ounce
4 tablespoons equal (¼) standard cup
16 tablespoons equal 1 standard cup
1 standard cup equals ½ pint
2 standard cups equal 1 pint
4 standard cups equal 1 quart
16 standard cups equal 1 American gallon

DRY INGREDIENTS

Almonds—4 cups equal 1 lb.
Apricots (dried)—3 cups equal 1 lb.
Barley (pearl)—2 cups equal 1 lb.
Beans (limas)—2⅔ cups equal 1 lb.
Bread crumbs—2 cups equal 1 lb.
Butter—2 tablespoons equal 1 oz.
Butter—2 cups equal 1 lb.
Cheese (freshly grated)—4 cups equal 1 lb.
Cheese (dry grated)—8 cups equal 1 lb.
Chocolate—16 squares equal 1 lb.
Cocoa—¼ cup equals 1 oz.
Coffee—4⅓ cups equal 1 lb.
Corn (canned)—2 cups equal 1 lb.
Corn meal—3 cups equal 1 lb.
Cornstarch—3 cups equal 1 lb.
Cranberries—5 cups equal 1 lb.
Currants—2¼ cups equal 1 lb.
Eggs—9 medium-sized equal 1 lb.
Figs (whole, dried)—2½ cups equal 1 lb.
Flour (ordinary)—4 tablespoons equal 1 oz.
Flour (Graham)—4½ cups equal 1 lb.
Flour (pastry)—4 cups equal 1 lb.
Flour (wheat)—3⅞ cups equal 1 lb.
Hominy (blanched)—1 cup equals 6 oz.
Macaroni (uncooked)—4 cups equal 1 lb.
Meat (chopped)—2 cups equal 1 lb.
Oatmeal (uncooked)—2⅔ cups equal 1 lb.
Oats (rolled)—4¾ cups equal 1 lb.
Peaches (whole, dried)—3 cups equal 1 lb.
Pecan (kernels)—3 cups equal 1 lb.
Prunes (whole, dried)—2½ cups equal 1 lb.
Raisins—2 cups equal 1 lb.
Rice—1⅞ cups equal 1 lb.

Rye (meal)—4⅓ cups equal 1 lb.
Spinach (cooked)—2½ cups equal 1 lb.
Sugar (granulated)—4 tablespoons equal 1 oz.
Sugar (granulated)—2 cups equal 1 lb.
Sugar (brown)—2⅔ cups equal 1 lb.
Sugar (confectioner's)—3½ cups equal 1 lb.
Sugar (powdered)—2½ cups equal 1 lb.

TABLE OF OVEN TEMPERATURES

Very slow equals 250°   Moderate equals 350°
Slow equals 300°   Moderately hot equals 375°
Moderately slow equals 325°   Hot equals 400° to 425°
          Very hot equals 450° to 500°

WATER

Simmering equals 180–182°
Boiling equals 212°

MARINADES

Marinades soften and render the meat and fish to which they are submitted and increase their natural sapidity through the action of penetration, and sometimes ensure their preservation. For further details and information, *see* VOLUME I.

ABOUT WINE

Although this book is altogether concerned with the methods of preparing fish, the author deems it necessary to place here a few words about an unexcelled ingredient that enters so often in good cookery.

WINE, the most pleasing of drinks, whether we owe it to Noah, who planted the vine, or whether credit is due to Bacchus who squeezed juice from the grape, dates from the infancy of the world; and beer, said to have been created by Cairis, goes back to those times beyond which everything is uncertain. Wherever men are holding social intercourse, they are found to be provided with spirituous liqueurs, which they make use of at their meals, their banquets, their sacrifices, their marriages, their funeral rites; in short, whenever there is any feasting or solemn ritualism we find liqueurs and wine.

WHERE DID THE WINE COME FROM?

From India? Perhaps from China? Who knows? . . . In any event, legend speaks of these mysterious countries as the places where the "joy of living" was tasted for the first time.

It came through wild countries where brutal strength reigned. It came and life smiled anew as fear, which until then reigned over gloomy humanity, ran away ashamed and desolate. Wherever wine went, art flourished. Wine lingered in Persia, the Persia of roses, before making its private domain in the Helliades. The sun ripened the bouqueted wine vine, agreeable to the gods . . . and to men, who will ever exalt its grandeur in generous sentiments and graciously condone its weaknesses.

From Greece, the great god went to Italy where he exchanged his Greek name of Dionysius for the Latin name of "De Liber"—the god of the free men who liberates worries. Then he went to Gaul. On his entry, did he give Gaul the divine gift of wine? Nobody knows. Many centuries, doubtless, passed before a Phoenician colony was founded—the great Massilia (Marseille). The poetic myth of Dionysius appears as the symbol of the triumphal march of Civilization throughout the world. The God of Civilization is the God of Wine.

Civilization has died and its precious flowers and fruits disappeared wherever wine has been despised. Let us leave the millennial civilization of China which is very dim in world legend and return to Persia. Few nations can boast of such a glorious past. Its more recent past still dazzles us by the resplendency of its arts and the perfection of its poets. The roses of Ispahan seemed to be the only roses of the world. Suddenly the Koran turned away the faithful from the drinks of their forefathers, the arts were fed on narrow formulas, lost the subtle essence of life and grew dry and rigid as a cadaver. The more scrupulous the artisan to the abstentions of the law, the more obvious the sterility of his art. As art is the most exalted expression of life, life dies when inhibition and prohibition assail its essence; art ceases to exist.

Arabians, happy disciples of Persia, were creators as long as they didn't refrain from wine. What has been their contribution to the world since Mahomet? Desolation! What did they do to the wheat fields of Rome? North Africa? They became an arid, a joyless solitude!

Is it not significant that the disappearance of the use of wines was followed by the disappearance of creative genius? This makes us repeat that the inaptitude for vital production presupposes the servitude of the mind of the artist. How well now one realizes the significance of the Latin name, "De Liber," given to Dionysius! Liber, god of the wine, is the god who released the spirit of man from the sordid limitations of the material world and fortified his mind as well as his body, bringing forth a more highly civilized order of human beings.

Has not the legend—often more true than history, of which it is the essence—kept only what was worth keeping in the beautiful myth or fiction of Dionysius, throughout the centuries?

What Is Wine?

This term is usually applied only to the fermented juice of the grape; when other fruits, as currants, blackberries, gooseberries, and so forth, are used instead of grapes in making it, the product is generally distinguished as domestic fruit-wine or rather homemade wine.

Wines, however, are not consumed for their alcoholic content; they contain other ingredients derived from the juice of the grape, which give them taste and flavor. Thus, when fermentation of the grapejuice is not complete, a certain quantity of sugar is left, and according to the quantity of sugar left, wines are said to be sweet or dry. While hocks, clarets, and other light wines contain little sugar, port, sherry, and champagne always contain a large amount.

There are three points in wines which demand some consideration: (1) The first is what is called the bouquet and the flavor. These two are sometimes confounded, but they are really different. The vinous flavor is common to all wines, but the bouquet is characteristic of certain individual wines. The substance which gives flavor to all wines is oenanthic ester, and is formed during the fermentation of the grapejuice. The bouquet, as analysis proves, is a matter of "esters"—aromatic compounds soluble in alcohol. If a grape lacks the right "esters," no amount of aging will help the wine. Even a good claret or hock will spoil with age; its valuable "esters" will have been converted into something else. Very few wines may be kept for decades. Even 15 years is hoary for many a wine, be it Bordeaux, Burgundy, or other wines. It is only the sweet wines, the Madeiras, Malagas, ports, sherries, angelicas, Tokays and champagnes, that can be handed down to our children.

Bouquet and flavor are the attributes which make one wine more pleasant to drink than another. They are not detectable by any chemical agency, but by the taste and smell.

The second point (2) is their color. Some wines are what is called red, and others white. The various red colors of these wines have been analyzed with some care, but they do not seem to exert any harmful influence upon the system. The most important agent in them is tannic acid, or tannin, which is produced by the skins of the grapes used in making the wine. It gives an astringency to red wines which is not found in whites. The other coloring matters described by chemists are blue and brown. These also come from the skins of the grape and the latter is found in dark white wines as well as in red.

The third point (3) which gives a character to wine is the saline compounds. These substances, which constitute the ashes of all vegetable tissues, exist in a varying quantity in all fruits, and are found dissolved in the juices of fruits, hence we find them remaining in wine after fermentation of the juice. They do not make much difference in so far as the flavor or action of wines is concerned, but their presence or absence is one of the surest indications of the genuineness of the wine.

The Etiquette of Serving Wine

It takes a great deal of practice to learn how to drink wine. As to knowing how to make one's guests drink and appreciate it, this can only be accomplished by a host of cultivated tastes, and gifted with exquisite tact.

A master's picture needs a favorable light and suitable surroundings if the artist's talent is to be properly appreciated. No woman, however triumphant her beauty, is ignorant or contemptuous of the art by which her charms may be set off to greater advantage through harmonious accord or skilfully managed contrasts. In the same way there exists a science and an art of drinking fine wines. First you must know the distinguishing characteristics of each of those that are selected for your guests. Then, you must serve the wine with the particular dish—with such dish that is likely to make each fully appreciated—following this plan throughout the different courses, in a cleverly contrasted ascending scale of enjoyment and appreciation, equally distributed as to WINE *and* FOOD. The wine gains if served in large glasses of fine crystal.

It is only after a careful study of the menu that you can decide which wines are to be offered and in what order. RED WINES must be roomed (*chambré*), that is, gradually brought to the temperature of the dining room. The sweeter the WHITE WINES, the more iced they should be.

With reference to the tasting of sweet wines, such as those of the Sauternes district, the best judges are divided into two schools. One prefers having them at dessert, and the other, at the beginning of the meal, along with the FISH.

PROGRESSIVE ORDER TO SERVE RED AND WHITE WINES

The progressive order to be followed with WINES, places first the youngest and the least famous. Let us see how connoisseurs observe this rule.

A few spoonfuls of SOUP have, by infusing a pleasant warmth into the palate and the stomach, induced them to fulfill their useful and agreeable functions. Together with the OYSTERS, followed by SALMON or any other kind of FISH, Bordeaux GREAT WHITE WINES make their appearance. They may be dry, semidry, or sweet, but, to our mind, an excess of sweetness in the wines served at the beginning of the meal is detrimental to the enjoyment of the GOOD RED WINES, which are to succeed them. As soon as the FISH is removed, the hostess stops serving WHITE WINE.

When MEAT is brought on the table, wines belonging to the classes of GRAND ORDINAIRE, or BOURGEOIS DU MEDOC, full of flavor and of body, and purple hued, fill the glasses.

It is in company with the more solid joints: ROAST BEEF, GAME or VENISON, that the excellent racy and heady wines, from the first cru (Châteaux, Domains, Clos, etc.) of the Saint Émilion or Pomerol districts of France are served; or the selected and incomparable Burgundy region, or the Rhône or Drome wines, or the cru Italian red and highly robust and delicately perfumed Piedmont Barbera Wine, or the Castel Bracciano, from the Latium Province of Lazio, or the Chianti, the most famous of all the wines of sunny Italy, or the Lago di Caldaro, the Venetian wine originating in the pebbly soil on the shores of the beautiful lake of the same name, or perhaps a fiasco of red Valpolicella, from the foothills of the Lessini Mountains, or perhaps champagne throughout the meal.

It may be an American wine, some of which compare favorably with the imported kind, such as Catawissa, the excellent claret wine of very fine flavor or a Devereaux, with its dark-ruby-colored hue, fine flavor, and bouquet, similar to the French Burgundy type; or a Cinsaut, with its rich dark-ruby color, having a fine body, character, aroma, and flavor which rank this wine as one of the best in California, a Medoc type; or a Petite Sirah, a Burgundy type wine, housing the glorious hidden flavors of California's sun-ripened grapes, fruity, frank, dry, warm, and of agreeable perfume; or a Refosco, a Burgundy type wine, comparing most favorably with the French Burgundy, Mercurey, which says much, smelling fully of the California grape flavor; or a Zinfandel, the popular California Burgundy type, possessing body, a fine dark-ruby color, a generosity and vigor that can be compared with the French Saint Émilion.

It may be that our taste turns to the world-famous red wine of Valdepenas, the reputation of which dates back to the time of Pliny, a handsome, abundantly vinous and highly bouqueted extract of the vine from the plains of La Mancha, in Spain, or a wine such as the red Alvala Rioja, with its delicious and incomparable Spanish bouquet.

When, in the middle of the meal, the guests have reached by degrees that "happy condition" in which the stomach, now docile, no longer manifests imperious exigencies and the taste, brought to the proper pitch by a masterful progression of pleasurable sensation, is susceptible to the most delicate impressions, the GRAND RED WINES of the Medoc, or the velvety Burgundy, or Macon, or Beaujolais, without omitting the purple tinted, highly aromatized Rhône wine; unless we turn to such delicious Italian RED WINES as the Stefano de Cerignola, from the Apulia Province; the Lacrima Christi (Tears of Christ), the exceedingly rich wine from the Campania Province; or a Cremono, from the same province; or a Grumello, from the secluded valley of Valtellina; or a Nebiolo, from Piedmont, a wine which requires four years to mature, make a triumphal entrance and pride fills the hostess's voice when she proclaims illustrious names and dates.

After these wines, it is still possible to taste the sweet Sauternes, the king of the white wines and to empty a few foaming coupes or flutes of the wine of the wines—CHAMPAGNE—with the dessert, or select one of your favorite wine of liqueurs to close and crown the feast.

How To Buy Wine, Champagne, or Liqueur

It is useless to say that connoisseurs should not be biased at all by the persistent appearance of certain brands, labels, or names of wines, champagnes, or liqueurs on the market. The superiority is only due to the intensive and continuous publicity which raises the price tremendously. It must be borne in mind that the land-property division of the region of Champagne, France, to take this example, in fact all over France, bears evidence to the fact that the best champagne is produced *All at the Same Time by Thousands of Small Vineyard Proprietors,* and that no particular mark or brand entitles it to a monopoly on goodness and quality.

Did you ever notice how much more frequently the names of wines, champagnes, or liqueurs, or cordials come up in conversation than the characteristics of a given one, be it wine, champagne, liqueur, or cordial? We hear wine lovers say, "My cellar needs a Bordeaux, or a Burgundy, or an Italian wine"—or whatever wine it may be. We hear wine dealers say, "My store needs a brandy, or an Alpina Flora liqueur, or some Vodka." Names, names, names—always names—whether it may be stars of the wines, the stars of liqueurs, or cordials with the most famous name may prove a failure. On the other hand, the wine, liqueur, or cordial that you never heard of may win renown.

It is not the name itself which makes the wine or liqueur; it's the essential goodness, the characteristics, that really count and will make it popular. Don't be guided by names. Choose a wine or liqueur or cordial that warms the cockles of your heart, that delights your eye by its color, that seems to have some special inner message for you, and which may hold locked in secrecy many things which will be revealed to you, and disregard the fact of whether its manufacturer is famous or unknown.

There is a barren period in the career of every beverage, as in any human career. It is the period during the time when the manufacturer, the wholesalers, the retailers know its name, its quality, and its characteristics well enough to offer it everywhere while the public Does Not Know its name well enough to buy it.

Do not buy the name. Buy the particular wine, the special liqueur, or the new cordial that speaks to you, that appeals to you through its characteristics and qualities. The best-known beverage depends for its fame not on its name, but on innate qualities, individual choice and taste, as well as derived benefit. This applies to everything, food included.

IMPORTANT POINTS TO REMEMBER
IN WINE COOKERY

See Volume I.

DEFINITION OF TERMS USED
IN COOKERY

See Volume I.

FISH SAUCES

Unseen God of Gastronomy, Genius of Gustatory Delights, Sultan of Sauces, Director of Delectables, Caliph of the Culinary Art; seldom seen, his or her presence is manifested by the savory and bounteous offerings beneath which your dining-room table groans. He or she is a cook, a master of the fine art of cookery as the real cooks practice it—the accepted standard with epicures throughout the world.

HOT FISH SAUCES

AMERICAN SAUCE

This sauce is ordinarily made in the preparation of LOBSTER À LA NEWBURG, page 302, and used with such.

ANCHOVY SAUCE I

(Suitable for Any Fish in Any Style)

Place ¾ of a cup of cream sauce in a saucepan and heat to the boiling point. Do not boil. Add off the fire ½ teaspoon anchovy paste or 2 or 3 fillets of anchovy, well washed and sponged and finely chopped.

ANCHOVY SAUCE II

(Suitable for Any Fish in Any Style)

To a cup of HOLLANDAISE SAUCE II, page 41, add ½ teaspoon anchovy paste. Stir and mix well. Do not boil.

ANNA SAUCE

(Suitable for Any Kind of Fish in Any Style)

Melt 3 tablespoons of butter, add 3 tablespoons of flour; blend well and pour on gradually 1½ cups of cream, mixed with 1 scant tablespoon of meat extract. Season with salt and pepper, add 1 tablespoon of lobster coral, and 1 scant half cup of cooked diced lobster meat.

AROMATIC SAUCE

(Well Adapted for Large Boiled Fish of Any Kind)

Into a cup of fish stock brought to the boiling point, but not practically boiling, put a few thyme leaves, a small pinch each of sweet basil, savory, marjoram, and sage, a teaspoon of finely chopped chives, 1 teaspoon of finely chopped shallots, a few grains of nutmeg, and 3 bruised peppercorns. Season to taste with salt and pepper and let infuse 15 minutes on the side of the range. Meanwhile blend 1 teaspoon each of butter and flour, moisten with the strained infusion, and boil 5 minutes, stirring once in a while. Remove from the fire and finish with 1 tablespoon of strained lemon juice and a tablespoon each of chervil and tarragon herbs, finely chopped.

BAVARIAN SAUCE

(Foamy)

(Suitable for Any Kind of Filleted Fish)

To a cupful of tarragon vinegar, add a few thyme leaves, 1 tiny bit of bay leaf, 1 sprig parsley, 2 slightly bruised peppercorns, 1 scant teaspoon grated fresh horseradish. Place on a hot fire and operate as for HOLLANDAISE SAUCE II, page 41; add one by one 3 egg yolks, alternating with 3 or 4 tablespoons of butter and a few drops of water, the butter being added bit by bit, stirring continually until the mixture thickens a little. Strain through a fine cloth or sieve and finish off the fire with a teaspoon of lobster butter (*see* COMPOUNDED BUTTERS) and 2 tablespoons of whipped cream. Finally fold in a tablespoon of crayfish or lobster meat, finely diced.

BÉARNAISE SAUCE

(Suitable for Any Kind of Fish Broiled or Grilled)

Reduce over a hot fire to ⅔ volume the following ingredients: 1 cup white wine to which add 1 scant tablespoon tarragon vinegar, 1 tablespoon finely chopped shallots, a small sprig of parsley, 1 small sprig of tarragon herbs, coarsely chopped, a small pinch of chervil, finely chopped, 2 peppercorns, bruised. Let cool a little; then add 2 or 3 egg yolks gradually and stirring vigorously all the while, alternated with as much melted butter as the sauce can hold or until of the consistency of a soft ball. The blending is produced by the egg yolks which gradually cook on a low fire. Finish with a dash of Cayenne pepper and a teaspoon of very finely chopped mixed tarragon herbs and chervil. This sauce cannot be served very hot and is usually placed on the fish, which should be piping hot, just when serving.

BERCY SAUCE

(Suitable for Any Kind of Boiled Fish, also Baked, Braised, and Especially Filleted Fish. May Be Used with Very Good Results with Grilled Dark Fish)

Sauté in a skillet one tablespoon of finely chopped shallots in 1 tablespoon butter. When getting brown, moisten with 1 wineglass of white wine mixed with ½ cup of stock made with the trimmings of the fish. Add ½ cup of rich CREAM SAUCE III, page 37, bring to a boil and set aside on the range to simmer a few minutes. Finish off the fire with a generous tablespoon of butter and a little finely chopped parsley.

BONNEFOY SAUCE

(Suitable for Broiled Fish)

To a cup of white wine, add 2 scant tablespoons of finely chopped shallots, 2 crushed peppercorns, 4 or 5 thyme leaves, and a tiny bit of bay leaf. Reduce to half volume over a hot fire. Add 1 cup of CREAM SAUCE I, page 36. Bring to a boil and set aside to simmer 5 minutes. Strain through a fine sieve; season with salt and pepper and finish with a teaspoon of finely chopped tarragon herbs.

CANOTIÈRE SAUCE

(Suitable for Any Kind of Boiled Fresh Water Fish)

Reduce over a hot fire 2 cups white wine court bouillon (*see*

How To Boil Fish) to ½ volume. Remove from the fire and thicken with a tablespoon of kneaded butter (*see* Compounded Butters). Place on the fire again and boil once or twice. Rectify the seasoning and finish with a few grains of Cayenne pepper.

CAPER SAUCE

(Suitable for Any Kind of Boiled Salt- or Fresh-water Fish)

To a cup of Drawn Butter Sauce, page 38, add ½ cup of well-washed and well-drained capers.

CREAM SAUCE I

(Also Called White Sauce)

(Suitable for Boiled Fish of Any Kind)

Melt in a saucepan, a tablespoon of butter, add 1 tablespoon of flour and season with salt and pepper to taste, being parsimonious with the pepper and using only white pepper; then pour on gradually, while stirring constantly, a cup of scalded milk, bring to the boiling point and let boil 2 or 3 minutes.

To Scald Milk

Place the milk in the top of a double boiler, having water boiling beneath; cover and let stand on top of the range until the milk around the edge of the pan has a beadlike appearance.

To obtain a richer sauce, use cream instead of milk.

CREAM SAUCE II

(Suitable for Boiled Fish of Any Kind)

Prepare and cook exactly as indicated for Cream Sauce I, above, using 2 tablespoons each of butter and flour. This sauce is, of course, much richer and thicker.

CREAM SAUCE III

(Suitable for Boiled Fish of Any Kind)

Prepare and cook exactly as indicated for CREAM SAUCE I, above, using 3 tablespoons each of butter and flour instead of 1 tablespoon. This sauce is much used in compounded sauces. If it is desired to have a smooth and richer sauce, one or two egg yolks may be stirred in either one of the three CREAM SAUCES.

CREOLE SAUCE

(Suitable for Fish Prepared in Any Style)

Cook in 4 tablespoons of butter, 4 tablespoons of sliced (not chopped) onions and 8 tablespoons of sliced green pepper, seeds and white parts removed, over a gentle fire for about 5 minutes, stirring gently once in a while; then add ½ cup of sliced mushrooms and a dozen and a half small green olives, stoned and quartered. Cook 5 or 6 minutes longer and pour over 1 cup of strained fish stock and 1 large can of tomatoes, liquid and solid. Season with salt, pepper from the mill, a few grains of Cayenne pepper, a tiny pinch of thyme leaves, a small bay leaf, and a crushed clove. Let simmer very gently for 20 long minutes. Serve.

As a variation, you may add a tablespoon of sherry wine or white wine. The sauce should be highly spicy, although with a sweet taste. If to be served with meat, use brown sauce instead of fish stock.

DIPLOMATE SAUCE

(Suitable for Any Kind of Boiled Fish)

Reduce over a hot fire to half volume 2 cups of fish stock and add a scant cup of white wine. Remove from the fire and thicken with a generous tablespoon of lobster butter (*see* COMPOUNDED BUTTERS); then add ½ cup of scalded fresh cream, stirring all the while. Rectify the seasoning and finish, off the fire, with 2 tablespoons of coarsely chopped shrimps and same quantity of lobster. Finely chopped truffle may be added if desired.

DRAWN BUTTER SAUCE

(Suitable for Any Kind of Boiled or Broiled Fish)

Melt 3 tablespoons of butter and blend with 3 tablespoons of flour, adding ½ teaspoon of salt and pepper to taste, and, when well blended, pour on gradually, while stirring constantly, 1½ cups of hot water. Boil 5 minutes, then add an additional 3 tablespoons of butter bit by bit, stirring gently and interspersing with a teaspoon of strained lemon juice, added little by little.

DUTCH BUTTER SAUCE

(Suitable for Any Kind of Boiled or Broiled Fish)

Cream 8 tablespoons of butter and add 4 egg yolks gradually and alternating with a cup of sour cream, stirring meanwhile. Cook, stirring constantly until mixture thickens. Season with salt and pepper to taste, add a tablespoon lemon juice and the rind of ½ lemon, finely chopped. Fold in gently 3 stiffly beaten egg whites.

EGG SAUCE I

(Suitable for Large Pieces of Boiled Fish)

To 1 cup of DRAWN BUTTER SAUCE, page 38, add 2 hard-boiled eggs, chopped coarsely.

EGG SAUCE II

(Suitable for Large Pieces of Boiled Fish)

To 1½ cups of DRAWN BUTTER SAUCE, page 38, add 2 beaten egg yolks gradually, while stirring constantly, 1 teaspoon of strained lemon juice, and 2 hard-boiled eggs, coarsely chopped.

EGG SAUCE III

(Suitable for Large Pieces of Boiled Fish)

To 1½ cups of DRAWN BUTTER SAUCE, page 38, add 2 egg yolks, stirring meanwhile, 3 hard-boiled eggs coarsely chopped, a tablespoon of finely chopped parsley, and a teaspoon of strained lemon juice. Finish with a few grains of Cayenne pepper and salt to taste.

EGG SAUCE IV

(Scotch)

(Suitable for Large Pieces of Boiled Fish)

To 1½ cups of CREAM SAUCE I, page 36, add 2 egg yolks, stirring meanwhile, the coarsely chopped whites of 5 or 6 hard-boiled eggs, and, just before serving, add 5 or 6 hard-boiled yolks forced through a sieve.

EPICUREAN SAUCE

(Suitable for Fish Prepared in Any Style)

Cook 5 tablespoons of butter until well browned and add in the order named, stirring after each addition: 1 teaspoon prepared mustard, 1 generous tablespoon strained lemon juice to which is added a few grains of Cayenne pepper, 1 tablespoon of Worcestershire sauce, and a small can of strained tomatoes. Bring to a boil and add ½ cup of strained fish stock to which is added 2 tablespoons of white wine. Season with salt and pepper to taste and finish with a tablespoon of sweet butter.

FENNEL SAUCE

(Suitable for Boiled Mackerel, Spanish Mackerel, Eel, Bluefish, Swordfish, Shad, Herring, and All the Fish Having Fat Distributed Throughout the Flesh)

Peel 3 or 4 branches of fennel as you would for parsley and chop fine; there should be a tablespoon. Parboil, cool in cold water, and drain well in a sieve. Place in a saucepan 2 tablespoons of melted veal fat and ½ cup of melted butter and heat to the boiling point; add the fennel, stir and season with salt, pepper and a little nutmeg to taste.

FIGARO SAUCE

(Suitable for Large Pieces of Boiled Fish)

To 1½ cups of HOLLANDAISE SAUCE I, page 40, add 3 tablespoons of tomato purée, 1 tablespoon finely chopped parsley, and a few grains of Cayenne pepper, with salt to taste.

GOOSEBERRY SAUCE

(Suitable for Oily Fish Which Have the Fat Secreted Throughout the Flesh, such as Mackerel, Eel, Salmon, and Spanish Mackerel)

Blanch a generous cup of cleaned and washed gooseberries (not quite ripe), boil 5 minutes; drain and add 1 tablespoon, or less according to taste, of granulated sugar melted in 3 tablespoons of good white wine and well stirred. Strain through a fine sieve with a little pressure so as to obtain as much of the fruit as possible. Heat over hot fire, and finish with ½ cup of DRAWN BUTTER SAUCE, page 38, stirring meanwhile.

HOLLANDAISE SAUCE I

(Suitable for All Kinds of Boiled Fish)

Place ½ cup of butter in a bowl, cover with cold water and wash, using a spoon. Divide in 3 parts; put one part in a saucepan with 2 egg yolks and 1 tablespoon of strained lemon juice; place the saucepan in a large one containing hot water (or use a double boiler), stirring constantly with a wire whisk until the butter is melted; then add the second part of butter, and, as the mixture thickens, add the third part. When the butter is well mixed, add ⅓ cup of boiling water, pouring slowly and stirring meanwhile. Cook over the fire one or two minutes and season with salt and Cayenne pepper to taste.

NOTE: If the mixture curdles, add 2 tablespoons of heavy cream or 2 tablespoons of boiling water, pouring slowly and beating all the while.

HOLLANDAISE SAUCE (MOCK) II

(*Suitable for Any Kind of Boiled Fish*)

Melt 2 tablespoons of butter, add 2 tablespoons of flour and stir until well blended; then add ¾ cup of scalded milk, stirring meanwhile, and salt, pepper, and a few grains of Cayenne to taste. Bring to the boiling point, while continuing to stir; remove from fire and stir in 2 or 3 egg yolks, and bit by bit, ½ cup of butter. Finish with a tablespoon of strained lemon juice.

HORSERADISH SAUCE I

(*Suitable for Boiled and Broiled Fish*)

Cook in 1 cup of fish stock 4 tablespoons of freshly grated horseradish and after the first boil, let simmer gently for 20 minutes on the side of the range. Add ½ cup of DRAWN BUTTER SAUCE, page 38, a tablespoon of fresh thick cream, and a cupful of freshly made soft bread crumbs. Boil once. Season with salt and pepper to taste and finish off the fire with 2 egg yolks, added one by one while stirring gently and constantly. A tablespoon of prepared mustard may be added as a variation, but this is more suitable for boiled meat.

HORSERADISH SAUCE II

(*Suitable for Boiled and Broiled Fish*)

Cook 3 tablespoons of saltine cracker crumbs with ⅓ cup freshly grated horseradish and 1½ cups of milk in a double boiler for 25 minutes. Add 3 generous tablespoons of butter, stir, and season with salt and pepper.

LAGUIPIERE SAUCE

(A Fine Sauce for Boiled Fish of Any Kind)

Place on a hot fire a pan containing 2 cups of white wine court bouillon (*see* How To Boil Fish) and reduce to half volume; this done, add the size of a walnut extract of meat (Liebig, Oxo, etc.), stirring well until the liquid reaches the boiling point. Thicken with a tablespoon of kneaded butter. Boil 3 or 4 minutes longer. Serve.

LAWRENCE SAUCE

(Suitable for Fish Prepared in Any Style)

Melt 2 tablespoons of butter and add 3 tablespoons of flour, stir until well blended; then pour on gradually, while stirring constantly, ½ cup of scalded milk and ½ cup of white wine court bouillon in which the fish was cooked. Bring to the boiling point, add 2 tablespoons of grated young American cheese, salt, pepper, and a few grains of Cayenne pepper to taste and the yolks of 3 eggs slightly beaten, stirring meanwhile. Finish with the size of a walnut of anchovy paste and one tablespoon of sweet butter. The addition of a scant tablespoon of sherry wine adds to the flavor.

LEMON BUTTER SAUCE

(Suitable for Boiled and Grilled Fish)

Cream ¼ cup of butter with a tablespoon of strained lemon juice. NOTE: When using for boiled fish soften a little near the fire.

LOBSTER SAUCE

(Suitable for Boiled and Grilled Fish)

To a cupful of HOLLANDAISE SAUCE II, page 41, add ⅓ cup of

lobster meat cut in small dices. For economy's sake, cream sauce may be substituted for Hollandaise sauce.

MAÎTRE D'HÔTEL BUTTER SAUCE
(Suitable for Any Kind of Broiled Fish)

Soften 5 tablespoons of butter slightly and mix with a teaspoon of finely chopped parsley, salt and pepper to taste, and a teaspoon of strained lemon juice.

NOTE: It is a mistake to add onion juice to this butter.

MORNAY SAUCE
(Suitable for Any Kind of Fish, Especially Those Prepared "au Gratin")

To one cup of CREAM SAUCE I, page 36, add ¾ cup of white wine court bouillon (*see* How To Boil Fish) and reduce to ⅓ over a hot fire, stirring all the while. Add then a generous tablespoon of grated Parmesan cheese mixed with a scant tablespoon of grated Swiss cheese. Stir well and finish, off the fire and just before using add a tablespoon of sweet butter.

MUSTARD SAUCE
(Suitable for Boiled and Broiled Fish, Especially Dark-fleshed Fish)

To a cup of DRAWN BUTTER SAUCE, page 38, add, just before serving, a tablespoon of prepared mustard. If the sauce is not served at once, keep in a double boiler, but do not boil.

VARIATION

To a cup of HOLLANDAISE SAUCE II, page 41, add, just before serving, a tablespoon of prepared mustard and a few leaves of tarragon herbs finely chopped.

VARIATION (*Russian Style*)

Place in a double boiler ⅓ cup each of granulated sugar, tarragon vinegar, butter, prepared mustard, and cold water and season with salt and a few grains of Cayenne pepper. Mix and beat thoroughly and boil a few minutes until thick and creamy, stirring constantly. Finish, off the fire with 2 egg yolks, added one by one, while stirring. A fine sauce for broiled fish.

NORMANDE SAUCE

(Suitable for Baked and Boiled Fish, Especially Fillets)

To 2 cups of white wine court bouillon reduced to half, add a scant tablespoon of kneaded butter and cook a few minutes; then add off the fire, 2 egg yolks, one by one, stirring gently and constantly. Finish with sufficient butter to bring to the consistency of rich cream, operating as for HOLLANDAISE SAUCE I, page 40. Finish with a little lemon juice and rectify the seasoning.

OLIVE SAUCE

(Suitable for Any Kind of Boiled Fish)

Stone 2 dozen small green olives, cover with fish stock and cook 5 minutes; drain, discard the liquid, and add to 1 cup of DRAWN BUTTER SAUCE, page 38. Finish with a tablespoon of finely chopped parsley.

VARIATION

To a cup of rich CREAM SAUCE III, page 37, add 3 tablespoons of finely chopped black olives, 1 tablespoon of finely chopped parsley, and a few tarragon leaves also chopped fine.

VARIATION

To a cup of HOLLANDAISE SAUCE II, page 41, add 2 tablespoons of coarsely chopped black olives. Finish with ½ teaspoon each of finely chopped parsley and tarragon herbs.

OYSTER SAUCE

(Suitable for Boiled, Grilled, and Steamed Fish)

Cook the oysters in their own liquor until plump, drain and cut in small pieces. Save the liquor. Blend 2 tablespoons of flour with 2 tablespoons of butter and pour in gradually, stirring meanwhile, a cup of scalded milk to which has been added the oyster liquor. Season to taste with salt, pepper, a few grains of Cayenne pepper and a few grains of nutmeg; add a teaspoon of strained lemon juice, then the oysters which have been kept hot and bring to the boiling point. Sprinkle over a teaspoon of finely chopped parsley and finish with a tablespoon of butter.

VARIATION

Place in a saucepan a dozen freshly opened small oysters with their liquor and a tablespoon of white wine; cover and cook until plump over a very low fire. Remove at once, otherwise they will be tough and stringy. Prepare a sauce as indicated in paragraph above, using the oyster liquor, which pour slowly while stirring constantly; add 2 yolks of eggs, slightly beaten, keeping on stirring and finish with a tablespoon of butter, beating with a wire whisk. Add the oysters, stir gently, and let stand a few minutes.

RED BURGUNDY WINE SAUCE

(Suitable for Braised, Roasted, or Baked Fish of Any Kind)

Have ready 1 small carrot, 1 small onion, 1 small celery root, all cleaned, peeled, and cut into very small pieces. Brown in a little butter (2 tablespoons), adding a very few thyme leaves and a tiny bit of bay leaf; do not cook, simply brown. Pour over a generous cup of red Burgundy wine and ½ cup of fish stock with a very tiny bit of garlic. Cook over a hot fire until reduced to half. Add then 1 cup of fish stock and let simmer for 15 to 20 minutes; strain through a fine sieve, pressing a little and finish, off the fire, with a generous tablespoon of sweet butter. One teaspoon of anchovy butter may be used instead of sweet butter.

RED WINE SAUCE

(Suitable for Any Kind of Braised, Boiled or Baked Fish)

Proceed exactly as indicated for preceding recipe, using ordinary red wine instead of Burgundy wine.

RIALTO SAUCE

(Suitable for Fish Prepared in Any Style)

Mix together a generous ½ cup of blanched and chopped almonds and 1 tablespoon of finely chopped capers. Pour over 2 cups of white-wine fish stock and let reduce to 1 cup over a hot fire. Finish off the fire with 2 egg yolks, added one by one, while stirring constantly, 1 generous tablespoon of butter, and the size of a hazelnut of anchovy paste. Season to taste with salt and pepper and, when ready to serve, add a teaspoon of finely chopped orange rind.

SAN SEBASTIAN SAUCE

(Suitable for Boiled, Fried, or Sautéed Fish of Any Kind)

To a cup of HOLLANDAISE SAUCE II, page 41, add 3 sponged fillets of anchovy chopped in small pieces, 1 teaspoon of chopped green olives, and a tablespoon of chopped walnuts. Stir gently.

SHALLOT SAUCE

*(Suitable for Boiled, Broiled, Sautéed, and Fried Fish
of Fine Texture)*

Place in a saucepan a tablespoon of finely chopped shallots with 2 tablespoons of tarragon vinegar and reduce to half over a hot fire; then add a tablespoon of tomato purée and a cup of strained fish stock (use beef broth if the sauce is the accompaniment of meat). Stir in a tablespoon or two of cold fish stock, a teaspoon of cornstarch, and add to the sauce. Season to taste with salt and a few grains of Cayenne pepper and finish with a teaspoon of finely chopped parsley.

SHRIMP SAUCE

(Suitable for Any Kind of Boiled, Broiled, or Fried Fish)

To a cup of Drawn Butter Sauce, page 38, add 1 egg yolk and ½ can of shrimps, cleaned, and cut in small pieces.

Variation I

To a cup of Hollandaise Sauce II, page 41, add, just before serving, a tablespoon of shrimp butter (*see* Compounded Butters) and ½ can of shrimps, cleaned, and cut in small pieces.

Variation II

To a cup of Cream Sauce I, page 36, add ½ small can of shrimps, cleaned, and cut in small pieces. Color with a little red vegetable coloring to the desired hue.

Variation III

To a cup of Drawn Butter Sauce, page 38, add the size of a hazelnut of anchovy paste and ½ can of shrimps, cleaned, and cut in small pieces. Color as indicated above.

SPANISH SAUCE

(Suitable for Boiled or Sautéed Fish of Fine Texture)

Melt 3 tablespoons of butter and blend with 3 tablespoons of flour; then pour on gradually, while stirring constantly, a cup of scalded milk (or cream, if a richer sauce is wanted). Bring to the boiling point; season to taste with salt, pepper, a few grains of Cayenne, and a few grains of nutmeg. Finish with ½ cup of pimento purée.

Pimento Purée

To obtain pimento purée, drain canned pimentos and force through a fine sieve.

TARTARE SAUCE

(Hot)

(Suitable for Boiled, Fried, or Steamed Fish)

To ½ cup of hot CREAM SAUCE I, page 36, add ⅔ cup of mayonnaise dressing and the following ingredients, well mixed and finely chopped: ½ teaspoon each of shallot, capers, sweet pickles, olives, and parsley. Finish with ½ teaspoon of heated tarragon vinegar. Mix and season to taste with salt and pepper.

WESTOVER ORANGE SAUCE

(Suitable for Boiled, Baked, or Broiled Fish of Oily Flesh)

Put into a saucepan ½ pint (1 cup) of white wine court bouillon, 1 small onion (finely sliced), and 4 or 5 strips of orange peel. Let simmer very gently 15 to 20 minutes, the longer the better. Strain and reduce to half and add the strained juice of a small orange, salt and white pepper to taste. Boil 2 or 3 times and finish with 2 tablespoons of port wine; let heat through and when on the point of boiling remove and add a generous tablespoon of sweet butter.

WHITE BUTTER SAUCE

(Suitable for Any Kind of Fish Cooked in White Wine Court Bouillon)

Chop up a shallot fine, wrap in a fine cloth previously immersed in cold water, wring and twist (the purpose of this important operation is to extract and reject the volatile oil of the shallot), then place in a saucepan with ½ cup of cold water and a teaspoon of white vinegar, salt and pepper to taste. Reduce on a hot fire to ⅔ volume, strain through a fine cloth over another saucepan and set on the side of the fire to keep hot. Do not boil. Add gradually and systematically the size of a walnut of sweet butter, rocking and tossing the pan, but not stirring. When this first piece of butter is entirely absorbed by the liquid, add another, let it be absorbed, then another and so on until a good half pound of sweet butter has been thus incorporated. You will have an unctuous, white, lightly foamy sauce, slightly piquant, redolent of sweet butter.

Note: This is the original recipe as prepared in Touraine, France. No pastelike butter, no flour, no egg, no wire whisk, no wooden spoon forming the *mise en scène*. Shallot, butter, salt, and white pepper, a pot, a fire, and the sleight of hand. This is all. Well worth trying.

WHITE WINE SAUCE

(Suitable for Fish Cooked in Any Style, but Especially for Fillets, Fine-textured Fish Boiled, and Small Fish Sautéed in Butter)

Place in a saucepan 2 cups of strained white wine court bouillon, reduce to half over a hot fire; pour in a little more wine if desired strong; add, when reduced, a generous teaspoon of tomato purée. Finish with a tablespoon of kneaded butter, boil once or twice. Let simmer a few minutes and serve.

VARIATION

Blend a tablespoon of butter with one of flour, add the wine used for cooking the fish (there should be a cup), bring to a boil, stirring constantly until well mixed and thick and add, off the fire, 2 or 3 egg yolks, one by one, while stirring constantly. Finish with a tablespoon of sweet butter, season with salt and pepper, and add ½ teaspoon of strained lemon juice.

COLD FISH SAUCES

AIOLI SAUCE

(Suitable for Any Kind of Cold Cooked Fish)

Pound in a mortar 2 small cloves of garlic (more if you desire a sharp, strong sauce) very smooth and add the yolk of a fresh egg, 6 or 7 tablespoons of olive oil, which add drop by drop at first, increasing gradually in a thin streak as soon as the sauce begins to thicken, and blend, stirring constantly as for mayonnaise; when half the oil has been incorporated, alternate with a scant teaspoon of strained lemon juice and a few drops of cold water. Season to taste with a little salt and pepper. Serve.

NOTE: Should the mixture curdle start over with another egg yolk, using the curdled part as is done for fallen mayonnaise.

ANDALOUSE SAUCE

(Suitable for Any Kind of Cold Boiled Fish and Shellfish and Crustaceans)

To a cup of mayonnaise, add ⅓ of a cup of thick tomato purée and a tablespoon of finely chopped green pepper.

BOHEMIAN SAUCE

(Suitable for Any Kind of Cold Boiled Fish, Crustaceans, or Shellfish)

Place in a bowl ⅓ of a cup of cold CREAM SAUCE I, page 36, 2 fresh yolks, salt and pepper to taste, and a few drops of tarragon vinegar and beat well with a wire whisk, pouring in meanwhile, very slowly and drop by drop, 2 tablespoons of olive oil. Finish with a tablespoon of prepared mustard.

GENOISE SAUCE

(Suitable for Any Kind of Cold or Hot Fish)

Pound in a mortar 3 large blanched bitter almonds and 3 large sweet ones with ½ teaspoon of CREAM SAUCE II, page 36, or a little unbeaten egg white. Force this paste through a fine strainer, add 2 fresh egg yolks, salt and pepper to taste, and beat thoroughly with a wire whisk; then add gradually and drop by drop until the sauce begins to thicken, one cup of olive oil alternating with the juice of a small lemon while continuing stirring and beating. Finish with a tablespoon of mixed fine herbs, such as chervil, parsley, tarragon, chives, and pimpernel, in equal quantities, previously blanched one or two minutes in plain water, drained, and squeezed through a cloth.

GRIBICHE SAUCE

(Suitable for Any Kind of Cooked Cold Fish)

Pound in a mortar 2 hard-boiled egg yolks with a scant teaspoon of prepared mustard, salt, and pepper to taste. Pour on gradually, and alternating, ⅔ cup of olive oil and a scant teaspoon of tarragon vinegar. Finish with a generous tablespoon each of capers and sour gherkins, finely chopped, a teaspoon of mixed parsley, chervil, and tarragon herbs, finely chopped, in equal parts and, when ready to serve, fold in the white of a hard-boiled egg, cut julienne-like.

HORSERADISH SAUCE WITH WALNUT

(Suitable for Cooked White-fleshed Fish)

Mix in a bowl 3 tablespoons of freshly grated horseradish, same amount of finely chopped walnut meats; add salt and pepper to taste, a small pinch of granulated sugar, and a cupful of fresh thick cream.

HORSERADISH SAUCE

(Suitable for Cooked White-fleshed Fish)

Place in a bowl 4 tablespoons of freshly grated horseradish; add a pinch of granulated sugar, pepper and salt to taste, and a little vinegar so as to obtain a rather thick purée. Mix with 4 tablespoons of tomato catsup.

RAVIGOTE SAUCE

(Hungarian Recipe)

(Suitable for Cold Boiled Fish)

Force through a sieve 3 hard-boiled egg yolks, and add 2 fresh egg yolks, a small pinch each of paprika, dry English mustard, and granulated sugar, a teaspoon each of finely chopped onion, shallots, parsley, and chives. Beat the whole thoroughly and fold in ⅔ cup of mayonnaise.

REMOULADE SAUCE

(Suitable for Any Kind of Cold Cooked Fish)

To one cup and a half of mayonnaise, add a teaspoon of prepared mustard, a scant tablespoon of finely chopped sweet gherkins, a teaspoon of finely chopped capers, all pressed together through a cloth to extract the liquid, a scant teaspoon each of finely chopped parsley and chervil, and a third of a teaspoon of finely chopped tarragon herbs. Finish with the size of a small hazelnut of anchovy paste.

RUSSIAN SAUCE

(Suitable for Any Kind of Cooked Cold Fish or Crustaceans)

Pass through a meat chopper sufficient cooked cold lobster meat to obtain a generous tablespoon, place in a bowl, add a scant tablespoon of caviar and mix thoroughly and gently. Force the mixture through a fine sieve and add ⅔ cup of mayonnaise. Finish with a third of a teaspoon of prepared mustard and same quantity of Derby sauce (if not available, substitute Worcestershire).

TARTARE SAUCE

(Cold)

(Suitable for Any Kind of Cold Cooked Fish and Crustaceans)

Pound in a bowl, 2 hard-boiled yolks to a paste; season with salt and pepper to taste, using pepper from the mill if available as the sauce should be highly seasoned, and incorporate gradually, as for mayonnaise, a cupful of olive oil, interspersed with a teaspoon of tarragon vinegar, added gradually. Finish with a pinch of the green top of an onion (chives may be used), pounded in a mortar, to which is added a generous teaspoon of mayonnaise.

VARIATION I

To a cup of highly seasoned mayonnaise, add a generous teaspoon each of finely chopped capers and sour gherkins.

VARIATION II

Mix together in a bowl, a teaspoon each of finely chopped parsley, shallots, tarragon herbs, sweet gherkins, olives, salt and pepper to taste (pepper from the mill), a teaspoon of prepared mustard and fold in a cupful of mayonnaise.

VARIATION III

Mix together in a bowl, a teaspoon each of capers, sweet pickles, olives, parsley, shallots (or onion), salt, pepper and a few grains of Cayenne, and fold in a cup of mayonnaise.

VALENCIA SAUCE

(Suitable for Any Kind of Cold Cooked Fish)

Reduce to a paste 4 hard-boiled egg yolks with a few drops of olive oil and add a small clove of garlic, pounded in a mortar. Pour on gradually 4 tablespoons of olive oil and add a tiny pinch of saffron, salt and pepper from the mill to taste, a tablespoon of tarragon vinegar, and 2 tablespoons of tomato catsup. Stir well and finish with 2 tablespoons of thick fresh cream.

VINCENT SAUCE

(Suitable for Any Kind of Cold Cooked Fish and Crustaceans)

Parboil 2 or 3 minutes a handful of sorrel, 5 or 6 leaves of fresh parsley, an equal amount of tarragon, chives, and pimpernel, and strain. Cool in cold water, drain, and sponge. Pound in a mortar with a few sprigs of young watercress, adding gradually 2 hard-boiled egg yolks, freshly cooked. Force this mixture through a sieve, add salt and pepper from the mill to taste, and beat in, one by one, 3 whole fresh eggs, alternating with a cup of olive oil. Finish with a little tarragon vinegar to taste and add a few drops of Derby sauce or Worcestershire sauce. Very appropriate for cold salmon and cold trout.

VARIATION

Prepare the aromatic herbs as indicated above and fold in a cupful of mayonnaise.

COMPOUNDED BUTTERS

Compounded butters in cookery are the finishing touch to a sauce, a soup, or a dish, as is powder to the face of a beautiful woman.

They may be prepared in advance and stored in the refrigerator for use when necessary.

The complete list of compounded butters would be too lengthy to be given here. The author will simply describe those most used in present-day cookery, and especially those adapted to fish cookery.

ALMOND BUTTER

Pound in a mortar 6 sweet almonds, peeled, well washed, then sponged, adding a few drops of water or egg white to prevent their turning into oil and mix well with a generous tablespoon of salted butter.

ANCHOVY BUTTER

Pound a tablespoon of sweet butter with a hazelnut-sized portion of anchovy paste.

BERCY BUTTER

Reduce to half volume a scant cup of white wine to which has been added a pinch of finely chopped parsley. Let cool and mix thoroughly with salted butter in sufficient quantity to obtain a solid mass.

BLACK BUTTER

This butter is principally used for fish and eggs and is made as required. Its preparation consists in browning well a little butter and mixing with a little vinegar and coarse pepper (pepper from the mill). Black butter may also be prepared in advance and heated when necessary. Capers and chopped parsley may be used in proportion, being placed on the food calling for this butter and the latter poured piping hot over it.

CAVIAR BUTTER

Pound fine, one tablespoon of caviar; place in a fine cloth and twist to remove the oily liquid and briny water, then mix with 2 tablespoons of sweet butter.

CHIVRY BUTTER

Mix together in a mortar a scant ½ teaspoon each of previously finely chopped parsley, chervil, tarragon herbs, chives, and a very small shallot with 2 tablespoons of salted butter.

COLBERT BUTTER

To a tablespoon of MAÎTRE D'HÔTEL BUTTER, page 57, add the size of a hazelnut portion of extract of meat (Liebig, Oxo, Armour, etc.) and a small pinch of finely chopped tarragon herbs.

CRAYFISH BUTTER

In a mortar mix finely the meat trimmings of crayfish (about a tablespoon) with the same amount of salted butter.

GARLIC BUTTER

Blanch in a few drops of water a clove of garlic. Remove, dry, and pound with 2 tablespoons of salted butter.

GREEN BUTTER

Consists of butter mixed with sufficient green vegetable coloring to obtain the desired hue.

HERRING BUTTER

Mix well a walnut-sized portion of herring with 2 tablespoons of sweet butter.

HORSERADISH BUTTER

In a mortar mix a teaspoon of freshly grated horseradish with a tablespoon of salted butter.

KNEADED BUTTER

This butter is usually employed for quick blending and thickening. It consists of one tablespoon of salted butter thoroughly mixed with a generous teaspoon of flour.

LOBSTER BUTTER

Pound together the equivalent of a tablespoon of cooked lobster trimmings such as coral, milky meat, roe, etc., with two tablespoons of salted butter.

MAÎTRE D'HÔTEL BUTTER

Consists of softening a tablespoon of salted butter, then adding a scant teaspoon of finely chopped parsley and a few drops of lemon juice (onion juice may be added if desired), and kneading all these ingredients mixed together thoroughly. Keep on ice until wanted.

MARCHAND DE VIN BUTTER

(*Wine Dealers' Butter*)

Reduce to half volume over a hot fire, ½ cup of red wine in which a very small shallot finely chopped is added and 2 pounded peppercorns; then add a hazelnut-sized portion of meat extract, a small pinch of finely chopped parsley, 2 or 3 drops of lemon juice, and knead with 3 tablespoons of sweet butter. Keep on ice until wanted.

MEUNIÈRE BUTTER
Should be prepared as required. Butter is melted until it acquires a brown color, a few drops of lemon juice are placed on the food, with a pinch of finely chopped parsley; when ready to serve, the piping-hot browned butter is poured over.

MUSTARD BUTTER
To a tablespoon of sweet butter, add a half teaspoon of prepared mustard, mix well, and keep on ice until wanted.

PAPRIKA BUTTER I
Is a tablespoon of salted butter kneaded with ½ teaspoon of paprika.

PAPRIKA BUTTER II
Cook together a tablespoon of salted butter, ½ teaspoon of paprika, and ½ teaspoon of finely chopped onion. Strain and, when cold, knead with a generous tablespoon of salted butter.

POLISH BUTTER
Consists of mixing 2 tablespoons of salted butter with ⅔ cup (more or less) of fine bread crumbs, cooking until well browned.

SHALLOT BUTTER
Mix in a mortar a small shallot previously blanched in a little butter; strain, cool, and knead with a generous tablespoon of salted butter.

SHRIMP BUTTER
Pound finely in a mortar a half dozen cooked shrimps, then knead with 2 tablespoons of salted butter.

SMOKED SALMON BUTTER

Consists of kneading 2 tablespoons of sweet butter with a teaspoon of salmon paste.

TARRAGON BUTTER

In a mortar pound finely 1 teaspoon of chopped tarragon leaves and knead with 2 tablespoons of salted butter.

FISH AND SEA FOOD COCKTAILS
CLAM

CLAM COCKTAIL ON HALF SHELL

Only littleneck clams are used for cocktails. Arrange on plates of crushed ice, six littleneck clams, placing in center a small flat goblet containing in equal parts tomato catsup and prepared horseradish and a few drops of lemon juice. Serve with a quarter of lemon and oyster crackers or small finger sandwich of brown bread and butter.

CLAM COCKTAIL FRAPPÉ

Wash and scrub with a brush 2 quarts of clams, changing water several times; put in a kettle with ½ cup of cold water and a teaspoon of lemon juice and steam until the shells are opened. Remove the clams from the shells and strain the liquor through a very fine cloth. Season highly with pepper and a few grains of Cayenne pepper to taste. Cool and, when thoroughly cold, shake as you would an ordinary cocktail. Serve in cocktail glass and top with a tablespoon of whipped cream, dusted with a little paprika or nutmeg.

CLAM COCKTAIL CRYSTAL PALACE

Proceed as indicated for recipe above, using one-half quantity of ingredients. Measure. Add an equal amount of tomato juice, shake, pour in a cocktail glass; top with whipped cream dusted with nutmeg and a few grains of Cayenne pepper.

CLAM COCKTAIL NELSON MORRIS

Place in the bottom of a cocktail glass a generous teaspoon of flaked, boned crab meat and over this 6 littleneck clams. Pour over both, a mixture of tomato catsup with prepared mustard and prepared horseradish to taste. Serve with saltine crackers.

LOBSTER

LOBSTER COCKTAIL I

Allow ¼ of a cup of lobster meat cut in small pieces for each cocktail and season with 2 tablespoons each of tomato catsup and sherry wine, ½ teaspoon lemon juice, a few drops of Tabasco sauce, a small pinch of finely chopped chives and salt, pepper, and Cayenne pepper to taste. Chill thoroughly and serve in cocktail glasses.

LOBSTER COCKTAIL II

Equal parts of lobster meat cut in small pieces and small dices of cucumber. Mix with the same sauce as indicated for LOBSTER COCK-TAIL I and serve in cocktail glasses.

LOBSTER COCKTAIL III

Equal parts of lobster meat cut in small pieces and small diced cucumber with a few capers, mixed with thin mayonnaise, adding prepared mustard to taste. Dress in cocktail glasses, top with tomato catsup, and in center place a small dot of thick mayonnaise forced through a pastry bag with small fancy tube.

OYSTER

OYSTER COCKTAIL ON HALF SHELL I

(Serves One)

Served dressed on half shell as indicated for CLAM COCKTAIL ON HALF SHELL.

OYSTER COCKTAIL II

(Serves One)

Combine a tablespoon of tomato catsup, ½ tablespoon of tarragon vinegar or lemon juice, 2 drops Tabasco sauce, dash of salt to taste, a teaspoon of finely diced cold celery, and a few drops Worcestershire sauce. Fold in six medium-sized oysters and dress in a cocktail glass.

OYSTER COCKTAIL III

(Serves One)

Combine a scant teaspoon lemon juice, ½ tablespoon tomato catsup, ½ (scant) teaspoon of finely chopped shallot, 2 drops of Tabasco sauce, ½ teaspoon prepared horseradish, and a tablespoon of finely diced celery. Season with salt and Cayenne pepper to taste and place 6 small oysters in a cocktail glass and pour over the mixture. Top with a stuffed olive.

OYSTER COCKTAIL IV

(Serves One)

Prepare a marinade as follows: 1 tablespoon of sherry wine, salt and Cayenne pepper to taste, 1 tablespoon tomato catsup, a few drops of Worcestershire sauce, and a teaspoon of finely diced celery. Place the oysters (6) in it and let stand half an hour. Dress in a cocktail glass with a border of thin slices of sweet gherkins, cut in two and arranged scallop-like around edges of glass. Top with a green olive.

SCALLOP

SCALLOP COCKTAIL I

Clean 3 dozen scallops, put in a saucepan and cook in their own liquor until they begin to shrivel. Drain; chill and dress over finely shaved ice in scallop shells, allowing six for each shell. Serve on individual plate covered with a doily, with a small glass containing cocktail sauce as indicated for OYSTER COCKTAIL ON HALF SHELL.

SCALLOP COCKTAIL II

Combine in a bowl the following ingredients: 8 tablespoons tomato catsup, 2 tablespoons tarragon vinegar, 1 tablespoon prepared horseradish, 1 teaspoon prepared mustard, salt and pepper to taste and a few grains of Cayenne pepper, 1 teaspoon finely chopped chives, 1 teaspoon very finely chopped shallot, 3 or 4 drops Tabasco sauce, 1 generous tablespoon of olive oil and 1 teaspoon Worcestershire sauce. Mix well by beating with a wire whisk and chill thoroughly. Clean and cook 3 dozen scallops 5 minutes; drain, cut in two, and chill, add to the mixture and let stand ½ hour in refrigerator. Dress in 6 cocktail glasses and top each with a dot of thick mayonnaise, forced through a pastry bag with small fancy tube, and dust lightly with paprika.

SHRIMP

SHRIMP COCKTAIL I

Allow 8 shrimps for each portion. Cut in two and mix with same dressing as OYSTER COCKTAIL III, page 62.

SHRIMP COCKTAIL II

Allow 8 shrimps for each portion. Cut in two and mix with a teaspoon of finely diced celery, a tablespoon tomato catsup, a teaspoon mayonnaise, a few drops Worcestershire sauce and a few drops of Tabasco sauce, salt, pepper, and a few grains of Cayenne pepper. Serve in cocktail glasses.

SEA FOOD

SEA FOOD COCKTAIL I

Mix together ½ cup each of cooked diced shrimps; ½ cup cooked diced lobster, ⅓ cup of cooked diced scallops, and ⅓ cup of diced celery. Season to taste with salt and pepper and a few grains of Cayenne pepper and stir in the following dressing: 1 teaspoon lemon juice, ½ teaspoon onion juice, 1 tablespoon tomato catsup, a scant teaspoon prepared horseradish, 3 drops Tabasco sauce and a few drops of tarragon vinegar. Dress in cocktail glass and top with an olive.

SEA FOOD COCKTAIL II

Mix together ½ cup each of diced shrimps, cooked salmon, cooked diced codfish, or diced finnan haddie, and ⅓ cup of diced celery. Season to taste with salt, pepper and a few grains of Cayenne pepper and stir in the dressing indicated for LOBSTER COCKTAIL I, page 61. Dress in cocktail glass and decorate with slices of hard-boiled eggs, cut in two and topped with a caper.

BOUILLON, BROTH, FISH CREAM SOUPS, CHOWDERS, FISH SOUPS, AND COMPOUNDED FISH STEWS

BOUILLON, BROTH, FISH CREAM SOUPS, CHOWDERS, FISH SOUPS, AND COMPOUNDED FISH STEWS

BOUILLON and BROTH

CLAM BOUILLON

Wash and scrub with a brush ½ peck of clams, changing the water several times. Put in a kettle with 3 generous standard cups of water, cover tightly and steam, until the shells are well opened (10 minutes or thereabouts), over a hot fire. Strain through a very fine cloth, cool and clear.

CLAM BROTH

Prepare and cook the same amount of clams as indicated for above recipe. Strain through a fine cloth over another saucepan; reheat to the boiling point; season to taste with a little salt, pepper, and celery salt and serve, hot or cold, with saltine crackers.

CLAM BROTH WITH POACHED EGG

Prepare, cook and strain as indicated in recipe for CLAM BROTH. Reheat to the boiling point and place a freshly poached egg in each cup just before serving.

CLAM CONSOMMÉ

Wash 2 quarts of clams in shell. Put in a kettle with ¼ of a cup of cold water, cover and cook until the shells open. Strain the liquor through a very fine cloth and add to 4 cups of clear beef or chicken consommé.

CLAM CONSOMMÉ WITH WHIPPED CREAM

Prepare, cook, and serve as indicated in recipe for CLAM CONSOMMÉ, adding just before serving a tablespoon of whipped cream to each cup.

TOMATO BOUILLON WITH OYSTERS

Place in soup kettle one large can of tomatoes, 1 quart of fish stock, 2 tablespoons of butter, 1 tablespoon of finely chopped onion, a tiny bit of bay leaf, 2 crushed cloves, ½ teaspoon celery seed, and 6 crushed peppercorns and boil continuously for 15 minutes. Strain through a very fine sieve and clear. Just before serving, parboil 6 large oysters until plump and the gills curl and place one in each cup with a teaspoon of whipped cream. Serve with saltine crackers.

FISH CREAM SOUPS
(Called also "Coulis" or "Bisque")

CREAM OF CLAM CORINTHIAN

Wash 3 dozen clams, put in a kettle, and add ¼ cup of cold water, bring to the boiling point and cook until the shells open. Lift out the clams and remove from the shells. Chop finely and add to the liquor in the kettle then add one medium-sized onion, coarsely sliced, a sprig of parsley, a little blade of mace, salt, and a few grains of Cayenne pepper. Let simmer very gently for 20 minutes. Add to a quart of scalded milk, 2 scant tablespoons of cornstarch, diluted in 2 tablespoons of cold water or cold milk and pour on the clams. Cook 10 minutes longer; strain through a fine cloth, rectify the seasoning and finish just before serving with 2 or 3 egg yolks, added gradually, while beating constantly. Serve with a side dish of small dices of bread fried in butter.

You may serve in cups, adding a tablespoon of whipped cream to each cup with small brown-bread and butter sandwiches or saltine crackers.

CREAM OF CLAM AND OYSTER

Clean and pick over a pint of small oysters, reserving the liquor; do likewise with a pint of clams and chop together very finely. Place in a kettle with the liquor, add ½ cup of cold water, bring to a boil and set aside to simmer very slowly for 5 minutes. Pour on a quart of milk to which is added 2 tablespoons of cornstarch diluted in 2 tablespoons of cold milk and bring to a boil; season to taste with celery seed, salt, and white pepper and let simmer 5 minutes longer. Strain through a fine cloth over another pan, add a table-spoon of kneaded butter, and cook for 10 minutes. Finish off the fire with 3 egg yolks slightly beaten and add gradually, while stirring constantly, a tablespoon of sweet butter and a few drops of onion juice. Serve in cups with a teaspoon of whipped cream over each cup.

CREAM OF CLAM SARAH BERNHARDT

Proceed as indicated in recipe for CREAM OF CLAM AND OYSTER, above, omitting whipped cream, and pouring in, while boiling violently, 4 fresh eggs well beaten, through a fine sieve. Serve with caviarettes.

CREAM OF CLAM MANHATTAN

Wash thoroughly 2 quarts of clams in shell, put in a kettle and add ½ cup of cold water, cover and cook until shells are partially open. Strain the liquor through a very fine cloth and add enough water to make 5 standard cups. Brown 3 tablespoons of butter, add 3½ tablespoons of flour, and continue browning, while stirring constantly. Pour on the liquid gradually, stirring meanwhile. Bring to the boiling point and let simmer very gently for 15 minutes, season with salt, pepper, and a few grains of Cayenne pepper and nutmeg. Boil once, remove aside, add 3 egg yolks gradually, stirring meanwhile, and finish with 1 cup of heated cream.

CREAM OF CRAYFISH BOURGEOISE

Cook in 3 tablespoons of butter, 1 small carrot, 1 small onion, a small stalk of celery, very finely chopped with a small bouquet of parsley, 1 tiny bit of bay leaf, 1 crushed clove, and 4 peppercorns also crushed, until nearly done, stirring frequently, and pour over a wineglass of white wine. Let the liquid reduce to half, add 25 or 30 crayfish, well cleaned and washed and cook for 10 minutes. Remove aside, lift out the crayfish and shell. Set the meat aside with the shells, which pound finely in a mortar. Place this mixture in a soup kettle, add 1 quart and a half of fish stock or white consommé with a small pinch of nutmeg, boil once, and let simmer very gently 10 minutes. Strain through a very fine cloth. Replace on the fire and add 2 tablespoons of butter. Do not boil. When ready to serve, finish with 3 egg yolks, added gradually, while stirring constantly, and a tablespoon of sweet butter. Just before serving a dozen of small balls of fish forcemeat (*see* FISH FORCEMEAT AND STUFFING) may be added. Rectify the seasoning and serve.

CREAM OF CRAYFISH DROUANT

"Nothing is too complicated or too tedious in cookery when the results are the production of a satisfactory and delectable dish which responds to the anticipation produced by the reading of the recipe, as the pleasures of the table are second to none."

BRILLAT-SAVARIN

INGREDIENTS

Thirty living crayfish, a small carrot, chopped fine, a small onion also chopped fine, a small stalk of celery, diced small, 3 tablespoons of butter, a teaspoon of meat extract, 1 wineglass of white wine, 1 pony glass of brandy, ½ cup of cooked rice, 1 scant cup of fresh cream, 1 additional tablespoon of sweet butter, and 3 egg yolks, salt, pepper, and a few grains of Cayenne pepper.

Cook the carrot, onion, and celery for 5 or 6 minutes, stirring often, in 3 tablespoons of butter, adding a small bouquet garni and a tablespoon of meat extract. Meanwhile sauté in a little butter the well-washed and cleaned crayfish and remove the center shell which will automatically pull with it the green filament which it holds; add the wine and brandy, cover and let simmer very gently for 15 minutes. Add then the crayfish to the vegetables and pour over a quart of water. Boil once and let simmer 10 minutes. Lift out the crayfish; remove the meat from the shell, saving the tails. Pound the shell and meat in a mortar, adding the cooked rice gradually; return this compound to the court bouillon, stir well and bring to a boil. Set aside to cool a little, strain through a very fine cloth, place again on the fire, and bring to the boiling point; then pour in the cream to which has been added the beaten egg yolks, while stirring constantly. Rectify the seasoning and, just before serving, add the additional tablespoon of sweet butter and the crayfish tails set aside. Serve with triangles of freshly made toast.

CREAM OF CRAYFISH ITALIAN STYLE

Prepare, cook, and serve as indicated in above recipe, adding just before serving 3 tablespoons of cooked macaroni cut in small pieces with a side dish of grated Parmesan cheese and a poached egg for each serving.

CREAM OF LOBSTER HOME STYLE

Remove the spines from a generous cup of lobster meat, chop coarsely. Melt 2 tablespoons of butter in a double boiler, stir in 2 tablespoons of flour, blend well, and moisten with a quart of rich milk or 3 cups of milk and one cup of cream, added gradually, while stirring constantly, until thickened. Add the lobster meat and let cook for 15 minutes; strain through a fine cloth and pound the lobster meat to a paste, adding 2 egg yolks gradually. Return this paste to the milk and bring to the boiling point, but do not boil; season with salt, pepper, and a blade of mace; strain through a fine cloth again and finish with a tablespoon of sweet butter. Serve with a side dish of triangles of toasted bread or saltine crackers.

CREAM OF LOBSTER

Remove the meat from the shell of a 2-lb. live lobster. Place the shell, claws, and bones broken to pieces in a saucepan and cover with 2 cups of cold water; bring slowly to the boiling point, then set aside to simmer gently for 25 minutes. Drain and strain through a very fine cloth and place the liquor on the fire. Blend ¼ cup of butter with ¼ cup of flour and moisten with the liquor, while stirring constantly; let simmer very gently for 5 or 6 minutes; then add a quart of scalded milk containing the lobster meat, finely chopped, season with salt, pepper, and a few grains of Cayenne pepper and bring to a boil. Let simmer 5 minutes and strain through a fine sieve or, better, a fine cloth. Add gradually and off the fire, 3 egg yolks, one by one, stirring meanwhile, and finish with a tablespoon of sweet butter.

If a richer soup is desired, white stock may be used instead of water. When coral is found in lobster, wash, wipe, force through a fine sieve, put in a mortar with a tablespoon of butter, work until well blended, and add to the soup. If color is desired, add a little red vegetable coloring.

CREAM OF OYSTER PILGRIM

Parboil a quart of oysters in their own liquor, remove the oysters; chop and pound them in a mortar, then press or force through a fine sieve. Melt 2 tablespoons of butter and blend with 2 tablespoons of flour, moisten with a quart of scalded milk, then add the purée of oysters and bring to a boil. Let simmer very gently for 15 minutes and add a cup of heated cream. Strain through a fine cloth and add salt, white pepper, and a few grains of Cayenne pepper to taste. Finish with 3 egg yolks added one by one, while stirring constantly.

CREAM OF OYSTER NEW ENGLAND

Clean and pick over a quart of oysters, reserving the liquor, re-move the soft portions, and chop the gills and tough muscles. Place 2 cups of white stock in a saucepan (water may be substituted), add 1½ cups of bread crumbs, oyster liquor, chopped gills, and tough muscles, 1 medium-sized onion, finely chopped, 2 stalks of celery also finely chopped, a large sprig of parsley, a tiny bit of bay leaf, 1 small clove and a blade of mace, and cook over a moderately hot fire for 25 minutes. Force through a sieve, rubbing hard so as to extract as much of the hard parts as possible and place again on the fire, bringing to the boiling point. Add 2 tablespoons of kneaded butter mixed with 2 cups of scalded milk and ½ cup of thick cream. Boil 2 or 3 minutes, season to taste. Serve.

CREAM OF SCALLOP

Clean a quart of scallops, reserve one half and finely chop re-mainder. Add the latter to 4 cups of scalded milk, season to taste with salt, pepper, and a few grains of nutmeg and add a small pinch of ground clove, a tiny bit of bay leaf, 6 peppercorns (bruised), 1 small onion (finely chopped), and cook very slowly for 25 to 30 minutes; strain, thicken with a tablespoon of butter and a table-spoon of flour kneaded together. Boil once or twice, remove aside, add 2 or 3 egg yolks, one by one, while stirring constantly, and finish with a generous tablespoon of sweet butter. When ready to serve, parboil the reserved scallops and add to the soup.

CREAM OF SALMON

Force through a sieve 2 cups of cooked salmon and mix with ½ cup of cold milk, stirring well so as to obtain a fine paste, adding more milk if necessary. Scald 1 quart of milk, add to salmon paste, add a small bit of bay leaf, a teaspoon of finely chopped onion, a sprig of parsley, a small clove, and a blade of mace, season with salt and pepper to taste and a few grains of nutmeg and add a tablespoon of kneaded butter. Bring to the boiling point and let simmer for 15 minutes. Remove aside and finish with 2 yolks of eggs well beaten and poured slowly, stirring meanwhile, and 2 tablespoons of butter.

CHOWDERS

CLAM CHOWDER HOME STYLE I

Clean and pick over a quart of clams, separate the hard and soft parts and chop the former. Strain the liquor through a fine cloth. Try out a 2-inch cube of pork fat cut in small pieces, fry in it one tablespoon of finely chopped onion until brown and turn into a large kettle. Boil enough potatoes to obtain 4 cupfuls, cut in small dices and put into the kettle; add the clams, soft parts and chopped hard parts, 1 quart of milk, 3 tablespoons of butter, and 6 soda crackers broken into small pieces, a small pinch of thyme leaves, a small bay leaf, a clove, and a sprig of parsley. Let cook 5 minutes, set aside, and let simmer very gently for 15 to 20 minutes. Just before serving, add the strained clam liquor heated. Remove the bay leaf, sprig of parsley, and serve with a side dish of toasted crackers.

CLAM CHOWDER HOME STYLE II

Clean and pick over a quart of clams, separate hard parts from soft, put the hard parts through meat chopper, then the soft parts, keeping them separate. Fry a 1½- to 2-inch cube of salt pork, well minced, in which brown a tablespoon of finely chopped onion, turn into a kettle, in which place a layer of cooked potatoes, diced small, hard part of clams, salt, pepper, and a few grains of nutmeg, and sprinkle with 2 tablespoons of flour; pour in the potato water and simmer gently for 15 minutes; then add a quart of scalded milk with a small pinch of thyme leaves, a small bit of bay leaves, and a tablespoon of kneaded butter. Bring to a boil and simmer gently for 10 minutes. Just before serving, add the soft parts of the clams heated with the liquor, rectify the seasoning, and serve with crackers.

CLAM CHOWDER NEW ENGLAND

Clean and pick over a quart of clams, using ⅔ cup of cold water; drain and reserve the liquor, which heat to the boiling point and strain. Chop finely the hard part of the clams, cut a scant ¼ of a pound of fat salt pork into small dices and fry, adding one small onion, chopped fine, which fry 5 minutes; turn into a kettle and add 3 cups of cubed raw potatoes, the chopped hard parts of the clams, salt, pepper, and a few grains of Cayenne pepper, a few grains of nutmeg, a small pinch of thyme leaves, a small bit of bay leaf, and sprinkle over with 2 tablespoons of flour. Cover with 2 cups of water and bring to a boil. Simmer for 20 minutes over a low fire and add one quart of scalded milk, to which is added 2 tablespoons of butter and a tablespoon of kneaded butter. Bring to a boil and, when ready to serve, parboil the soft parts of the clams in their own liquor and add to the chowder. Serve with hard pilot crackers.

CLAM AND OYSTER CHOWDER

Clean and pick over one pint of oysters, reserve the liquor, chop the oysters and add to the liquor; clean and pick over one pint of clams, reserve the liquor, remove the hard parts and add, finely chopped, to the liquor, putting aside the soft parts. Heat slowly clams and oysters with liquor of both and let simmer 15 to 20 minutes; strain through a fine cloth and thicken with 2 tablespoons of kneaded butter. Scald 1 quart of milk with a sprig of parsley, a tiny bit of bay leaf, a generous blade of mace, 2 slices of onion, and a small pinch of thyme leaves and strain over the clams and oysters.

Season with salt and pepper and a few grains of Cayenne pepper. Boil once more and finish with a tablespoon of butter.

CODFISH CHOWDER NAPOLITAINE

(*Zuppa di Baccala*)

Two pounds salted codfish, soaked in cold water overnight, 3 tablespoons olive oil, 3 small onions, finely sliced, 2 small leeks (white only), sliced fine, 2 bruised small cloves of garlic or a large one, 1 quart cold water, ½ bottle of white wine (optional) which may be substituted by 2 cups of rich fresh cream, 1 generous tablespoon of finely chopped parsley, salt, 6 coarsely pounded peppercorns (taking into consideration that the codfish may still be salted), 1 generous pinch saffron, 1 bouquet garni, 4 large potatoes, sliced thick, 4 additional tablespoons of olive oil, and Jocko toast, which consists of toast made in the oven, then rubbed lightly with garlic.

Sauté in the 3 tablespoons of olive oil, onion, leeks, and garlic; when half done, pour in the water, wine and seasonings; add saffron, then bouquet garni, and bring to a boil. At this time, put in the potatoes, codfish cut in small pieces, and additional olive oil. Continue cooking over a moderately hot fire until potatoes and fish are done, which should be simultaneous (½ hour or thereabouts). A few minutes before it is done, add the parsley, let simmer very gently a few minutes longer and pile in center of a hot, round, deep platter. Serve with a side dish of Jocko toast.

CRAB CHOWDER

Remove the meat from 7 or 8 hard-shelled crabs and chop finely (or use a can of crab meat, boned and flaked, then chopped finely), place in a soup kettle and pour over a quart of fish stock, a cup of stale bread crumbs, 1 small onion, finely sliced, a large sprig of parsley and a small pinch of thyme leaves with a tiny bit of bay leaf. Bring to a boil, then let simmer for 20 minutes over a very low fire or on the side of the range. Strain, forcing a little through a fine sieve, place again on the fire, add 2 tablespoons of kneaded butter, bring to a boil; add a cup of thick cream and season to taste with salt, pepper, and a few grains of Cayenne pepper. Just before serving, add a tablespoon or two of flaked crab meat or 2 tablespoons of cooked, diced shrimps and a tablespoon of sweet butter. Serve with saltine crackers.

EEL CHOWDER
(Netherland Soup)

Sauté in 3 tablespoons of butter for 3 or 4 minutes, 3 small leeks, using only the white part, with 3 thin slices of onion; then pour over a quart of boiling water and add 1½ lbs. of small eels, skinned, cleaned, and well washed; then cut in 1-inch pieces. Boil once and let simmer very gently for 25 minutes. Lift out the fish, remove the bones; keep hot. Strain the cooking broth through a fine sieve, pressing a little. Clean a cupful of finely chopped, uncooked spinach and a cupful of finely chopped uncooked lettuce and cook in 2 tablespoons of butter for 5 minutes, stirring once in a while; moisten with a little of the cooking broth and add ½ cup of stale bread crumbs. Let blend well on the side of the range, then add to the broth; cook 10 minutes, remove aside, add gradually 3 egg yolks, one by one, while stirring constantly and ⅔ cup of heated thick cream. Finish by adding 1 tablespoon of butter, salt, pepper, and a few grains of nutmeg. Serve with crackers.

FISH CHOWDER NEW ENGLAND STYLE

Cut in 2-inch pieces, 1 lb. of codfish and 1 lb. of haddock; place in a fish kettle after washing and sponging, and cover with 3 cups of water; then add 2 cups of diced raw potatoes, 1 medium-sized onion sliced and cooked with 1½-inch cube of fat pork, cut in small dices, a pinch of thyme leaves, a bouquet garni, a blade of mace, and 6 crushed peppercorns and cook over a moderately hot fire for 25 minutes. Drain the liquor, reserving the solid parts, and reduce to 3 cups; pour over the solid parts in the kettle and let simmer gently for 5 minutes; then add 2 cups of rich scalded milk, or 2 cups of milk and one cup of cream; bring to a boil, season with salt to taste and a few grains of Cayenne pepper, and finish with 2 tablespoons of butter and 5 or 6 saltine crackers, soaked in milk. Let stand a while and serve with pilot crackers on the side.

FISH CHOWDER HOME STYLE I

Wipe 2½ lbs. of any uncooked fish (white fleshed) with a damp cloth and place in kettle with 5 cups of cold water and salt; slowly bring to a boil; then remove aside to simmer 20 to 25 minutes very gently. Strain the fish and return the broth to the kettle; skin and bone the fish, set aside, and keep hot. Fry 1½-inch cube of salted fat pork with 2 onions, finely chopped, and add to the broth with 2 cups of diced raw potatoes; cook until the potatoes are done and return the fish to the kettle; add 2 cups of strained scalded milk with a pinch of thyme leaves, a small bit of bay leaf, 1 clove, a sprig of parsley, salt, pepper, a few grains of nutmeg, and a tablespoon of finely chopped parsley. Let heat through and, just before serving, add a tablespoon of butter. Serve in plates each containing a toasted cracker and bit of minced parsley.

FISH CHOWDER HOME STYLE II

Wipe with a damp cloth 2½ lbs. of any white-fleshed, uncooked fish and cut in 1-inch pieces; place in a soup kettle, cover with 5 cups of salted cold water, and add 2 tablespoons of finely diced carrots, 1 cup of diced small potatoes, ½ cup of finely chopped leeks (green and white), ¼ cup of diced small fat salt pork, 1 large onion, finely sliced, 1 tablespoon of finely chopped parsley, a bouquet garni, and a pinch of thyme leaves. Season with salt, 6 crushed peppercorns, a blade of mace, and a few grains of nutmeg. Bring to a boil and remove aside to simmer very gently for 25 to 30 minutes; then add 6 hard crackers soaked in milk and 2 tablespoons of butter and cook 10 minutes longer. Rectify the seasonings and serve in plates each containing a cracker.

FISH CHOWDER MARINE WITH CHEESE

Make a roux with 2 tablespoons of butter and 2 of flour and, when light brown and well blended, pour in a cup of white wine and 4 cups of water, well salted, and add 1 large onion, sliced fine, 2 small leeks, sliced fine, 1 crushed clove, 1 bouquet garni, 6 crushed peppercorns and a few grains each of Cayenne pepper and nutmeg and boil violently for 15 minutes; then add the well-cleaned, washed trimmings and bones of several fish together weighing 2 pounds. Reduce the fire and let simmer for 25 minutes, strain through a fine sieve, correct the seasonings, add 2 tablespoons of kneaded butter, and cook 10 minutes longer. Serve on plates each containing a piece of toast and a teaspoon of grated cheese.

FISH CHOWDER FLEMISH STYLE

(*Waterzoi Flamand*)

Cut the heads and tails from 1 lb. each of perch, carp, and eel (pike may also be used), wash and sponge well and place in a large skillet with 3 tablespoons of butter, 1 small carrot (finely sliced), 1 small onion (finely sliced), 2 crushed cloves, 1 parsley root (diced), 1 bouquet garni, a small pinch of thyme leaves, salt, and 6 crushed peppercorns and brown over a moderately hot fire for 10 minutes; then add 5 cups of salted water and 1 cup of white wine and boil violently 5 minutes. Remove aside and let simmer for 20 minutes. Strain through a fine sieve over another soup kettle and add 2 tablespoons of kneaded butter, a small lemon, peeled, seeded, and sliced. Boil once, rectify the seasoning and serve in plates containing a piece of toast, and a side dish of brown-bread and butter sandwiches.

HADDOCK CHOWDER CONNECTICUT STYLE

Cut a 2-lb. piece of haddock in 2-inch pieces, with 2 heads and the large bone or more bones procured from the fish dealer. Make a fish stock in the usual way, i.e., place the bones, heads, tails, skin in a saucepan with cold salted water, bringing slowly to the boiling point, simmering 20 minutes, and straining; a few slices each of carrot and onion, a bay leaf, a clove, and a few thyme leaves are added. Place the cut-up fish in a kettle and add 1 cup of diced raw potatoes, a small can of tomatoes, a small onion fried with 1½-inch cube of fat salt pork, diced small, 3 tablespoons of butter, and ⅓ cup of cracker crumbs, salt and pepper and a few grains of nutmeg to taste, and cover with the strained fish stock made from trimmings. Bring to a boil and let simmer gently for 25 minutes. Finish with 2 tablespoons of kneaded butter, cooking 5 minutes longer; rectify the seasoning and serve in plates each containing a pilot cracker.

HADDOCK CHOWDER GERMAN STYLE
(*Delicious*)

Clean, skin, and bone a 3-lb. haddock. Make a fish stock with bones, skin, and trimmings, which, after the first boil, let simmer on the side of the range for 20 minutes. Meanwhile chop the fish meat, then pass through meat chopper, mix well with 6 rolled saltine crackers, salt, pepper, Cayenne pepper and nutmeg to taste, 2 tablespoons of melted butter, 1 beaten egg, and pass again through meat chopper; then shape in small balls. Fry 2 tablespoons of salt fat pork with 4 or 5 slices of onion for 10 minutes over a low fire and add to the strained fish stock (there should be 2 cups); then add the fish balls and 1 cup of small dices of raw potatoes and cook until potatoes are tender. Scald a quart of rich milk or 3 cups of milk and 1 cup of cream with a few thyme leaves, a tiny bit of bay leaf, a sprig of parsley, and 2 tablespoons of kneaded butter and strain over the fish stock. Rectify the seasonings, seasoning highly, boil once or twice, and serve very hot with a side dish of brown-bread and butter finger sandwiches.

LOBSTER CHOWDER

Remove the meat from a 2-lb. live lobster and cut in small dices. Cream 2 tablespoons of butter, add the liver of the lobster (green part) and 2 ordinary soda crackers, finely rolled. Scald a quart of milk with 3 small slices of onion, a small pinch of thyme leaves, a bit of bay leaf, a small crushed clove, 4 crushed peppercorns, and a sprig of parsley and strain over the creamed butter, stirring constantly, while pouring slowly. Cook the shells in a cup of cold water for 10 minutes over a hot fire, strain over the milk through a fine cloth, season to taste with salt, paprika (generously), and a few grains of nutmeg; then add the diced lobster meat. Boil once or twice, set aside and let simmer 10 minutes. Serve with toast.

OYSTER CHOWDER HOME STYLE

Strain a quart of freshly opened oysters and pour the liquor into a deep dish; let settle 5 minutes and pour very carefully into a double boiler, adding 3 cups of fresh milk and 2 cups of thin cream or 3 cups of fresh milk, 1 cup of water, and 1 cup of thick cream, a small pinch of thyme leaves, a bouquet garni, a tiny pinch of ground clove, 4 or 5 drops of onion juice, and a blade of mace. Bring to a boil, strain, and add the chopped oysters, reserving the soft parts. Boil again once or twice and strain. Just before serving, add the soft parts of the oysters parboiled in their own liquor, a tablespoon of kneaded butter, and 2 tablespoons of finely chopped parsley.

OYSTER GUMBO CHOWDER

Clean and pick over a quart of oysters, strain the liquor into a deep dish, let settle 5 minutes. Cook a generous tablespoon of finely chopped onion in ¼ cup of butter for 2 minutes, then add ½ can of okra, a small can of tomatoes, season with salt, pepper, and a few grains of Cayenne pepper and boil 5 minutes; add the strained oyster liquor and 5 cups of fish stock, boil once and let simmer gently for 10 to 15 minutes. Rectify the seasoning, add a tablespoon of sweet butter, and, just before serving, the parboiled whole oysters. Serve in plates each containing a saltine cracker.

SHRIMP OKRA GUMBO CREOLE

Heat 3 tablespoons of bacon drippings in a saucepan and cook in it 3 celery stalks, leaves minced fine, 6 small new green onions, minced fine, and 2 tablespoons of finely chopped cooked ham for 5 minutes, stirring once in a while; sprinkle with 2 tablespoons of flour, stir well, and moisten with 5 cups of boiling water, adding a small can of tomatoes, the strained liquor from a can of crab meat, and the strained liquor from a can of shrimps. Cook very gently, stirring often. Bone the crab meat and clean the shrimps, add to the mixture, then cook 15 minutes. Add a can of okra with the liquid and cook 10 minutes longer; season wth salt and pepper to taste and finish with a generous tablespoon of butter after rectifying seasonings of salt, pepper, and Cayenne pepper to taste. Serve in bowls with a side dish of hot steamed rice. This dish is even more delicious when reheated.

WHITEFISH CHOWDER

Boil a 2½-lb. piece of whitefish in 3 cups of salted water with a large onion finely chopped, a tablespoon of finely chopped celery, a bouquet garni, a small pinch of thyme leaves, and a small can of tomatoes. As soon as boiling, remove aside and let simmer for 20 minutes. Meanwhile, scald 1 cup of milk and 1 cup of thick cream with 2 tablespoons of kneaded butter and strain over the fish. Let continue simmering for 10 minutes. Strain, pressing a little through a fine sieve to obtain as much as possible of the solid parts, after removing the bouquet garni and the large bones. Place over the fire again and boil once, rectify the seasoning and finish with a generous tablespoon of shallot butter. Serve in plates containing each a crisp piece of toast.

FISH SOUPS

CLAM SOUP HOME STYLE

Remove a peck of clams from the shells as soon as opened, in a warm place, until the juice is prepared. Add 2 cups of hot milk to 2 cups of juice, well strained, thicken with a roux made from 1 tablespoon each of butter and flour; then add the hard parts of clams, chopped very fine, reserving the soft parts; season to taste with salt, pepper, and a few grains of Cayenne and nutmeg and bring to a boil, set aside and let simmer for 15 minutes. Strain through a fine cloth, set over the fire, and add a tablespoon of kneaded butter, boil once and add, just before serving, the soft parts in the boiling soup; sprinkle with finely chopped parsley and serve in plates each containing a toasted saltine cracker.

OYSTER SOUP DUTCH STYLE

Clean, pick over, chop, and parboil one quart of oysters in their own liquor; strain through a very fine cloth and add to the liquor enough water to make a quart of liquid. Brown 3 tablespoons of butter and add 3½ tablespoons of flour, blend well and pour on gradually, while stirring constantly, the oyster liquor; set over a hot fire, bring to a boil and remove aside to simmer slowly for 20 minutes. Skim thoroughly, season with salt, paprika, and celery salt and, just before serving, add a cup of scalded cream, seasoned to taste, and one tablespoon of sweet butter. Serve with crackers.

MOCK TURTLE SOUP I

1 calf's head	2 cups brown stock
5 cloves	½ cup butter
½ teaspoon peppercorns	½ cup flour
6 allspice berries	1 cup stewed and strained to-
2 sprigs of thyme	matoes or a small can
½ cup sliced onion	Madeira wine to taste
⅓ cup diced small carrot	Juice of ½ lemon

Clean and wash the calf's head; soak one hour in cold water to cover; cook until tender in 3 quarts of boiling salted water to which are added cloves, peppercorns, allspice berries, thyme, onion, and carrot. Lift out the head and reduce the cooking liquor to one quart; strain and cool. Melt and brown the butter, add flour and stir until well browned; then pour the brown stock on slowly and bring to the boiling point; add the reduced liquor, tomato, and lemon juice, simmer 10 minutes and add Royal Custard cut in small dices and six forcemeat balls (*see* FORCEMEAT AND FISH STUFFING). Finish with Madeira wine to taste, then season with salt and pepper and add a cup of diced meat from the face of the calf's head.

ROYAL CUSTARD

Beat 3 yolks and 1 whole egg slightly, add gradually, while stirring constantly, ½ cup of consommé seasoned to taste with salt, a tiny pinch of nutmeg, and a few grains of Cayenne pepper and pour into a small buttered square shallow mold and place in a pan containing hot water and set in a moderately hot oven until firm. Cool, remove from mold, and cut in small squares.

MOCK TURTLE SOUP II

1 calf's head	½ teaspoon peppercorns, slightly
4 lbs. knuckle of veal	bruised
1 lb. marrow bones	1 tiny pinch celery seed
4 quarts cold water	4 allspice berries
1 small sliced carrot	2 blades of mace
2 small sliced onions	½ teaspoon salt
3 sprigs of thyme	1½ tablespoons of butter
2 sprigs of marjoram	1½ tablespoons flour
1 small bay leaf	1½ tablespoons lemon juice
½ teaspoon ground clove	¼ cup sherry wine

Salt and pepper to taste

Clean and wash the calf's head, put in a kettle with veal and marrow bones, add cold water, cover, bring slowly to boiling point, and let simmer gently until the meat leaves the bones. Cut the meat from the face of the head in small dices—there should be a cupful—and set aside with the brains to use as a garnish. Put the tongue, remaining calf's head meat, and veal through the food chopper and return to the kettle containing the stock; then add the vegetables and seasonings and let simmer very gently for 2 hours. Strain, cool, remove all the fat from the surface of the broth, reheat, and add butter and flour browned together. Then add the meat, lemon juice, sherry wine, and salt and pepper to taste. Finish with Egg Balls and Royal Custard made as indicated in recipe above.

EGG BALLS

Mash the yolks of 3 hard-boiled eggs and add an equal measure of mashed calf's brains. Season highly with salt, pepper, and a few grains of Cayenne pepper and add enough slightly beaten egg to hold mixture together so that it may be shaped into small balls. Roll the balls in flour and sauté gently in plenty of butter.

COMPOUNDED FISH STEWS

BOUILLABAISSE MARSEILLAISE STYLE

AUTHOR'S NOTE

No wine or liquor enters into the concoction of this delightful chowder, or stew, whatever it may be called, which was first prepared in Marseilles, France. The original recipe calls for 12 different kinds of fish, the list of which follows with corresponding name in English between parentheses, and the name of the fish which may be substituted for those not available in any part of America.

RASCASSE (unknown in America). Sea Bass may be substituted.
SARD (unknown in America). Substitute Haddock or Codfish.
LANGOUSTE (Spiny Lobster).
GRONDIN (Red Gurnard).
GALIENTTE (unknown in America). Substitute Grouper.

DORADE (Dory, also sometimes called John Dory).
BAUDROIE (Frog-Fish, also sometimes called Sea-Devil).
CONGRE (Conger, Conger Eel).
TURBOT (Turbot, often erroneously called Halibut; Turbotin, a young Turbot).
MERLAN (Whiting).
FIELAN (unknown in America). Small eel may be used.
ROUQUIER (unknown in America). Eel may be used.

Assuming you have all the necessary fish or substitutes, which must be of a firm flesh, the procedure is as follows.

Take about 6 pounds of the above-mentioned fish or their substitutes in approximately equal amounts for each variety. Cut the large fish into pieces, leave the small ones entire. Place in a pan a generous ½ cup of good olive oil and add to it 4 ozs. of minced onions, 2 ozs. chopped fine leeks (white only), 2 medium-sized fresh tomatoes (pressed, peeled, and slightly crushed), 4 whole cloves of garlic (crushed), 1 teaspoon of finely chopped parsley, 1 generous pinch of saffron (drugstore), 1 bay leaf, 1 small sprig of sarriette (common marum savory found in the field or drugstore), 1 pinch of the top of fresh fennel, salt and pepper to taste.

Place all the above ingredients in the pan with the exception of the whiting and red gurnard, which being very tender should be added when the bouillabaisse has been boiling from 8 to 10 minutes.

Pour in sufficient cold water to cover the fish; season with salt and pepper to taste and let cook on a hot fire for 12 to 15 minutes. *The Bouillabaisse Is Ready.*

Dress up some slices of plain bread, not toasted or fried, but plain slices, on a hot deep platter, preferably round; pour the liquid over these slices and, on another platter, dress up the fish, surrounding the whole with pieces of langouste or spiny lobster.

This recipe is the one used in Marseilles where the writer has been a Chef; is identical to that followed by Maître Escoffier; exactly the same as the one given by Master Caillat and identical to the one given by Maurice Graillot, Chef of the Touring Club of France, and also to the formula of Urbain Dubois, onetime Chef to the former King of Prussia, who became the Kaiser.

> . . . Horaça, se l'avies tastado,
> Ben luen de l'ave blastèmado,
> L'auries douna toun amitié
> Auries mies estima ta testa courounado
> D'un rez d'ayet que de lauzié.
>
> FABRE

Which translated into English means:

> Horace had you tasted it,
> Far from speaking ill of it,
> You would have been better adorned
> And might have been on friendly terms
> With a chain of garlic instead of laurel.

BOUILLABAISSE PARISIAN STYLE

Into the preparation of the Bouillabaisse Parisian Style, the following fish enter:

MOULES, Mussels.
ROUGETS, Red Gurnard.
GRONDIN, a specie of Red Gurnard.
SOLES (unknown in America, unless imported). Lemon Sole or Flounder may be substituted.
VIVES (unknown in America, except a short Wever). Eel may be substituted.
MERLANS, Whiting.
CONGRE, Conger Eel.
LANGOUSTE, Spiny Lobster.

Place in a large skillet 6 tablespoons of good olive oil and add the following ingredients: 2 large onions, finely chopped, 2 small leeks, using only the white parts, finely minced. Cook over a hot fire, taking care not to color; then add one bottle of good white wine; season with salt and pepper, and add a small pinch of saffron, 1 bouquet garni, 3 medium-sized fresh tomatoes, peeled, pressed, and then crushed, or use the equivalent of thick tomato purée, 2 small cloves of garlic, bruised. Bring to the boiling point, then reduce the fire and cook for 15 to 20 minutes longer. Meanwhile, select the fish, allowing 1 lb. of fish for each guest and in approximately equal amounts from each variety; place 6 tablespoons of olive oil in a deep skillet, add the fish well-cleaned, washed, sponged, and cut in 2-inch pieces, mussels included, after being scraped and well washed, but not removed from the shells, in other words "shell and all"; sprinkle over, 1 tablespoon of finely chopped parsley and cook about 5 minutes, tossing the skillet once in a while; then turn into the hot broth. Boil 10 minutes over a hot fire, set aside, thicken the liquid with a generous tablespoon of kneaded butter, stir gently, while simmering for a while, dress the fish on a hot round platter with a little of the broth, serving the remainder aside. Serve with a side dish of Jocko toast, which consists of bread toasted in oven, lightly rubbed with garlic, and slightly moistened with the fish broth.

FISH STEW CANOTIÈRE

Clean, wash 1½ lbs. of carp; skin, wash 1½ lbs. of small eels; cut both in 2-inch pieces and place in a kettle; cover with equal parts of white wine and fish stock, light a pony glass of good brandy and pour over the wine, let it burn until exhausted; season to taste with salt and pepper and add a tiny bit of bay leaf, 1 small onion, cut in slices, 3 or 4 slices of carrot, 1 bouquet garni, 1 clove, and a small stalk of celery diced small. Cover, bring to a boil, and remove aside to simmer gently for 15 to 20 minutes. Lift out the fish, dress on a hot round platter; keep hot while reducing the cooking liquor or broth to half, rectifying the seasoning and incorporating 4 table-spoons of butter (more or less) gradually, while beating with a wire whisk, until the sauce is creamy and unctuous. Garnish with small white onions, glazed in butter, small fried whitebait, fried in butter, mushrooms also fried in butter, shrimp and crayfish cooked in white wine court bouillon (*see* How To Boil Fish). This garnishing is optional.

FISH STEW HOME STYLE

Clean, wash, and cut in 2-inch pieces 1 lb. each of pike, halibut, or any other similar fish, sponge well and roll in salted, peppered flour. Place in a kettle ¼ cup of diced celery, ½ cup sliced carrot, ¼ cup sliced onion, 1½ cups of diced raw potatoes, barely cover with cold water and add a bouquet garni, 2 small cloves, a sliver of garlic, and a dash of nutmeg. Cover and bring rapidly to a boil, cook for 5 minutes, then add the fish with a small can of shrimps, cleaned and well drained, and cook very gently on the side of the range until the fish is done and vegetables are tender. The liquid will have reduced during the cooking process. Rectify the seasoning. Reduce the liquor a little or, better, remove a little if too thin and add a tablespoon of kneaded butter. Boil once or twice, add a tablespoon of finely chopped parsley, and dress on a hot deep round platter.

FISH STEW MARINIÈRE

Cut in 2½-inch pieces 1 carp, 1 pike, 1 eel (skinned) so as to obtain 3 lbs. of cleaned, washed, and sponged fish. Place in a copiously buttered kettle, barely cover with equal quantities of red and white wine (either kind alone may be used, but the mixture is much preferable because of the tannin contained in red wine), and add 1 small onion (sliced), 2 small cloves, 1 small carrot (sliced), 1 bouquet garni, 6 peppercorns, a blade of mace, a few thyme leaves, a small stalk of celery (diced small), and salt and a few grains of Cayenne to taste. Cover and bring rapidly to a boil; remove aside and let simmer slowly for 15 to 20 minutes. Lift out the fish, dress on a hot platter, keep hot. Strain the cooking broth, place over the fire, add a tablespoon of kneaded butter, boil once or twice, remove aside and add a drained small can of small mushrooms. Return the fish to the sauce, let stand a few minutes, rectify the seasoning, finish with a generous tablespoon of sweet butter, and pour fish and sauce over a hot round platter. Sprinkle a little finely chopped parsley over and serve very hot.

FISH STEW NORMAND STYLE

Clean, wash, and sponge well 1 lb. each of flounder, eel, red gurnard or any other kind of white-fleshed fish available—there should be 4 lbs. Cut in 2½-inch pieces and place in a copiously buttered kettle, sprinkle with salt and pepper to taste, and barely cover with cider. Burn over a pony glass of Calvados or applejack, and add 1 tiny bit of bay leaf, a few thyme leaves, 1 clove, a small onion (sliced), a small carrot (also sliced), a tablespoon of diced white celery, and a small bunch of tied parsley. Cover and bring rapidly to a boil, remove aside and let simmer slowly for 15 to 20 minutes. Lift out the fish, dress on a hot platter, keep hot. Reduce the cooking broth to half, and add 4 or 5 tablespoons of fresh heavy cream. Boil once or twice, rectify the seasoning, and pour over the fish. It is optional to garnish with small mushrooms cooked in butter and well drained, mussels and small oysters cooked in fish stock, and small triangles of bread fried in butter.

FISH STEW RUSSIAN STYLE

(Cold)

(A Fine Summer Dish)

Put in a kettle 2 quarts of cold water, 2 cups of wine vinegar, 1 large onion (sliced), 2 small cloves, 1 teaspoon of peppercorns (crushed slightly), a generous blade of mace, a small pinch of thyme leaves, 1 small bay leaf, and about 2½ lbs. of fish trimmings. Season to taste with salt and a few grains each of Cayenne pepper and nutmeg. Cover, bring to a rapid boil, then set aside to simmer for 2 or 3 hours. Strain through a fine cloth and if the weather is hot and you desire to keep the preparation for a week, add a tablespoon of granulated gelatin, softened in a little cold water.

Meanwhile, cut in 2½-inch pieces, 1 lb. each of skate, small turbot, flounder, and salmon, and cook in salted water, not to excess, but to the point where the fish is firm and the gelatin remains in the fish and is not distributed in the cooking water. Drain, pour a little of the still hot liquor of the first cooking in the bottom of a deep earthenware dish; place a layer of fish, then a layer of the liquor and a few cooked shrimps or pieces of lobster, crayfish tails, slices of gherkins, thin slices of peeled lemon, capers, etc., as available, according to taste and fancy and repeat layers until the dish is full. Let cool and set in Frigidaire or refrigerator until wanted. Serve with a salad of your choice.

FISH RECIPES

"What is understood by food?

"The popular answer is: Food is everything that nourishes us. The scientific answer is: We understand by food the substances which, submitted to the stomach, can be assimilated by digestion, and repair the losses which the human body suffers by the wear and tear of life.

"The human body is a machine far more complicated than the most expensive automobile. It deserves at least as much care as you give your car. Probably you know a lot about automobiles. You have driven them, tinkered with them, tested them, to see how much mileage they will give on a gallon of gas. Have you ever asked yourself how much 'mileage' you get out of yourself? What kind of 'fuel' is best for you? Whether you need an overhauling now and then so your gears don't click? You can buy a new car for a few hundred dollars. You can't buy yourself a new body, or trade your old one in. It is a good plan, therefore, to take care of your body, and to be especially careful of the 'fuel' you run on. Many don't do that. It is not surprising that after a few years they end up on the scrap heap. . . . You are careful to use the best oil and fuel you can get for your automobile. But—you will pile stuff into your body that you wouldn't throw into an iron pot."

HAL COFFMAN

BASS

The following recipes may be adapted to any kind of bass, such as black bass, lake bass, sea bass, and others.

BAKED FILLET OF BASS
(*Serves One*)

Sprinkle a fillet of bass (*see* MEANING OF THE WORD "FILLET" IN COOKERY) with salt and pepper to taste and arrange in an individual shallow pan, copiously buttered. Cover with a buttered paper and bake 12 to 15 minutes, according to size, in a hot oven (400°), basting often with melted butter. Dress on a hot platter, garnish with a small bunch of crisp young watercress and a quarter of a small lemon. Serve with any kind of sauce desired, or simply as is.

BOILED BASS NEW ENGLAND

Use vinegar court bouillon, enough to cover 3 lbs. of bass, adding a blade of mace. Sew up the fish in a piece of clean mosquito netting, or cheesecloth. Heat slowly for the first 20 minutes, then boil rapidly for a few minutes. Unwrap the fish, dress on a hot platter, remove the skin and pour over a cup of DRAWN BUTTER SAUCE, page 38, based upon the broth in which the fish was boiled, garnish with sliced lemon and green, crisp, curled parsley. Serve with a side dish of plain boiled potatoes.

FILLET OF BASS MEUNIÈRE

Salt, pepper, and roll the fillets in flour. Sauté in 3 tablespoons of hot butter until light golden brown on both sides. Dress on a hot service platter. Heat 3 tablespoons of butter until brown, squeeze the juice of a medium-sized lemon over the fish, sprinkle finely chopped parsley, and pour the brown butter rapidly over the fish. The dampness of the parsley added to the acid of the lemon juice will cause the butter to foam, which will disappear rapidly if not served immediately.

FILLET OF BASS AU GRATIN

Clean, fillet, wash, and sponge the fish well, there should be 3 lbs. Roll in salted, peppered flour. Place in a well-buttered earthenware baking dish a generous teaspoon of finely chopped parsley and one generous teaspoon of finely chopped onion, well mixed; lay the fillets on this and moisten with ⅓ cup of fish stock made from the trimmings of the fish, dot here and there with a tablespoon of butter. Cover with bread crumbs mixed with grated cheese, sprinkle lightly with melted butter, cover with buttered paper, and set in a hot oven for 15 to 20 minutes. Remove the paper and cook 5 minutes longer to brown. Serve right from the baking dish.

FILLET OF BASS MORNAY

Parboil as many fillets as required in sufficient fish stock made out of the trimmings and heads barely to cover the fish. Drain. Dress the fish on a well-buttered baking dish, cover with MORNAY SAUCE, page 43, and set in a hot oven to glaze. Serve right from the baking dish.

FILLET OF BASS SUZETTE

Operate as indicated in recipe for FILLET OF BASS MORNAY, above, laying the fish on a small layer of crab meat mixed with a teaspoon of finely chopped shallots, first browned lightly in butter. Just before glazing, lay strips of red pimento across the top lattice-like and a well-washed caper in each space.

FILLET OF BASS CREOLE

Prepare and cook 6 fillets as indicated in recipe for FILLET OF BASS MORNAY, page 43. Dress on a hot platter, covered with a layer of

CREOLE SAUCE, page 37, and top each fillet with a small mushroom cooked in butter and well drained.

BROILED FILLET OF BASS

Marinate the fillets—there should be 6—in 3 tablespoons of seasoned oil, turning once in a while for 15 minutes. Place the fillets on a double broiler which set on the rack of the broiling oven, broil, turning and basting often. Serve with plain melted butter.

BLACKFISH

In addition to the following recipes, the various methods of preparation of bass may be adapted to this fine fish, as well as those of mackerel, pompano, and similar fish.

BAKED BLACKFISH IN MILK
(OR CREAM)

Clean, trim, remove the head and tail, wash and sponge a 3½-lb. blackfish. Season with salt and pepper to taste. Place in a well-buttered baking dish, dot here and there with 2 tablespoons of butter and add 1 small bay leaf, 1 crushed clove, 3 slices of onion, and 1 sprig of parsley. Cover with cold milk and bake in a hot oven for 20 to 25 minutes. Lift out the fish; dress on a hot platter, keep hot. Prepare CREAM SAUCE I, page 36, using the milk in which the fish has been baked.

BAKED BLACKFISH CREOLE

Prepare a 3½-lb. blackfish as indicated for BAKED BLACKFISH IN MILK, above. Slice a small onion, 1 small green pepper and brown lightly in 2 tablespoons of butter. Add a small can of tomatoes to the onion. Season with salt, pepper, a few grains of Cayenne pepper, a few thyme leaves, and a tiny pinch of nutmeg. Bring to a boil, pour into a buttered baking dish, and lay the fish on this. Cover with a buttered paper and set in a hot oven for 20 to 25 minutes. Remove the paper and add 1 tablespoon of butter and continue cooking 5 minutes longer. Rectify the seasonings and serve right from the baking dish.

BAKED BLACKFISH WITH MUSHROOMS

In a well-buttered baking dish, place ½ cup of finely sliced raw mushrooms and sprinkle with a tablespoon of parsley and onion chopped together finely. Lay the 3½-lb. blackfish, cleaned, washed, and trimmed on this, moisten with ½ cup of fish stock made of the trimmings; dot here and there with 2 tablespoons of butter and a teaspoon of kneaded butter; cover with a buttered paper and set in a hot oven for 20 minutes. Remove the paper, season to taste with salt, pepper, and a few grains of nutmeg and continue cooking for 10 minutes, basting once in a while. Serve right from the baking dish with a side dish of your preferred salad with French dressing.

BROILED FILLET OF BLACKFISH
TARTARE SAUCE

Operate as indicated in recipe for BROILED FILLET OF BASS, page 97. Serve with a side dish of TARTARE SAUCE, page 52, and a side dish of cucumber salad with French dressing.

FRIED FILLET OF BLACKFISH JULIENNE

Cut in small strips (julienne-like) of ½-inch width, a cleaned, filleted, washed, and well-sponged 3½-lb. blackfish; dip in salted and white peppered milk, roll in flour, and, when ready to serve, place in a wire basket and plunge into very hot deep fat for not quite a minute; lift out rapidly, drain, dress bushlike on a hot platter covered with a napkin, garnish with fried curled parsley and quartered lemon. Serve with a side dish of DRAWN BUTTER SAUCE, page 38, or LEMON BUTTER SAUCE, page 42, or a cold sauce such as TARTARE SAUCE, page 52, and a salad of your choice.

BLUEFISH

BAKED BLUEFISH RICHARDIN

Clean, trim, remove the collar bone, and wash a 3½-lb. bluefish. Place in a buttered baking dish. Season with salt and pepper mixed with a little curry powder to taste and add a tablespoon each of onion, parsley, chives, and shallots, finely chopped and well mixed. Work in 2 tablespoons of butter until creamy, add the size of a hazelnut portion of anchovy paste and spread over the fish. Set the dish covered with a buttered paper into a hot oven (400°) and cook for half an hour, basting often with the butter. Meanwhile, to half a cup of fish stock made from the trimmings, add ⅓ cup of almonds, blanched and chopped coarsely, and 1 tablespoon of washed capers; bring to a boil and set aside on the range to simmer gently. When the fish is ready, pour the mixture over and sprinkle with freshly made coarse bread crumbs and continue cooking until crumbs are browned. Serve the fish in the baking dish set on a platter covered with a napkin.

BAKED BLUEFISH COMMODORE BENEDICT

Split and bone a bluefish of 3 to 3½ lbs., place in a well-buttered baking pan and set in a moderately hot oven covered with a buttered paper, basting once in a while with extra butter. Meanwhile, cream ¼ cup of butter, add the yolks of 3 eggs, and, when well mixed, 2 tablespoons each of onion, capers, sweet and sour gherkins, all finely chopped; 2 tablespoons of strained lemon juice, 1 tablespoon of tarragon vinegar, salt and paprika to taste. Sprinkle the fish with salt, then spread with the mixture and continue baking until done. Remove the fish to a hot platter, pour over the sauce after rectifying seasonings and surround the edges with small plain boiled potato balls, cucumber ribbons, lemon slices, and a small bunch of green parsley.

BAKED BLUEFISH CREOLE

Clean, cut off fins, remove the large bone, and wash a 3-lb. fish and place in a buttered baking dish, the bottom of which is covered with CREOLE SAUCE, page 37. Cover with a buttered paper and set in a moderately hot oven (350°) for 30 long minutes. Remove the paper, sprinkle over buttered bread crumbs, and cook 10 to 15 minutes longer. Serve right from the baking dish.

BAKED BLUEFISH KNICKERBOCKER

Prepare a 3-lb. bluefish as indicated above. Rub with salt and pepper. In a buttered earthenware baking dish, place the following well mixed: ⅔ cup of sliced raw mushrooms, a tablespoon of finely chopped green pepper, a teaspoon of finely chopped shallots and as much parsley; lay the fish on this and barely cover with strained fish stock made from the trimmings of the fish and to which is added a half wineglass of white wine. Dot here and there with 2 tablespoons of butter. Set covered with a buttered paper in a moderately hot oven (350°) and cook 25 minutes. Remove the paper, add 1 tablespoon of kneaded butter and cook 10 minutes longer, basting constantly. Dress the baking dish on a platter covered with a napkin and serve with a side dish of baked stuffed cucumber.

BROILED BLUEFISH MAÎTRE D'HÔTEL

Split open from the back, remove the large bone, trim, wash, and sponge well a 3-lb. bluefish. Roll in oil or melted butter; place on a double broiler which set on the rack of the broiling oven and broil, turning and basting often with melted butter. Turn onto a hot platter, dot here and there with MAÎTRE D'HÔTEL BUTTER, page 57, garnish with quartered lemon and fresh parsley.

BLUEFISH BONNE FEMME

Sprinkle the bottom of a well-buttered baking dish with a scant ½ cup of sliced raw mushrooms mixed with ½ teaspoon of finely chopped shallots and same amount of finely chopped parsley. Lay on this the 3-lb. bluefish prepared as indicated for above recipe, seasoned with salt and pepper to taste and moistened with 4 or 5 tablespoons of white wine (use lemon juice if desired) and a scant half cup of stock made from the trimmings and thickened with ½ teaspoon of flour. Set in a moderately hot oven, covered with a buttered paper, for 25 minutes. Remove the paper and cook 5 minutes longer. Dress the fish on a hot service platter, keep hot while adding, bit by bit to the sauce on the range, 3 tablespoons of butter, stirring gently meanwhile. Pour the sauce over the fish and glaze under the flame of the broiling oven. Serve at once without garnishing.

BROILED BLUEFISH

Prepare a 3-lb. bluefish as indicated in recipe for BROILED BLUEFISH MAÎTRE D'HÔTEL, page 101, and marinate in salted, peppered oil or melted butter for 15 minutes. Cook as indicated and served with a side dish of your favorite sauce.

BROILED BLUEFISH OYSTER SAUCE

Prepare, cook, and dress a 3-lb. bluefish as indicated in recipe for BROILED BLUEFISH MAÎTRE D'HÔTEL, page 101. Serve with a side dish of OYSTER SAUCE, page 45.

BAKED FILLET OF BLUEFISH AU GRATIN

Place 6 salted and peppered fillets of bluefish in a well-buttered baking dish. Prepare a stock from the trimmings of the fish, adding 1 teaspoon of finely chopped shallots and 1 teaspoon of finely chopped parsley, sprinkle with a teaspoon of flour and boil once, let simmer gently 10 minutes, and strain over the fillets. Surround the fish with a drained small can of mushrooms, pour over 3 tablespoons of white wine and sprinkle with bread crumbs sprinkled with melted butter. Set, covered with a buttered paper, in a moderately hot oven (350°) for 20 minutes, remove the paper and continue cooking for 10 minutes or until crumbs are brown. Serve right from the baking dish, sprinkling over a few drops of lemon juice, and a little finely chopped parsley. A side dish of plain boiled small potato balls will not be amiss.

CATFISH

BOILED CATFISH BUNGALOW

Pound in a mortar 2 small cloves of garlic with a scant teaspoon of salt, pepper, and nutmeg, moisten with a glass of white wine and a scant ½ cup of stock made from the trimmings of the fish and well strained. Pour the mixture into a fish kettle and add 3½ to 4 lbs. of cleaned, trimmed, and washed catfish. Bring to a rapid boil, reduce the fire or set aside on the range and let gently simmer for 10 to 15 minutes. Meanwhile, prepare a roux with a tablespoon of butter and one of flour, moistening with as little fish stock as possible; add to the fish in the fish kettle and cook very slowly for 5 or 6 minutes. Dress the fish carefully on a hot platter; keep hot; strain the cooking liquor and reduce to half volume over a very hot fire, incorporate gradually and stirring meanwhile 4 tablespoons of butter and off the fire 2 egg yolks alternately with the butter. Pour this sauce, after rectifying the seasoning, over the fish; garnish with small triangles of bread fried in butter and serve with a side dish of French fried potatoes.

BOILED CATFISH ENGLISH STYLE

Clean, wash, and marinate for 2 hours 3½ to 4 lbs. of catfish in MARINADE I (*see* MARINADES, Volume I). Drain and put the fish in a fish kettle, cover with stock made from the trimmings of the fish and add a tiny bit of crushed garlic, 6 small white onions, a small bouquet garni, a teaspoon each of finely chopped shallot and chives, and set over a hot fire to come to a boil. Remove aside and let simmer very gently for 15 minutes. Dress the fish on a hot platter and keep hot. Melt 4 tablespoons of butter, cook in it a scant cup of peeled, finely sliced fresh mushrooms and add the strained cooking liquor, reduced to half volume. Boil once, finish with ½ cup of heated thick cream, stirring well until boiling. Pour part immediately over the fish and serve the rest aside with plain boiled potatoes and a cucumber salad with French dressing.

BAKED FILLET OF CATFISH BONNE FEMME

Prepare the fish and operate as indicated in recipe for BLUEFISH BONNE FEMME, page 101.

BOILED CATFISH IN CREAM

Clean, trim, split in two from the back, remove the large bone, and wash thoroughly 3½ lbs. of catfish or more, taking into consideration that 50 per cent loss in weight occurs in this fish. Rub well with mixture of salt and pepper and a few grains of nutmeg, lay flat in a buttered baking dish and barely cover with one cup of thin cream or as much unsweetened milk; then add a bouquet garni, a clove, and a small blade of mace. Place cover on the pan, bring to a boil over a hot fire, reduce the heat, and continue cooking very slowly for 15 minutes. Dress the fish on a hot platter and keep hot while preparing CREAM SAUCE III, page 37, using the liquid in which the fish has been cooked. Pour the sauce over the fish, decorate with slices of hard-boiled eggs, and serve with a side dish of plain boiled potatoes.

BROILED CATFISH MAÎTRE D'HÔTEL

Operate exactly as indicated in recipe for BROILED BLUEFISH MAÎTRE D'HÔTEL, page 101, covering the fish with slightly melted MAÎTRE D'HÔTEL BUTTER, page 57.

BROILED CATFISH ANCHOVY SAUCE

Operate exactly as indicated in recipe for BROILED BLUEFISH MAÎTRE D'HÔTEL, page 101, using ANCHOVY SAUCE II, page 33, instead of Maître d'Hôtel Butter.

FRIED CATFISH HOME STYLE

Clean, trim, fillet, wash, and sponge well 4 lbs. of catfish; rub with salt and pepper and sauté over a moderate fire in 4 tablespoons of butter or bacon drippings, turning often to golden brown both sides. Lift out well drained; dress on a hot platter covered with a large can of tomatoes, heated and strained. Squeeze over the fish a small lemon, sprinkle with finely chopped parsley and pour over only the well-heated butter from the frying pan.

SAUTÉED FILLET OF CATFISH WITH MUSHROOMS

Prepare and cook the same amount of fish as indicated in recipe for FRIED CATFISH HOME STYLE, above, and dress on a hot platter covered with a layer of sautéed sliced mushrooms. Mix up the butter from the pan in which the fish was cooked with that of the mushrooms, heat well and add a tablespoon of finely chopped shallot and parsley. Pour over the fish.

SAUTÉED FILLET OF CATFISH CREOLE

Prepare and cook the same quantity of fish as indicated in recipe for FRIED CATFISH HOME STYLE, page 106. Dress on a hot platter. Garnish with tomatoes stuffed with crab meat and serve a side dish of SHRIMP SAUCE, page 47.

CODFISH

Codfish may be prepared in a thousand and one ways by boiling, frying, sautéing, baking, roasting, grilling, or steaming, and all the sauces which are applied to the halibut, flounder, or turbot, may be used for this healthful, inexpensive, delicious, and universally known fish.

BAKED FRESH CODFISH IN CREAM
(Use Leftover)

A good way to utilize remnants of cooked fish. Prepare a cup and a half of CREAM SAUCE I, page 36. Cover the bottom of a small buttered baking dish with 1½ cups of flaked cooked fish, sprinkle with salt and pepper to taste and pour over ⅔ cup of the cream sauce. Repeat this operation with the rest of the fish and cream sauce. Cover with buttered bread crumbs and bake in a hot oven until the bread crumbs are brown.

NOTE: Haddock, halibut, or any other kind of cooked fish, especially the white-fleshed fish, may be prepared in this way. For variation, individual baking dishes or ramekins may be used, or the fish may be spread in scallop shells or in patty shells. In the latter case a few sliced cooked mushrooms may be added.

BAKED CODFISH OYSTER STUFFING

Clean and sponge with a damp cloth, a 3½- to 4-lb. fish; slit open the side; brush the inside with vinegar or lemon juice and fill with a stuffing made as follows: To a cup of cracker crumbs, add half a cup or more of melted butter or bacon drippings, mixed with ½ teaspoon salt and pepper to taste and a tablespoon of finely chopped parsley; then add a tablespoon (optional) of finely chopped raw mushrooms, 1 tablespoon of finely chopped green peppers. Clean the oysters, removing the tough muscles, and add the soft parts of the oysters to the crumbs, moistening with oyster liquor. Pack this well-mixed stuffing into the opening of the fish, sew up, place the fish in a well-buttered baking pan and cover with a small can of tomatoes. Place cover on the pan and set in a moderately hot oven (375°) for 25 minutes; reduce the heat (to 325°) and cook 15 minutes longer. Serve right from the baking dish with a side dish of OYSTER SAUCE, page 45.

BAKED CODFISH NEW ORLEANS

Prepare and stuff a 3½- to 4-lb. codfish as indicated for recipe above, using FISH STUFFING IV (*see* FORCEMEAT AND FISH STUFFING). Place the fish in a well-buttered baking dish and pour over a small can of tomatoes with a teaspoon of finely chopped shallots, 1 teaspoon of finely chopped parsley, and ½ cup of sliced raw mushrooms. Adjust cover and set in a hot oven (400°) and cook for 20 minutes; lift the cover and add a tablespoon of kneaded butter and 1 tablespoon of butter. Cover and cook 20 minutes longer in a moderately hot oven (325°). Serve right from the baking dish.

BAKED CODFISH NEW ENGLAND

Lay a 3½-lb. piece of fresh codfish in cold salted water for ½ hour; then wipe dry and stuff with a fish forcemeat made of a generous half cup of bread crumbs, salted and peppered, 2 tablespoons of chopped salt pork, 1 tablespoon of mixed aromatic herbs (parsley, marjoram, thyme, a few leaves of tarragon herbs, etc.), a suggestion of onion chopped very fine, 1 scant tablespoon of butter, and a hazelnut portion of anchovy paste mixed together and the whole bound with a well-beaten egg. Lay the stuffed fish in a buttered baking pan and pour over 3 tablespoons of melted butter, mixed with the juice of half a lemon. Bake in a moderate oven (350°) for 35 minutes, more or less, until the fish is done, basting frequently, lest the fish brown too fast. Add a little butter and water or fish stock if the sauce thickens too much. When the fish is done, remove to a hot platter, strain the gravy over after rectifying seasoning, and stir in, off the fire, 2 egg yolks, one by one, 1 tablespoon of finely chopped parsley, and a tablespoon of capers. Serve piping hot.

CODFISH INDIAN STYLE

Wipe dry, place a 3½-lb. fish in a fish kettle and cover with cold salted water, adding 1 small onion, sliced, a bouquet garni, 1 small clove, ½ dozen thin slices of carrots, and 6 peppercorns. Bring to a rapid boil and remove immediately aside. Let simmer gently allowing 8 to 10 minutes for each pound of fish. Drain well. Dress on a hot platter, on which there is a border of plain boiled rice and pour over the fish CREAM SAUCE I, page 36, to which is added, during its preparation, a scant tablespoon of curry powder (more or less according to taste), diluted with a little cold milk. Dust over the rice a little paprika mixed with very finely chopped parsley.

CODFISH À LA LYONNAISE

Sauté in 3 tablespoons of butter, 2 small onions (finely chopped), and 4 raw potatoes (peeled and thinly sliced) until beginning to color; then add 2½ to 3 lbs. of codfish already boiled in plain salt water as indicated for recipe above, then flaked. Cook together five minutes; then sprinkle over salt and pepper to taste and a little finely chopped parsley. Cook 5 minutes longer and when ready to serve, sprinkle over all a tablespoon of tarragon vinegar. Dress on a hot round platter; surround the fish with small triangles of bread fried in butter.

CODFISH PIE ENGLISH STYLE

(Use Fresh or Leftover Cooked Codfish)

NOTE: This dish is a favorite one in Cornwall and Devonshire and a huge pie is often served at festivities. It is also an unusual way to use leftover cooked codfish or any kind of fish similar to the cod, as haddock, halibut, etc.

Cut in portion sizes 2 lbs. of fresh codfish or have the equivalent of cooked codfish. Add to the fish ¾ of a pound of diced fat pork, ½ cup of finely sliced cooked mushrooms, and ½ cup of plain boiled small white onions. Mix well and gently and pour over 1½ cups of CREAM SAUCE I, page 36, well seasoned with salt, pepper, and a few grains of Cayenne pepper. Pour in a well-buttered deep earthenware baking dish or deep pie dish, dot here and there with 2 tablespoons butter, cover with a layer of pie dough, making a few incisions to let the steam escape, and set in a moderately hot (350°) oven until the crust is golden browned. Serve right from the dish.

CODFISH PUDDING

(Use Fresh or Leftover Cooked Codfish)

Flake carefully and bone thoroughly 2 cups of cooked codfish, mix well with 2 or 3 tablespoons of melted butter, to which add, one by one, 3 whole eggs, beating meanwhile, 2 tablespoons of fine bread crumbs, a dash of nutmeg, salt and pepper to taste, and a scant teaspoon each of finely chopped parsley and chives. Fill a well-buttered border mold and sprinkle the top lightly with buttered crumbs. Set in a pan containing hot water in a moderately hot oven (350°) for 45 minutes. Unmold on a hot round platter. Serve with a side dish of ANCHOVY SAUCE II, page 33.

CODFISH FLEMISH STYLE

Clean, cut in 1-inch thick slices, wash, sponge, and rub with salt and pepper a 3-lb. piece of codfish. Arrange in a well-buttered baking dish and sprinkle over a little nutmeg to taste. Barely cover with fish stock, to which add a scant wineglass of white wine and spread over the fish a teaspoon each of shallots, parsley, chives, and onions, all finely chopped and well mixed with a teaspoon of tarragon herbs, also finely chopped. Set on each end a ring of peeled lemon. Place the baking dish on a very hot stove, bring to a boil, remove aside immediately, dot here and there with 2 tablespoons of butter, cover with a buttered paper, and set in a hot oven for 15 minutes.

Remove the paper and cook 5 minutes longer. Drain the fish and dress on a hot platter. Keep hot. Pour the cooking liquor in a saucepan, set on a hot fire, and add 2 or 3 tablespoons of coarsely crumbed saltine crackers. Boil once or twice, stirring once in a while and pour over the fish. Serve with a side dish of plain boiled potatoes.

CREAMED CODFISH AU GRATIN

Prepare and cook the fish as indicated in recipe for CODFISH IN-DIAN STYLE, page 109, adding to the fish 3 hard-boiled eggs, chopped coarsely. Turn the mixture into a well-buttered baking dish, sprinkle with fine bread crumbs, then generously with melted butter. Brown rapidly under the flame of the broiling oven. Serve right from the baking dish with a side dish of your favorite salad.

FILLET OF CODFISH BAMBOCHE

Cut in strips, lengthwise and ½ inch in width, julienne-like, 6 fillets of codfish (see MEANING OF THE WORD "FILLET" IN COOKERY). Season with salt and pepper to taste; dip in cold milk, then roll in flour, and twist carefully each strip in spiral shape. When ready to serve, place in a wire basket and plunge rapidly in boiling-hot deep fat for one minute or until brown and crisp. Lift out, drain, and dress pyramid shape in the center of a hot round platter, covered with a ring made of a mixture of leftover cooked vegetables, heated in CREAM SAUCE I, page 36, and well drained. Garnish with quartered lemon and surround the edge of the platter, close against the ring of creamed vegetables, with plain boiled potato balls, well buttered, and rolled in finely chopped parsley. Serve with a side dish either of Cream Sauce I or plain, hot, melted butter.

FRIED CODFISH STEAK ENGLISH STYLE

Cut a 3-lb. piece of fresh codfish in equal-sized slices. Season with salt and pepper to taste, roll in melted butter, then in fine cracker dust. Melt in a deep skillet 4 or 5 tablespoons of butter and place the fish steak in it. Cook, turning often to prevent scorching and ensure uniformity. Dress the slices on a hot platter, overlapping one another, garnish with fried green parsley and quartered lemon, and serve with a side dish of MAÎTRE D'HÔTEL BUTTER, page 57, and a side dish of diced cucumber salad with sour cream dressing.

FRIED CODFISH STEAK CREOLE

Prepare and cook the fish as indicated in recipe for FRIED CODFISH STEAK ENGLISH STYLE, page 111. Dress on a hot platter, overlapping, and surround with CREOLE SAUCE, page 37. Serve with a side dish of your favorite salad, with French dressing.

GRILLED DEVILED CODFISH STEAK

Have six slices of fresh codfish of equal size, 1-inch thick, sprinkle with salt and pepper and marinate for ½ hour in the following mixture: ¾ cup of oil, 1 tablespoon prepared mustard, a few grains of Cayenne pepper, a small pinch of curry powder, a tablespoon of wine vinegar, a tiny bit of crushed garlic, ½ teaspoon paprika, and a teaspoon of prepared horseradish, the whole well mixed. Lift out the fish, roll in bread crumbs, sprinkle with oil, place on a double broiler, set on the rack of the broiling oven, and grill slowly, turning often and sprinkling oil over often. Dress on a hot platter, propped up, and garnish with fresh parsley and quartered lemon. Serve with a side dish of ANCHOVY SAUCE II, page 33.

STUFFED BAKED CODFISH RIVIERA

Clean, wash, sponge, cut open from the side a 3½-lb. codfish, and remove the large bone. Rub with salt and pepper inside and out and fill the opening with the following stuffing:

STUFFING

A half cup of bread crumbs, 6 crushed and well-crumbed saltine crackers, ½ cup bacon drippings, 1 tablespoon of finely chopped parsley, 1 teaspoon lemon juice, 1 teaspoon onion juice, the finely chopped rind of a small lemon, salt, pepper, 4 or 5 thyme leaves and paprika to taste. Mix the above ingredients together and moisten with 3 (more or less) tablespoons of fish stock, so as to obtain a soft filling of uniform consistency.

Sew the fish securely, set in a well-buttered baking pan, and pour over a full can of tomatoes, juice and pulp, add a tablespoon of lemon juice, 1 cup of raw, sliced, fresh mushrooms, a teaspoon each of parsley, shallots, and green pepper, finely chopped and well mixed, a bouquet garni, 4 peppercorns, crushed, and salt to taste. Cover the fish with 6 slices of bacon, adjust cover of pan, and set in a hot oven (400°) for 35 minutes; remove the cover and cook 10 minutes longer, basting often. Remove the fish to a hot platter. Place the baking pan containing the cooking liquor and vegetables over a hot fire, add ½ cup of fish stock, a tablespoon of kneaded butter, and reduce to nearly half volume over a hot fire; rectify seasoning, and pour over the fish after removing the bacon. Serve with a side dish of plain boiled potato balls.

EEL

In the following recipes either conger eels or fresh-water eels or salt-water eels may be used.

BAKED LARDED EEL OLD FASHION

Skin, clean, and wash a large eel; rub with salt and pepper, and lard with strips of fat pork all over the back part. Place the fish in a well-buttered baking dish, larded part up, rolled on itself, ringlike, and secure with skewers. In a skillet containing 3 tablespoons of butter, well heated, throw one small onion, finely chopped, 5 or 6 thin slices of carrots, a small bouquet garni, a very tiny pinch of basilic, 3 or 4 peppercorns slightly bruised, and salt to taste and cook the whole together over a low fire, stirring once in a while. Moisten with 2 cups of fish stock and a tablespoon of strained lemon juice. Cook 20 minutes or until the liquid is reduced to half volume. Strain, rectify seasoning and pour over the fish, cover tightly, set in a hot oven (400°), and cook for ½ hour. Dress the fish on a hot round platter covered with hot plain-cooked spinach, well drained; garnish with quartered hard-boiled eggs interspersed with quartered lemon and serve with a side dish of SHALLOT SAUCE, page 46.

BOILED EEL TARTARE SAUCE

Skin, clean, cut in 3-inch pieces, wash, and sponge well 3 lbs. of eel and cook in a vinegar court bouillon (*see* How To BOIL FISH) for 25 minutes. Lift out the fish. Dress on a hot platter; garnish with green crisp parsley and quartered lemon and serve with a side dish of hot TARTARE SAUCE, page 52, and a side dish of French fried potatoes.

BROILED MARINATED EEL MUSTARD SAUCE

Skin, cut in 2-inch pieces, wash, and sponge well 3 lbs. of eel, place in a bowl, and cover with Marinade No. I (*see* Marinades, Volume I), turning often. Let stand for an hour. Drain well but do not sponge, and sauté the fish in 3 tablespoons of butter or olive oil on a very low fire, turning often, for about 15 minutes. Lift out, roll in melted seasoned butter, then in bread crumbs, place on a double broiler, set on the rack of the broiling oven, not too near the flame, turning often and sprinkling frequently with melted butter. Dress on a hot platter covered with a little Mustard Sauce, page 43; garnish with quartered lemon and strips of sweet gherkins and serve aside a dish of the remainder of the sauce.

EEL À LA POULETTE IN PATTY SHELL

Skin, clean, cut in 1-inch pieces, bone, wash, sponge, and rub with salt and pepper 3 lbs. of eel and sauté in 4 tablespoons of butter until beginning to color (about 5 or 6 minutes); then add nutmeg to taste, a bouquet garni, and moisten with 2 cups of fish stock. Let simmer very slowly 20 minutes over a low flame. Blend 2 tablespoons of butter with the same quantity of flour over a low fire, stirring meanwhile until the mixture begins to brown lightly. Moisten with the cooking broth of the fish (strained); stir and let simmer gently 15 minutes; skin and add, one by one and off the fire, 3 or 4 egg yolks, stirring all the while. Set on the fire to heat, but do not boil and add the strained juice of a medium-sized lemon. Strain through a fine sieve and finish with a tablespoon of butter, one of finely chopped parsley, and ½ cup of sliced mushrooms, cooked in butter and well drained. Strain the fish and add it to the sauce. Let stand a few minutes to blend with the sauce. Fill 6 heated patty shells and dress on individual plates. Garnish with a sprig of parsley and serve with a side dish of the remainder of the sauce and a side dish of plain boiled small potato balls.

EEL PIE FRENCH STYLE

Cut into pieces 1½ inches long, 2 lbs. of eel, skinned, cleaned, washed, and blanched in salt water for 10 minutes; drain, discard the water. Line a deep pie dish with a pie dough and place in it a layer of blanched fish, season to taste with salt, pepper, and a few grains of nutmeg, then a layer of hard-boiled eggs, sliced or coarsely chopped. Sprinkle over a little finely chopped parsley and repeat with a layer of fish, then a layer of eggs and parsley, seasoning each layer, and so on until the dish is filled to half an inch from the top. Dot profusely with kneaded butter (about a tablespoon). Pour over a wineglass of good white wine (lemon juice may be substituted, in which case use a tablespoon). Cover with a thin sheet of the same pie dough, slash here and there for the escape of steam, and set in a moderately hot oven (350°) for one hour. Serve right from the baking dish, placed on a platter covered with a napkin, after forcing under the crust half a cup of hot thick CREAM SAUCE II, page 36.

EEL PIE ENGLISH STYLE

Proceed as indicated for recipe above, adding after the layer of hard-boiled eggs a thin layer of sliced raw mushrooms and a tablespoon of finely chopped shallot. Just before serving, force under the piecrust a half cup of thick CREAM SAUCE II, page 36.

EEL PIE CREOLE

Prepare and parboil 2½ lbs. of eel as indicated in recipe for EEL PIE FRENCH STYLE, page 115. Lay in a well-buttered earthenware or Pyrex baking dish, a layer of diced cooked shrimps rolled in melted butter, and over the shrimps a layer of parboiled eels. Pour over this a layer of CREOLE SAUCE, page 37, sprinkle the sauce over another layer of shrimps and so on until the dish is nearly full. Dot here and there with a scant tablespoon of kneaded butter and pour over the whole a half cup of fish stock to which is added a tablespoon of lemon juice. Cover with a sheet of pie dough, slash here and there to let the steam escape. Set in a moderately hot oven (350°) for an hour. Serve right from the baking dish.

FRIED, BONED, AND FILLETED EEL
SICILIAN

Skin 3 lbs. of eel, clean, cut in 3-inch pieces, bone and fillet each piece (*see* MEANING OF THE WORD "FILLET" IN COOKERY). Twist each fillet spiral-like and roll in salted and peppered flour. When ready to serve, place the spiral-like fillet in a wire basket and plunge rapidly into boiling deep fat one minute or just the time to crisp-brown well. Dress on a hot platter covered with a napkin in pyramidal shape; garnish with fried curled parsley and quartered lemon and serve with a side dish of the following sauce:

SAUCE

Cook over a hot fire, 2 cups of red wine to which add 1 cup of stock made from the trimmings of the fish, a tablespoon of finely chopped shallots, 1 tablespoon of finely chopped parsley, salt to taste, and 3 peppercorns, roughly crushed. Reduce to ⅔ volume; strain through a very fine sieve or cloth, pressing a little, and finish off the fire with as much butter (nearly ¾ cup) as it will hold so as to be foamy and fluffy, stirring gently while adding the butter bit by bit, never adding another before the previous bit is entirely incorporated into the sauce. Finish with 3 drops of Angostura bitters.

FRIED EEL ENGLISH STYLE

Skin, bone, cut in 3-inch pieces, fillet, and wipe 3 lbs. of eel and marinate in MARINADE No. I (*see* MARINADES, Volume I). Lift the fish from the marinade, do not sponge, roll in fine bread crumbs and, when ready to serve, plunge into boiling-hot deep fat for 2 short minutes. Drain well. Dress on a hot platter covered with a napkin; garnish with fresh green parsley and quartered lemon. Serve with a side dish of CREAM SAUCE II, page 36, into which stir the size of a hazelnut of anchovy paste. Serve also a side dish of cucumber salad with French dressing.

FRIED EEL NORWEGIAN STYLE

Prepare as indicated for recipe above, the same quantity of eel and marinate also as indicated in that recipe, substituting lemon juice for vinegar and adding a small pony glass of brandy (may be omitted). Lift out and sponge well. Dip in BATTER IV (*see* BATTER FOR FRYING FISH) and, when ready to serve, fry in deep boiling fat. Drain. Dress on a hot platter covered with a napkin, garnish with cups of cucumber stuffed with crab meat in cream, fresh parsley, and quartered lemon. Serve with a side dish of RAVIGOTE SAUCE, page 52.

ROASTED, STUFFED, MARINATED EEL

Select a large eel of 3 to 3½ lbs. Skin, clean, cut in 3-inch pieces, and split in two, lengthwise (but do not separate), bone, wash, sponge, and rub the inside with lemon juice. Fill each piece with a thin layer of STUFFING VIII (*see* FISH FORCEMEAT AND FISH STUFF-ING), surround each piece with bacon, secure with string at both ends and in center. Place the pieces thus prepared in MARINADE II (*see* MARINADES, Volume I). Let stand for 2 hours. Lift out, drain, and place in a well-buttered baking pan, pour over a large can of strained tomatoes, mixed with ½ cup of sliced raw mushrooms, salt and pepper, and add 1 bouquet garni, a finely chopped onion, and 1 clove. Pour over this ⅓ cup of stock made from the trimmings of the fish. Set uncovered in a very hot oven (450°) for 15 minutes, basting often. Place cover on pan and cook 15 to 20 minutes longer in a moderately hot oven (350°). Dress the pieces of fish on a hot round platter, each on a freshly made piece of toast lightly spread with anchovy paste. Surround the fish with the hot cooking liquor and vegetables, the seasoning of which has been rectified. Serve with a side dish of plain boiled potato balls and a side dish of cucumber salad with French dressing.

FLOUNDER

Any one of the various methods employed in the preparation of cod, haddock, fillet of sole, whitefish, etc., may be adapted to this excellent and popular fish.

BAKED FLOUNDER BOURGEOISE

Clean, wash, sponge a flounder of 3 to 3½ lbs. Rub with salt and pepper and place in a copiously buttered earthenware or Pyrex baking dish. Sprinkle over the juice of a small lemon, and set covered with a buttered paper in a hot oven (400°) for 25 to 30 minutes, basting often with melted butter on hand for that purpose. Reduce the temperature to moderately hot (350°); remove the paper, dot here and there with 2 tablespoons of butter, sprinkle over the fish coarsely ground saltine crackers, then a little melted butter and continue cooking until well browned. Serve right from the baking dish with a side dish of plain boiled potatoes and another side dish of stewed tomatoes.

BAKED FLOUNDER FISHERMAN

Golden brown in 2 tablespoons of butter, 2 medium-sized onions sliced in ring, turn into a well-buttered baking dish, set over a 3-lb. flounder, cleaned, washed, and cut in portion sizes, season with salt, pepper, and a few grains of nutmeg to taste, a few thyme leaves, a bouquet garni, and squeeze over the juice of a whole lemon. Dot here and there with 3 tablespoons of butter and set, covered with a buttered paper, in a moderately hot oven (375°). The fish will give off sufficient liquid to keep moist, but should be basted often. Cook about 35 minutes. Ten minutes before serving pour over a level tablespoon of flour diluted in a little cold fish stock and continue the cooking until ready to serve, with a side dish of plain boiled potatoes. Serve the fish right from the baking dish.

BAKED FLOUNDER ROLL

Mix 1 tablespoon of mayonnaise with 1 teaspoon of prepared mustard and 2 tablespoons of slightly melted butter. Cut six flounder fillets in half, spread the mixture over and place 2 shrimps on each piece of fillet; roll up; fasten with toothpicks. Arrange the fish thus prepared in a buttered baking dish, surrounded with ¾ of a pound of cooked shrimps and pour over a small can of tomatoes. Sprinkle the top with buttered bread crumbs and bake slowly in a moderately hot oven (325°), covered with a buttered paper for 25 minutes; remove the paper and cook 10 minutes longer, or until the top is golden brown. Serve right from the baking dish with a side dish of plain boiled potato balls, rolled first in butter, then in finely chopped parsley.

BAKED FLOUNDER FINE HERBS

Clean a 3-lb. flounder, fillet, cut the fillets in three equal parts, roll in salt and pepper, and place in a well-buttered baking dish, the bottom of which is spread with a generous tablespoon of finely chopped parsley, ½ cup of fresh mushrooms, finely chopped, all well mixed after pouring over a small can of drained tomatoes. Cover the pieces of fish with another layer of the same preparation without the tomatoes and dot here and there with 3 tablespoons of butter. Cover the baking dish tightly, set it in a very hot oven (450°) for 20 minutes. Lift out the fish, well drained, and dress, crownlike on a hot round platter. Place the sauce over the fire and add one tablespoon of kneaded butter and the juice of a small lemon; boil once or twice and pour over the fish after rectifying the seasoning. Serve with a side dish of plain boiled potatoes.

BAKED FLOUNDER SPANISH STYLE

Peel and cut 1 medium-sized eggplant in thin slices. Cut 1½ lbs. of fresh tomatoes in rather thick slices; peel and slice 2 large Bermuda onions. Fry the eggplant in olive oil until brown on both sides, then place, well drained, in a buttered baking dish, lay in the cleaned, washed 3-lb. flounder rubbed with salt and pepper, and add a bouquet garni, 1 crushed clove (head removed), then a layer of sliced tomatoes, cover with a layer of sliced onions, dot here and there with 3 tablespoons of butter, cover with a thin layer of buttered crumbs, sprinkle melted butter over, adjust cover tightly and set, covered, in a very hot oven (450°) for 25 minutes; remove the cover and cook 10 minutes longer or until crumbs are well browned. Serve right from the baking dish.

BAKED FLOUNDER WITH MUSHROOMS

Clean a 3-lb. flounder, trim, wash, rub with salt and pepper mixed with a little flour, and place in a well-buttered baking dish, the bottom of which is covered with a cupful of sliced raw mushrooms and a tablespoon of finely chopped parsley. Place over the fish a few strips of bacon, pour over a tablespoon of strained lemon juice, spread over a half cup of finely chopped green peppers, and dot here and there with a generous tablespoon of kneaded butter. Cover tightly and set the baking dish in a very hot oven (450°) for 20 to 25 minutes, lift off the cover, sprinkle with rolled saltine crackers, then with melted butter, and cook 10 minutes longer or until the top is well browned. Serve right from the baking dish, with a side dish of your favorite salad with French dressing.

ROAST FLOUNDER PARISIENNE

Clean a 3½- to 4-lb. flounder, wash, rub with salt and pepper then with oil, and place on a crate the size of a roasting pan, adding 1 small onion sliced coarsely, 1 sliced small carrot, 1 small stalk of celery cut in small pieces, 1 bouquet garni, 2 cloves, a few thyme leaves, and pour in the bottom of the pan ⅔ cup of fish stock. Roast in a very hot oven (450°) as for a roast of beef, basting very often and turning once in a while. Dress the fish on a hot platter; pour the cooking liquor in a saucepan, add a generous tablespoon of flour; bring to a boil, stirring all the while, and let reduce a little. Strain through a fine sieve, pressing a little, rectify the seasoning and serve aside very hot. A dish of roasted small potatoes may be served aside.

STUFFED TURBAN OF FLOUNDER

Clean, skin, wash, and cut a 3½- to 4-lb. flounder into fillets. Trim and coil around inside of well-buttered rings, placed in a buttered pan. Cook ¾ of a cup of chopped fresh mushrooms in 3 tablespoons of butter, with a few drops of onion juice, for one minute or two, and add 4 tablespoons of flour, stirring until well blended; then pour on gradually, while stirring constantly, ½ cup of fresh cream. Bring to the boiling point and add 1 dozen, chopped, bearded oysters or ½ cup of flaked crab meat, then season with salt and pepper to taste. Fill the muffin ring with this mixture, cover with buttered paper, and bake in a hot oven (400°) 12 to 15 minutes. Remove the paper, sprinkle with buttered bread crumbs, then with melted butter, and continue baking until the crumbs are golden brown. Unmold on a hot round platter, ringlike, and garnish the center with one dozen oysters fried in BATTER I (*see* BATTER FOR FRYING FISH). Surround the platter with slices of lemon dipped in paprika interspersed with quartered hard-boiled eggs. Serve with a side dish of DIPLOMATE SAUCE, page 37.

HADDOCK

BAKED HADDOCK PORTUGUESE

Sauté in 3 tablespoons of olive oil 6 small slices of eggplant and lay flat in a well-oiled baking dish. Cover with a layer of onion rings also sautéed in oil, and over the onions lay half a cup of boiled rice mixed with 2 tablespoons of well-washed capers, finely chopped. Place on top of this a 3-lb. haddock, cleaned, trimmed, split along the back and large bone removed, washed and sponged, rubbed with salt, pepper, and a little paprika. Pour over a small can of tomatoes, pulp and juice. Dot here and there with 1 tablespoon of kneaded butter and squeeze a lemon over the whole. Cover tightly and set in a hot oven (400°) for 25 minutes, then remove cover, and cook 10 minutes longer. Serve right from the baking dish with a side dish of salad of your choice.

BAKED HADDOCK BOURGEOISE

Clean a 3-lb. haddock, trim, split along the back, removing the large bone, wash and sponge; sprinkle over a little lemon juice and rub with salt and pepper. Place in a well-buttered baking dish, skin down, and lay on the fish 6 thick slices of raw tomatoes spread lightly with anchovy paste, sprinkle over the tomatoes a mixture made of 2 tablespoons of finely chopped parsley and green pepper, a teaspoon of shallot and 3 tablespoons of chopped raw mushrooms. Cover with 6 lean slices of bacon over which pc · a scant ½ cup of stock made from the trimmings of the fish highly seasoned. Set covered tightly in a hot oven (400°) for 25 minutes, remove the cover, dot here and there with a generous tablespoon of kneaded butter, to which is added the size of a pea of anchovy paste, and continue cooking for 10 minutes longer in oven reduced to moderate. Rectify the seasoning and serve right from the baking dish.

BAKED HADDOCK AU GRATIN

Prepare a 3-lb. haddock as indicated above. Sauté ½ cup of lean cooked ham in small dices, 1 tablespoon of onion in 2 tablespoons of bacon drippings, and add a tablespoon of finely chopped parsley, a teaspoon of finely chopped shallots, and a cup of sliced fine raw mushrooms. Moisten with ½ cup of stock made from the trimmings of the fish, to which is added a tablespoon of strained lemon juice. Let simmer very gently for 15 minutes and pour in a buttered baking dish, previously rubbed with a clove of garlic. Lay the fish, skin down, on this sauce, dot here and there with a tablespoon of kneaded butter, season with salt, pepper, and 4 or 5 thyme leaves, and set, tightly covered, in a hot oven (400°) for 25 minutes; remove the cover, rectify the seasonings, and spread over a cupful of bread crumbs mixed in equal parts with grated American cheese. Continue cooking 10 minutes longer, or until the top is well browned and sizzling. Serve right from the baking dish with a side dish of baked stuffed tomatoes.

BROWNED HADDOCK SHEPHERD STYLE

(Use Freshly Cooked or Leftover Cooked Haddock)

Take equal portions of cold, flaked, cooked haddock and cold boiled potatoes, finely chopped, as if for hashed brown potatoes. Season with salt, pepper, and a few grains each of Cayenne pepper and nutmeg. Heat 4 tablespoons of bacon drippings or lard and place the mixture of fish and potatoes in it, adding more bacon drippings or more lard, if necessary, to moisten sufficiently. Let brown slightly on one side, then mix well with a fork, stirring rapidly and let brown underneath. Fold, and turn on a hot platter, omelet-like, showing the well-browned part on top. Brush with bacon drippings, garnish with slices of tomatoes fried in bacon drippings, a small bunch of parsley, and serve with a side dish of lettuce salad with French dressing.

CREAMED HADDOCK FRENCH METHOD

(Use Freshly Cooked or Leftover Cooked Haddock)

Cover the bottom of buttered individual shirred egg dishes or large flat ramekins with ¼ of a cup of cold flaked haddock, highly seasoned, and sprinkle over scant teaspoon of green pepper, cooked in butter, and ½ teaspoon of slightly browned shallot in butter, mixed together and well drained; pour over this 2 tablespoons of CREAM SAUCE II, page 36. Repeat until dish is nearly full. Dot here and there with little bits of butter, sprinkle with fine buttered bread crumbs mixed in equal parts with grated Swiss cheese, then with a little melted butter; place in a pan containing hot water and set in a hot oven (400°) for 5 or 6 minutes, covered with a buttered paper. Remove the paper and cook 5 minutes longer or until the top is well browned and sizzling. Stick a small piece of parsley in the middle of each ramekin. Serve on individual plate covered with a doily and a side dish of French fried potatoes.

CUTLET OF HADDOCK BOURGEOISE

(Use Freshly Cooked or Leftover Cooked Haddock)

Cook in 3 tablespoons of bacon drippings a generous tablespoon of finely chopped shallots and 3 tablespoons of finely chopped pimento, previously well drained, for 5 minutes, stirring constantly. Do not brown at all; sprinkle over ⅓ cup sifted flour with salt, pepper, and a few grains each of Cayenne pepper and nutmeg. Blend well and pour over gradually and slowly, while stirring constantly, ½ cup scalded milk, then like amount of cream also scalded. Bring to the boiling point, set aside, and let simmer gently for 10 minutes, then add off the fire, 3 egg yolks, gradually, one by one, stirring meanwhile. Add to this mixture 2½ cups of flaked cooked haddock, stir and mix gently but thoroughly, pour into a flat buttered pan to cool. Shape in cutlet form, dip in finely seasoned bread crumbs, then in beaten eggs and again in bread crumbs. Let stand a moment and, when ready to serve, place in a wire basket and plunge 2 or 3 minutes in boiling deep fat or until well browned. Drain. Dress on a hot round platter covered with a layer of rather dry creamed spinach and garnish center with a can of asparagus tips, heated, and sprinkled with melted butter. Garnish between each cutlet (there should be 6) with quartered hard-boiled eggs dipped in paprika after being dipped first in butter. Stick a small piece of green parsley on each cutlet and serve with the following sauce:

BOURGEOISE SAUCE (*Cold*)

Mix 1 tablespoon of tarragon vinegar, 2 tablespoons prepared horseradish, 1 tablespoon prepared mustard, the size of a pea of anchovy paste, salt and pepper to taste, beating rapidly; then fold in ½ cup of whipped cream mixed with ½ cup of mayonnaise, stir gently and pour into a sauceboat and sprinkle with a little finely chopped parsley.

HALIBUT

In addition to the following recipes, the various methods of preparation of cod, haddock, whitefish, and in fact all the large white-fleshed fish, may be adapted to this popular fish.

BAKED HALIBUT SWEDISH STYLE

Wipe a 3-lb. halibut, remove the skin and place in an earthenware baking dish, copiously buttered; sprinkle with salt, pepper, and a few grains of nutmeg, and pour over 2 tablespoons of melted butter with a large can of drained tomatoes, over which sprinkle a teaspoon of granulated sugar. Spread over the tomatoes, ½ cup of fresh sliced mushrooms, 1 tablespoon of finely chopped onion, and moisten with a scant ½ cup of stock made from the trimmings of the fish and in which dilute a small hazelnut size of anchovy paste. Dot here and there with 1 tablespoon of kneaded butter. Cover tightly, set in a very hot oven (425°) for 20 minutes, remove the cover and cook 10 minutes longer, basting frequently. Rectify the seasoning and serve with a side dish of buttered peas.

BAKED HALIBUT HOLLENDEN

Arrange 6 thin slices of fat salt pork in a buttered baking dish, cover with 1 tablespoon of onion, finely sliced, and add a tiny bit of bay leaf and 5 or 6 thyme leaves. Wipe a 3-lb. piece of halibut and place over the pork and onion. Cover the fish with 2 tablespoons of kneaded butter (*see* Compounded Butters), sprinkle the whole with ⅔ cup of buttered cracker crumbs and arrange 6 thin strips of bacon over the crumbs. Cover with a well-buttered paper and set in a moderately hot oven (375°) for about 30 minutes, remove the paper and cook 10 minutes longer, or until the crumbs are well browned. Serve right from the baking dish with a side dish of Cream Sauce III, page 37.

BAKED HALIBUT PIERRETTE

Place a wiped 3-lb. piece of halibut, sliced in 6 equal pieces, in a well-buttered baking dish, season with salt, pepper, and a few grains each of Cayenne pepper and nutmeg. Arrange on top 6 thick slices of raw peeled tomatoes and sprinkle over ½ cup of green pepper, cut julienne-like, and a generous teaspoon each of finely chopped onion, parsley, and chives. Pour over ⅓ cup of tomato soup and dot here and there with 2 tablespoons of butter and 1 tablespoon of kneaded butter. Cover tightly and bake in a hot oven (400°) for 20 minutes, remove the cover, rectify the seasoning, add ½ cup of diced, cooked shrimps, and cook 10 minutes longer. Serve right from the baking dish with a side dish of plain boiled small potato balls.

BAKED HALIBUT VALERIA

Wipe a 3-lb. piece of halibut, slice in 6 equal parts, sprinkle over the juice of a lemon and season with salt and pepper to taste. Place the fish in a well-buttered baking dish and pour over a sauce, prepared as follows:

Sauce Valeria

Melt 3 tablespoons of butter and blend with the same amount of flour; moisten, pouring gradually, stirring constantly, with ⅔ cup of fish stock and a generous ½ cup of thick cream; season to taste with salt, pepper, and a dash of celery salt and add the size of a small walnut of meat extract. Boil once and pour over the fish. Cover tightly and set in a very hot (450°) oven for 10 minutes, remove the cover and add ⅔ cup of seedless Malaga raisins, softened in a little hot water. Cover again tightly and continue baking for 20 minutes in a moderately hot oven (350°). Serve right from the baking dish, sprinkled with finely chopped parsley and with a side dish of broiled green tomatoes.

BAKED FILLET OF CHICKEN HALIBUT VERONICA

Clean, wash, and fillet a 3½-lb. halibut to make 6 fillets. Spread over each fillet a thin layer of finely chopped olives mixed with a little anchovy butter and fold in two. Place in a well-buttered baking dish, the bottom of which is covered with ⅔ cup of the following mixture: a scant teaspoon of finely chopped parsley, a scant teaspoon each of finely chopped shallot and chives, and the balance of finely chopped raw mushrooms; place a slice of bacon across each fillet; barely cover with stock made from the trimmings of the fish, dot here and there with a tablespoon of kneaded butter and 1 tablespoon of sweet butter, season with Cayenne pepper and a few grains of nutmeg to taste—no salt at all—and set covered with bread crumbs sprinkled with melted butter, then covered with a buttered paper, in a moderately hot oven (375°) and cook 15 minutes; remove the paper and continue cooking until top is well browned. Serve with a side dish of SHALLOT SAUCE, page 46, and a side dish of cucumber salad with French dressing.

BAKED HALIBUT PARK AMERICAN

Sauté in 3 tablespoons of bacon drippings, 1 teaspoon each of finely chopped and well-mixed parsley, green pepper, onion, and chives. Do not brown. Sprinkle with 2 tablespoons of flour, blend well, and moisten gradually, with 1 cup of scalded milk and 1 cup of scalded cream, stirring meanwhile until the mixture thickens; then add ½ cup of small dices of cooked ham, stir, season with salt, pepper, and a few grains of nutmeg and pour into a well-buttered baking dish. Place in a buttered baking dish a 3-lb. piece of halibut cleaned, washed, large bone removed and well sponged, squeeze over the juice of a small lemon, cover with a buttered paper, and set in a moderately hot oven (350°) for 20 minutes. Remove the paper, sprinkle 2 tablespoons of grated American cheese over and continue baking until brown and sizzling. Serve right from the baking dish with a side dish of your favorite salad.

BAKED CHICKEN HALIBUT SUZANNE

Clean, split open the back, and remove the large bone, wash, and sponge well a 3-lb. halibut. Rub inside and out with salt and pepper and place the size of an ordinary egg of tarragon butter in the opening and secure with skewers. Set in a well-buttered baking dish, the bottom of which is covered with 2 tablespoons of finely chopped raw mushrooms, same quantity of green pepper, a teaspoon of finely chopped shallot, all well mixed and seasoned with salt, pepper, and a few grains of nutmeg. Lay over the fish 6 slices of bacon and pour over ½ cup of mushroom liquor and 1 tablespoon of white wine mixed with a teaspoon of lemon juice. Cover tightly and set in a hot oven (400°) for 20 minutes; remove the cover and add a scant tablespoon of butter and 1 teaspoon of kneaded butter and continue cooking for 10 minutes. Rectify the seasoning and serve right from the baking dish with a side dish of glazed small white onions and a cucumber salad with French dressing. Serve very hot.

BAKED CHICKEN HALIBUT DUTCH STYLE

Clean a 2½-lb. chicken halibut, split from the back, and remove the large bone, wash, rub well inside and out with lemon juice, then with salt and pepper, and fill the opening with stuffing prepared as follows:

STUFFING

Combine ¾ cup of bread crumbs, 2 tablespoons of finely chopped parsley, 1 teaspoon finely chopped chives, salt, pepper and nutmeg to taste, a few grains of Cayenne pepper and a scant ½ cup of butter. Sew up the fish, brush generously with melted butter and add a few drops of lemon juice and roll in fine, dry bread crumbs. Place in a well-buttered baking dish and set in a very hot oven (400°) for

15 minutes, while preparing a soft custard sauce with 3 eggs, a generous ½ cup of milk, salt, pepper and nutmeg to taste, and 2 tablespoons of butter. Beat the whole well and pour over the fish. Reduce the heat to 350°, cover with a buttered paper, and cook 15 to 20 minutes longer or until the soft custard is set. Meanwhile prepare a sauce as follows:

Dutch Sauce

Cook in a double boiler over a very hot fire a generous tablespoon of finely chopped onion in 1½ tablespoons of butter. Do not brown. Sprinkle over the onion 1 generous tablespoon of flour. Blend well and moisten with a cup of stock made from the trimmings of the fish, add 2 tablespoons of tarragon vinegar, stirring well until the mixture thickens, then ¾ of a cup of heated sour cream. Add ½ cup (scant) of finely chopped gherkins (sweet), 1 tablespoon of finely chopped parsley, season to taste with salt, pepper, and a few grains each of Cayenne and nutmeg. Finish by adding, bit by bit, 3 tablespoons of butter, or more if necessary, to make the sauce foamy, while beating thoroughly. Serve the fish from the baking dish.

BOILED CHICKEN HALIBUT GOURMET

Select a 2½- to 3-lb. halibut, clean, split along the back, remove the large bone, wash, rub with lemon juice inside and out, then with salt. Open the fish and lay small squares of bacon on one side and on the other side spread 3 tablespoons of flaked crab meat, boned thoroughly; reshape, wrap in cheesecloth, and place in a fish kettle, cover with white wine court bouillon, bring to a rapid boil, remove aside to simmer gently for 25 minutes. Lift out the fish, unwrap, dress on a hot platter, keep hot while preparing the following sauce:

Gourmet Sauce

Melt 3 tablespoons of unsalted butter and when very hot sprinkle over 2½ tablespoons of flour, blending well. Do not brown. Pour on gradually, while stirring constantly, ½ cup of strained cooking liquor in which the fish has been boiled, then ½ cup of thin scalded cream. Bring to the boiling point, seasoning with salt and Cayenne pepper; add 3 tablespoons of freshly grated young American cheese, stirring meanwhile so as to obtain a smooth, thick liquid sauce. Then add off the fire, stirring constantly, 2 egg yolks and finish with as many tablespoons of sweet butter as the sauce will hold, beating constantly with a wire whisk. This sauce should be very foamy. Pour over the fish just enough to cover with a thin coat, garnish the top of the fish with a dozen cooked large shrimps rolled in butter, and serve the remainder of the sauce in a side dish. Surround the edge of the platter with plain boiled small potato balls, rolled in butter then in finely chopped parsley, forming a sort of necklace of green hue.

BROILED HALIBUT MAÎTRE D'HÔTEL

(*Master Recipe*)

Clean a 3-lb. halibut, split open from the back, wash, remove the large collar bone, sponge well, and rub with salt and pepper. Roll in oil or melted butter; place on a double broiler, set on the rack of the broiling oven, and broil slowly under a low flame, turning often and basting frequently with melted butter. Dress on a hot platter and just before serving dot here and there with MAÎTRE D'HÔTEL BUTTER, page 57; garnish with green parsley and quartered lemon. Serve with a side dish of your favorite salad with French dressing. Any other kind of sauce may be substituted if desired.

FILLET OF CHICKEN HALIBUT
FIN DE SIÈCLE

Clean, wash, fillet, and wipe a 3-lb. halibut so as to have 6 fillets. Season with salt, pepper, and a few grains of Cayenne pepper, brush over with lemon juice and roll, securing with toothpicks. Set in a well-buttered earthenware or Pyrex baking dish, placing in the opening of each fillet a large piece of cooked lobster. Pour over a drained small can of mushroom buttons, sprinkle with a teaspoon of finely chopped parsley and 1 teaspoon of finely chopped shallots, barely cover with fish stock and add a tablespoon of lemon juice. Set covered with a buttered paper in a moderately hot oven (350°) for 15 minutes. Remove the paper and cook 5 minutes longer. Dress the fish, crownlike, on a hot platter and pour over LOBSTER SAUCE, page 42. Garnish with small triangles of bread fried in butter, interspersed with mushrooms cooked in butter and well drained, and, in center, place 6 small fried smelts.

FILLET OF CHICKEN HALIBUT
J. B. MARTIN

Split lengthwise 6 fillets of halibut so as to obtain 12 small fillets. Lay 6 of the fillets flat, salted and peppered and sprinkled with lemon juice, in a well-buttered baking pan; barely cover with mushroom stock in which has been cooked a tablespoon of finely chopped chives. Set, covered with a buttered paper, in a moderately hot oven (375°) for 10 minutes. Meanwhile, roll the remaining 6 fillets, secure with a small skewer or a couple of toothpicks, and place in the opening a small piece of cooked lobster or a stuffed olive. Season with salt and pepper and roll in crumbs, then in butter and again in crumbs and plunge 2 short minutes in deep boiling fat. Dress the first 6 fillets on a round hot platter, covered with a layer of cooked string beans (cut julienne-like and rolled a few minutes in hot melted butter forming a star), and place a fried fillet between each flat fillet. Cover the whole with MORNAY SAUCE, page 43, and glaze rapidly in a very hot oven (450°) or under the flame of the broiling oven; dust with paprika, garnish rapidly with a bunch of green parsley and quartered lemon, and serve at once with a side dish of French fried potatoes and a side dish of diced cucumber and artichoke bottom salad with French dressing.

FILLET OF CHICKEN HALIBUT JACQUELINE

Prepare and cook 6 fillets of chicken halibut as indicated in recipe for FILLET OF CHICKEN HALIBUT FIN DE SIÈCLE, page 132. Dress on a hot round platter, crownlike, garnish center with 3 dozen small oysters fried in deep fat, cover the fish with WHITE WINE SAUCE, page 49; garnish the edge of platter with small triangles of bread fried in butter, interspersed with 6 small tomatoes stuffed with creamed crab meat. Serve with a side dish of small potato balls fried in butter.

FILLET OF CHICKEN HALIBUT À LA RECTOR

Prepare 6 fillets of chicken halibut, sprinkle with salt, pepper, onion juice, and then with lemon juice; roll, secure with small skewers or a couple of toothpicks, and place in a well-buttered baking dish, the bottom of which is laid with a cupful of finely chopped fresh mushrooms, mixed with a teaspoon each of finely chopped parsley and shallots. Pour over a cupful of CREAM SAUCE I, page 36, and cover with a thin layer of sliced hard-boiled eggs and a cupful of parboiled small potato balls. Pour more cream sauce to cover and let stand 15 minutes on the side of the range, covered with a buttered paper, but not cooking, to permit blending of flavor of the different ingredients. Sprinkle over fine bread crumbs mixed with grated American cheese and set, covered with a buttered paper, in a hot oven (400°) for 15 short minutes; remove the paper and continue cooking until top is well browned and sizzling. Serve right from the baking dish with a side dish of your favorite salad.

FRIED FILLET OF CHICKEN HALIBUT RUSSIAN STYLE

Sprinkle 6 fillets of chicken halibut with salt and pepper. Let stand half an hour covered in half cup of white wine. Drain; dip each piece separately in thick fresh cream seasoned with salt and pepper to taste, then in flour, and, when ready to serve, plunge in deep boiling fat until golden brown. Dress on a hot platter, cover with a cupful of fresh mushrooms, peeled, then sautéed in butter and well drained, and pour over the following sauce:

RUSSIAN SAUCE (*Hot*)

Cook skin, bones, and all the trimmings of the fish with 4 or 5 thin slices of carrot, 3 slices of lemon, a small sprig of parsley, a bit of bay leaf, 4 or 5 thyme leaves, 4 peppercorns (crushed), and 2 cups of water until reduced to 1 cup liquid. Meanwhile melt 2 tablespoons of butter and combine with 2 generous tablespoons of flour. Blend well and moisten, stirring meanwhile with the strained fish stock, then with ½ cup of scalded thick cream (using the cream in which the fish has been dipped). Finish, off the fire, with 3 egg yolks, added one by one while stirring, season with salt, pepper, and a few grains of nutmeg and a couple of tablespoons of white wine, if desired. Serve with a side dish of plain boiled small potato balls and a side dish of green salad with French dressing.

FRIED FILLET OF CHICKEN HALIBUT
TARTARE SAUCE
(*Master Recipe*)

Clean 3 lbs. of chicken halibut, split open from the back, remove the large bone, and fillet in 6 pieces, lengthwise; wipe dry, season with salt and pepper, roll and fasten with small wooden skewers or toothpicks, dip in fine cracker crumbs, then in beaten eggs and again in crumbs. When ready to serve, dip in boiling hot fat; drain, dress on a hot platter; garnish with a bunch of parsley and quartered lemon and serve with a side dish of TARTARE SAUCE, page 52, and a side dish of freshly made French fried potatoes. Any other kind of cold sauce may be substituted if desired.

FRIED JULIENNE OF FILLET OF HALIBUT BOHEMIAN

Cut 6 fillets of halibut, lengthwise, in small strips ½ inch wide; season with salt and pepper and dip in BATTER II (*see* BATTER FOR FRYING FISH). When ready to serve, place in a wire basket and plunge in boiling frying fat until golden brown and crisp. Drain, dress on a hot platter covered with a napkin, garnish with fried curled parsley and quartered lemon, and serve with a side dish of BOHEMIAN SAUCE, page 50, and a side dish of shoestring potatoes.

KINGFISH

All the different methods of preparation, cooking, and serving of the mackerel, bluefish, herring, shad, and in fact all the fish having the fat distributed throughout the body, may be adapted to this excellent fish, which is essentially American, not being found elsewhere.

MACKEREL

The mackerel may be prepared in an endless variety of delicious ways and served with almost any kind of sauce, although when grilled and served with plenty of clarified or drawn butter it appears at the height of its glory.

In addition to the following recipes, the various methods of preparation of bluefish, herring, and shad may be adapted to this delicious fish.

BAKED MACKEREL IN MILK

Split open from the back 3 mackerel, wash, trim, and sponge well. Spread wide and put into a well-buttered baking pan, season with salt, pepper, and a few grains of nutmeg, dot with 2 tablespoons of butter here and there, barely cover with cold milk and set in a moderately hot oven (375°) covered with a buttered paper, for 30 minutes. Lift out and drain the fish; dress on a hot platter and keep hot. Strain the milk through a fine sieve into a saucepan placed over a hot fire and heat to the boiling point. Set aside on the fire and add 2 tablespoons of kneaded butter. Place again on the fire and boil 5 minutes, remove and add gradually 3 egg yolks beaten with the size of a hazelnut of anchovy paste and 4 drops of Angostura bitters, stirring meanwhile; rectify the seasoning, return the fish to the sauce, sprinkle 3 tablespoons of grated American cheese over, and set in a hot oven until well browned and sizzling. Serve right from the baking dish with a side dish of plain boiled small potato balls.

BAKED FILLET OF MACKEREL
TARRAGON BUTTER

Clean 3 large mackerel, split open from the back, and fillet; wipe dry and rub with lemon juice, then with salt and pepper. Place in a well-buttered baking dish, dot here and there with 3 tablespoons of tarragon butter (*see* COMPOUNDED BUTTERS), set, covered with a buttered paper, in a moderately hot oven (350°) for 20 to 25 minutes; remove the paper and cook 5 minutes longer. Dress on a hot platter, garnish with curled fresh parsley and quartered lemon, sprinkle the fish with finely chopped parsley and pour over the butter from the baking dish. Serve with a side dish of French fried potatoes and your favorite green salad with French dressing.

BOILED MACKEREL LONDON STYLE

Clean 3 large mackerel, remove the head and tail, wash, sponge well, and cut into 3½- to 4-inch pieces. Cook in highly seasoned white wine court bouillon (*see* How To BOIL FISH) to which is added a few sprigs of fennel. Dress on a hot platter; garnish with plain boiled potatoes, fresh parsley, and quartered lemon and serve with a side dish of GOOSEBERRY SAUCE, page 40.

BOILED MACKEREL PARISIENNE

Clean 3 large mackerel, remove the head and tail, wash and sponge well. Wrap and secure in cheesecloth and cook in vinegar court bouillon (*see* How To BOIL FISH). Unwrap, remove the skin carefully, dress on a hot platter, brush with melted butter, sprinkle lightly with fine bread crumbs, and brown slightly under the flame of the broiling oven; garnish with small sour gherkins, cut in two lengthwise and split fanlike, interspersed with quartered lemon and quartered hard-boiled eggs. Serve with a side dish of GOOSEBERRY SAUCE, page 40.

MUSKALLONGE

The muskallonge is a fresh-water fish, belonging to the pike and pickerel family, found in the Great Lakes of the North and the Upper Saint Lawrence River, and areas north of the Great Lakes in Canada are well supplied. It is seldom seen in the East, being consumed mostly in the Middle West.

BAKED MUSKALLONGE FORT MEIG

3½ to 4 lbs. of fish
2 cups cold water
6 slices carrots
6 slices onion
A small bunch parsley
6 crushed peppercorns
½ cup butter
3 tablespoons flour

½ teaspoon salt
Few grains Cayenne pepper
¾ cup heavy cream
2 tablespoons pimento purée
½ tablespoon finely chopped chives
More salt
¾ cup buttered coarse crumbs

Skin, bone, and cut the fish into slices for individual service. Cover the bones, skin, and trimmings with cold water and add carrot, onion, parsley, peppercorns, and salt. Bring to the boiling point and let simmer until reduced to half volume. Meanwhile, melt the butter, add the flour, and stir, blending well; then pour in the reduced fish stock, well strained, and boil once. Arrange the slices of fish in a well-buttered baking pan; brush with lemon juice, using 1½ tablespoons; sprinkle with salt and pepper and pour over the sauce. Cover with buttered paper, set in a moderately hot oven (375°), and cook 20 minutes; then add the cream, heated and mixed with the pimento purée, stir, cover with coarse bread crumbs, sprinkle with melted butter, and cook until well browned. Serve right from the baking dish.

PIMENTO PURÉE

To obtain pimento purée, drain a can of pimentos and force through a fine sieve.

BAKED MUSKALLONGE STEAK WITH TOMATO

Place in a well-buttered baking pan, ½ cup sliced raw mushrooms, 1 teaspoon chopped onion, 1 teaspoon chopped parsley, a few grains of nutmeg, salt and pepper to taste, and lay on this 6 slices of muskallonge steak ½ inch in thickness, skinned and wiped dry. Pour over a large can of tomatoes. Dot here and there with 1 tablespoon of kneaded butter, sprinkle with a tablespoon each of finely chopped parsley and onion, season to taste with salt and pepper and a few grains of Cayenne pepper and cover tightly. Set in a hot oven (400°) for 15 minutes, remove the cover and cook 10 minutes longer, after adding 2 tablespoons of butter. Rectify the seasoning and serve right from the baking dish with a side dish of plain boiled small potato balls.

BROILED MUSKALLONGE STEAK GOURMET

Marinate for 1 hour 6 slices of muskallonge, ½ inch thick, in salted and highly peppered oil to which ½ teaspoon of onion juice and minced parsley are added. Place the fish slices dripping from the marinade on a double broiler, set on the rack of the broiling oven, and broil in the usual way. Dress on a hot platter, the bottom of which is spread lightly with CREOLE SAUCE, page 37. Garnish with small bijou tomatoes, stuffed with creamed crab meat, topped with a little MORNAY SAUCE, page 43, and glazed under the flame or in a hot oven. Place over each slice of fish a large mushroom fried in butter and garnish with small triangles of bread fried in butter, quartered lemon, and green parsley. Serve aside a dish of small French fried potatoes.

GRILLED BREADED MUSKALLONGE STEAK

Marinate for 1 hour 6 slices of muskallonge, ½ inch thick, in salted and peppered oil, to which add a teaspoon of onion juice and 4 drops of Angostura bitters. Roll in bread crumbs, while dripping from the oil marinade, then in beaten egg, and again in bread crumbs. Place on a double broiler, set on the rack of the broiling oven, and sear both sides under a hot fire. Turn and baste often with butter. Turn onto a well-buttered baking pan and pour over a little melted butter mixed with finely chopped parsley and finish cooking in a moderately hot oven, basting frequently. Dress on a hot platter; garnish with quartered lemon, small green peppers, stuffed with creamed shrimps, and fresh curled parsley. Serve with a side dish of DRAWN BUTTER, page 38, and a side dish of O'Brien potatoes.

GRILLED DEVILED MUSKALLONGE STEAK SHALLOT SAUCE

Spread over 6 salted and peppered slices of muskallonge, ½ inch thick, 2 tablespoons of prepared mustard (more or less according to taste). Roll in fine cracker crumbs, then in butter and again in cracker crumbs, and broil in the usual way, first under a hot flame, to sear both sides, then reducing the heat and turning and basting frequently. Dress on a hot platter, the bottom of which is spread with a little SHALLOT SAUCE, page 46. Garnish with 6 cucumber cups stuffed with creamed crab meat and shrimps mixed together, quartered lemon, and fresh parsley and serve with a side dish of green salad with French dressing.

PERCH

The perch belongs to the bass family and is a common spiny-finned fresh-water fish found throughout the Northern Hemisphere where the bass belong.

The "yellow perch" found in the North is delicious and may be served in a thousand and one fine ways. As a general rule the small perch are fried, and the medium-sized baked, broiled, filleted; while the various methods employed in the preparation of bass, catfish, pike and pickerel, whitefish, and similar fish may be adapted to the large perch.

BAKED PERCH IN WHITE WINE

Clean, wash, sponge, and slash 2 or 3 times the sides of 3 medium-sized perch. Rub with salt and pepper and lay in a copiously buttered baking dish. Barely cover with white wine, mixed in equal parts with fish stock; dot here and there with 1 tablespoon of kneaded butter and set, covered with a buttered paper, in a hot oven (400°) for 20 minutes, basting often with butter kept for that purpose. Remove the paper, cook a few minutes longer, then lift out the fish, and dress on a hot platter and keep hot. Pour the cooking liquor in a saucepan over a hot fire and reduce to nearly half volume. Remove from the range and add the size of a small walnut of extract of meat, then gradually, bit by bit, 4 tablespoons of sweet butter, stirring all the while and a teaspoon of finely chopped parsley and rectify the seasoning. Pour this foamy sauce over the fish; garnish with triangles of bread fried in butter, interspersed with quartered lemon and green parsley. Serve with a side dish of your favorite green salad with French dressing.

BOILED PERCH DUTCH STYLE

Split open from the back, remove the collar bone, clean, wash, and sponge 3 perch of 1 lb. each. Place in a shallow baking pan, copiously buttered, and barely cover with stock made from the trimmings of the fish; then add 1 scant tablespoon of kneaded butter and season with salt and pepper. Cook over a low fire, uncovered, and at the first boil reduce the heat and let simmer very gently for 20 minutes. Lift out the fish, dress on a hot platter, keep hot. Meanwhile, cook a tablespoon of finely chopped onion in a tablespoon of butter in a double boiler until tender; do not brown. Sprinkle over a scant tablespoon of flour, blend well, and moisten with ¾ cup of the strained liquor; stir constantly, while pouring slowly and gradually, until it thickens, and add a tablespoon of tarragon vinegar, then ½ cup of sour cream, stir and place the top part of the double boiler directly over the fire and boil rapidly, stirring constantly. When boiling, add ⅓ cup of finely chopped sweet gherkins and a teaspoon of finely chopped parsley. Rectify the seasoning and finish with a tablespoon of butter. Pour this sauce over the fish; garnish with slices of lemon dipped in finely chopped parsley and small triangles of bread fried in butter. Serve with a side dish of cucumber salad with French dressing.

BOILED PERCH AU BLEU CÉCILE

Remove the gills and clean through the opening 6 small-sized perch. Place in a fish kettle, pour over ½ cup of boiling vinegar, then cover with white wine court bouillon (*see* How To Boil Fish), bring to a boil; remove aside and let simmer very gently for 15 minutes. Lift out and then, and only then, scale. Dress on a hot platter, garnish with quartered lemon and fresh parsley. Serve with a side dish of White Butter Sauce, page 48, and a side dish of plain boiled potato balls.

BOILED PERCH ORNAIN

AUTHOR'S NOTE

This unusual and heretofore unpublished recipe is the creation of the well-known French author Edmond Richardin and was served for the first time at a dinner given in September, 1873, at Vaucouleurs, Lorraine. The guests included other well-known authors such as Victor Hugo, Leo Claretie, Alfred Vicq, and the Comte de Sternberg.

Place in a fish kettle a generous bunch of tied parsley, 2 small cloves (heads removed), 2 very small cloves of garlic (slightly bruised), 2 large onions (sliced in thin rings), 1 small carrot (sliced thin), salt, pepper, and a few grains of nutmeg to taste, not forgetting the little sprig of thyme or 5 or 6 leaves if not available. Cover with 2 generous cups of white wine and bring to a boil. Meanwhile, clean and wash 6 small perch and place in this court bouillon or broth, while boiling rapidly. Set immediately on the side of the range and let simmer very gently, smiling, for about 15 minutes, according to size of the fish. Lift out, drain, place on a hot platter, and keep hot. Strain the cooking broth; place over a hot fire and let reduce to half volume. Force through a fine sieve 4 hard-boiled egg yolks and add to the reduced sauce, stirring rapidly, then add, bit by bit, 4 tablespoons of sweet butter, stirring all the while with a wire whisk. Finish with ½ cup of heated thick cream. Boil once, rectify the seasoning, add a few grains of Cayenne pepper, and pour over the fish, which should be carefully skinned. Garnish with fresh parsley and serve with a side dish of plain boiled small potato balls rolled in melted butter.

BOILED PERCH À LA MEUSE

Prepare a white wine court bouillon and cook 3 medium-sized perch which have been cleaned, washed, slashed in 2 or 3 places on the back to prevent retraction, and sponged as indicated under How To Boil Fish. Meanwhile, prepare the following sauce:

Sauce À La Meuse

Melt in a double boiler, 2 tablespoons of butter and 4 tablespoons of olive oil. Heat well. Separate the yolks from the whites of 4 fresh eggs; dilute the yolks with 1 generous tablespoon of tarragon vinegar, a little salt and black pepper to taste, and add gradually to the oil and butter in the double boiler, stirring constantly and until the mixture begins to thicken; then add ½ cup, more or less, of the strained cooking broth, stir and finish with a scant tablespoon of prepared mustard, mixing well. Pour this over the skinned fish and serve with a side dish of plain boiled small potato balls, rolled in finely chopped parsley. Garnish the dish with slices of lemon dipped half in paprika and half in chopped parsley.

BOILED MARINATED PERCH TOURAINE

Select 6 small perch of the same size; clean, wash, slash here and there slightly on the back, and marinate for 2 hours in olive oil, lemon juice, a few thin slices of onion, and salt, pepper, and a few grains of Cayenne pepper to taste. Drain. Cook in a red wine court bouillon (*see* How To Boil Fish) for 15 minutes. Lift out the fish, drain well, place on a hot platter, and keep hot. Meanwhile, melt in a saucepan, 4 tablespoons of butter, in which cook a scant cup of small mushrooms; moisten with ½ cup of the strained broth and add a scant ⅔ cup of heated fresh cream. Bring to a boil rapidly and let simmer gently for 10 minutes, rectify the seasoning and finish with 2 egg yolks, added one by one, while stirring all the while, and a tablespoon of sweet butter. Pour over the skinned fish; garnish with triangles of bread fried in butter, lemon slices dipped in finely chopped parsley, and a bunch of parsley. Serve with a side dish of cucumber salad with French dressing.

BOILED PERCH SAUVIGNY

Clean, trim, wash, and sponge 2 large perch of 1½ lbs. each, rub with salt and pepper, and place in a white wine court bouillon for 20 minutes. Cook as indicated under How To Boil Fish. Lift out the fish, drain, place on a hot platter, and keep hot.

SAUVIGNY SAUCE

Blend together 2 tablespoons each of butter and flour. Do not brown. Moisten with 1 cup (more if necessary) of strained fish broth, stir well, and boil once. Add ½ cup of heated thick cream. Boil once, remove from the fire and add, one by one, 3 egg yolks, stirring constantly, and the size of a small hazelnut of anchovy paste. Finish with a tablespoon of strained lemon juice and a tablespoon of sweet butter. Pour over the skinned fish, garnish with glazed small white onions, quartered lemon, and fresh parsley and serve with a side dish of plain boiled small potato balls rolled in finely chopped parsley.

BROILED PERCH WHITE BUTTER

Split open from the back, clean, remove the large bone, trim, wash, and sponge 3 medium-sized perch. Rub with salt and pepper, dip in melted butter mixed with a little paprika, place on a double broiler, well heated and well greased, and set on the rack of the broiling oven. Sear both sides under a hot flame, turning and basting frequently with melted butter; turn into a shallow baking pan, generously buttered, and finish cooking in a moderately hot oven, basting often with the butter from the pan. Dress on a hot platter, pour over the butter from the baking pan, surround with plain boiled small carrot balls, and cover with WHITE BUTTER SAUCE, page 48. Dust with a little paprika and serve with a side dish of cucumber salad with French dressing.

FRIED PERCH RAVIGOTE

(Master Recipe)

Clean, trim, wash, sponge well, roll in salted and peppered flour 2 dozen small perch and, when ready to serve, place in a wire basket, shake to remove the excess of flour and plunge in boiling deep frying fat until golden brown and crisp. Pile up on a hot platter covered with a napkin; garnish with fried curled parsley and quartered lemon and serve with a side dish of Ravigote Sauce, page 52. Any one of the cold sauces found in the Contents may be substituted if desired.

GRILLED MARINATED PERCH TARTARE

Marinate for 1 hour in olive oil, lemon juice, a few rings of onion, a bit of bay leaf, and 3 crushed peppercorns, salt and paprika to taste, barely to cover 3 medium-sized perch, cleaned, split from the back, large bone removed, washed and sponged well. Lift out dripping from the marinade, place on a double broiler, and set on the rack of the broiling oven. Sear both sides under a hot flame, turning and basting frequently, turn into a shallow baking pan, generously buttered, and finish cooking in a moderately hot oven, basting frequently with melted butter from the pan. Dress on a hot platter on which is spread the butter from the baking pan, sprinkle with finely chopped parsley, garnish with fresh parsley, quartered lemon, and fried slices of green tomatoes and serve with a side dish of hot Tartare Sauce, page 48, and a side dish of your favorite green salad with French dressing.

PERCH À LA POULETTE

Clean, trim, cut in 2½-inch pieces, wash, sponge well, 2 large perch of 1½ lbs. each. Place in a saucepan and add a small bunch of tied parsley, 1 tiny bay leaf, 1 crushed clove, the size of a pinhead of garlic, and 4 tablespoons of butter. Cook over a low fire, stirring often, and do not let brown. Moisten with 2 cups of stock made from trimmings of the fish and add ⅔ cup of sliced raw mushrooms. Bring to a boil and let simmer very gently for 15 minutes. Lift out the fish, drain well, dress on a hot platter, and keep hot.

Poulette Sauce (*For Fish*)

Strain the cooking broth and reduce to nearly half volume over a hot fire. Remove to the side of the range and add, one by one, 4 egg yolks, stirring meanwhile. Set again over the fire, but do not boil, and add the juice of a strained lemon. Strain the sauce through a fine sieve and add gradually, 2 tablespoons of butter and a generous tablespoon of finely chopped parsley. Add the fish, skinned carefully, let stand a few minutes to mellow, and dress on a hot platter. Garnish with small triangles of bread fried in butter, slices of lemon, one half dipped in paprika and the other half in finely chopped parsley or cinnamon for color contrast, and serve with a side dish of plain boiled potato balls.

PICKEREL

The various methods employed in the preparation and cooking of small bass, pike, smelts, and whiting may be adapted to this delicious and delicate fish of the pike family, known under various names in different localities.

BAKED PICKEREL LOUISIANA

Clean 3 pickerel of 1 lb. each, split open from the back, remove the large bone, trim, wash, and sponge well. Rub with salt and pepper mixed with a little nutmeg. Place in a well-buttered baking pan, side by side, and cover with a large can of drained tomatoes, lay on the tomatoes half a dozen large rings of onion, previously cooked for five minutes in a little butter, and sprinkle with salt and pepper to taste, a few thyme leaves and a teaspoon of finely chopped parsley. Dot here and there with 2 generous tablespoons of butter and 1 tablespoon of kneaded butter. Pour over a half cup of fish stock made from the trimmings. Adjust cover on pan and set in a very hot oven (425°) for 25 minutes. Lift out the fish and place on a hot platter. Set the baking pan over the fire and bring to a boil; correct the seasoning and surround the fish with the sauce and ingredients. Serve with a side dish of plain boiled small potato balls.

BRAISED STUFFED PICKEREL NORMANDE

Select 6 small pickerel, split on the side, remove the large bone, rub with salt and pepper inside and out, and fill the opening with the following stuffing:

STUFFING

To the 6 roe of the fish set aside and finely chopped, add a scant cup of freshly made soft bread crumbs, salt and pepper and a little

· 149 ·

nutmeg to taste, a teaspoon of finely chopped chives, a teaspoon of finely chopped parsley, same of chopped chervil, if available, all well mixed and blended together with 2 raw egg yolks. Sew up. Surround each fish with thin slices of larding pork and secure with string. Place the fish side by side in a well-buttered baking pan; barely cover with equal parts of white wine and strained fish stock (made from the trimmings of the fish) and set, covered tightly, in a hot oven (450°) for 20 minutes. Remove the cover and cook 5 minutes longer. Lift out the fish; dress on a hot platter and pour over NORMANDE SAUCE, page 44. Garnish with small triangles of bread fried in butter, alternating with slices of lemon dipped in finely chopped parsley.

BAKED STUFFED PICKEREL
GERMAN STYLE

Prepare 6 small pickerel as indicated for above recipe and fill the opening with stuffing made as follows:

STUFFING

Chop together 8 large oysters with the roe of the 6 pickerel and mix with a cupful of freshly made bread crumbs, a teaspoon each of finely chopped parsley, onion, and green celery leaves; add salt, pepper, and nutmeg to taste, and mix thoroughly. Blend with 2 raw eggs and a scant tablespoon of bacon drippings. Sew up. Place the fish in a well-buttered baking dish, the bottom of which is covered with ½ cup of sliced mushrooms and ⅓ cup of diced cooked ham. Cover the fish with a small wineglass of Moselle wine and ⅓ cup of stock strained through a cloth and made from the trimmings of the fish, and dot here and there with a tablespoon of butter and 1 tablespoon of kneaded butter. Set, tightly covered, in a hot oven and bake 20 minutes. Remove the cover, rectify the seasoning, and sprinkle over the whole a scant cupful of buttered bread crumbs; brown well and serve right from the baking dish.

GRILLED MARINATED PICKEREL
MARINIÈRE

Marinate in a cup of white wine for an hour 6 small pickerel previously split from the back, large bone removed, cleaned, washed, sponged, and rubbed with salt, pepper, and a little nutmeg to taste, to which is added 1 tiny bay leaf, a small clove, a slice of lemon, 2 thin slices of onion, 2 thin slices of carrot, a pinch of thyme leaves, and salt and pepper to taste, and a tablespoon of tarragon vinegar. Lift out, sponge, roll in melted butter, place on a double broiler, and set on the rack of the broiling oven. Broil, turning and basting frequently with melted butter. Dress on a hot platter; garnish with fresh parsley and quartered lemon and serve with a side dish of mayonnaise, to which is added 2 generous tablespoons of finely chopped walnut meats and a side dish of French fried potatoes.

Any one of the cold or hot sauces found in the CONTENTS may be substituted for mayonnaise if desired.

FRIED FILLET OF PICKEREL EN
BROCHETTE

Clean 6 small pickerel, fillet, wash, sponge, cut each fillet in two pieces, season with salt and pepper and arrange as follows: one piece of fish, then one mushroom cooked in butter and one slice of bacon, folded in three, all placed on a wooden skewer; repeat until the skewer contains four pieces of each of the three items for a service. Dip in melted butter, then in fine bread crumbs, again in butter and again in bread crumbs. Place in a wire basket and, when ready to serve, plunge in boiling deep frying fat. Drain and dress on a piece of toast dipped in melted butter, the size of the skewer; set on a hot platter; garnish with fresh curled parsley and quartered lemon and serve with a side dish of DUTCH BUTTER SAUCE, page 38, and place small mounds of small potato balls, cooked in butter and well browned, between each skewer.

VARIATION

Instead of frying in deep fat, you may broil under the flame or fry in plenty of butter. If broiled, the usual sauce is cold TARTARE SAUCE, page 52.

ROAST LARDED PICKEREL VALVINS

Skin carefully 2 or 3 large pickerel and wash thoroughly. By means of a larding needle, lard with fillet of anchovy, split in two lengthwise and passed through and through the fish. Sprinkle copiously with black pepper and use a little salt, taking into consideration that the anchovies are salted. Roll in oiled paper and place in a buttered baking pan. Cook in a hot oven (400°), basting over the paper often with oil or melted butter, for 20 minutes. Remove the paper, sprinkle melted MAÎTRE D'HÔTEL BUTTER, page 57, over the fish and continue cooking 10 minutes longer (more or less) in oven reduced to moderate. Dress on a hot platter; garnish with small mounds of small French fried potatoes, fresh parsley, and quartered lemon. Serve with a side dish of RAVIGOTE SAUCE, page 52.

STEWED PICKEREL BOURGEOISE

Clean, trim, wash, sponge, and cut in 3-inch pieces, 2 pickerel of 1½ lbs. each. Roll in salted and peppered flour and sauté slightly in 4 tablespoons of butter or, better, bacon drippings; when beginning to brown, sprinkle a little flour (about a teaspoon) over, add a small bouquet garni, a small clove of crushed garlic, a large onion, sliced thin, ½ cup diced cooked ham, salt and pepper to taste, a teaspoon of finely chopped shallot, and covered with strained fish stock, made from the trimmings. Close tightly and set on a hot fire. Cook for 10 minutes, remove the cover and add a generous cupful of small potato balls, and a drained small can of mushrooms. Cover and cook 15 to 20 minutes longer over a moderately hot fire. Rectify the seasoning and dress on a hot platter garnished with small triangles of bread fried in butter, sprinkle with finely chopped parsley, and serve with a side dish of your favorite green salad.

STEWED PICKEREL MARINIÈRE

Prepare 3 pickerel of 1 lb. each as indicated for above recipe and brown lightly in butter, turning often. Sprinkle over a tablespoon of flour, stir and moisten with the strained juice of a large can of tomatoes, stirring meanwhile, carefully, so as not to break the fish. Add ⅔ cup of strained stock made from the trimmings of the fish, a small bouquet garni, a small clove, salt, pepper, and a few grains of Cayenne pepper and 24 small white onions, parboiled in salted water. Pour over the pulp of the tomatoes and 6 slices of bacon, chopped finely. Cover, bring to a boil, and set aside to simmer very gently for 20 minutes. Five minutes before serving, rectify the seasoning and add a teaspoon of flour, diluted in a little cold water. Bring to a boil and cook a few minutes longer over a low fire. Dress on a hot, deep, round platter, sprinkle finely chopped parsley over, and serve with a side dish of freshly made dry toast.

PIKE

If the pike is a ferocious and cannibal fish, its flesh is of a supreme delicacy with which a good cook can work wonders and which any one of the thousand sauces known in culinary art may adorn and ennoble. In addition to the following recipes, all the methods of preparation of bass, eel, lamprey, carp, perch, and whitefish may be adapted to the pike.

BAKED PIKE ALSATIAN METHOD

Select a large pike of 3 to 3½ lbs. or two equaling the weight of 3 to 3½ lbs. Clean, wash under running cold water; sponge well, rub with salt and pepper. Place the fish in a fish kettle and pour over a white wine court bouillon (*see* How To Boil Fish). Remove the fish, cool a little, and bone thoroughly. Save the broth for other uses. Meanwhile, clean, wash, and sponge a small head of cabbage of 2 lbs. and blanch in salted water. Let cool a little, then remove the core of the leaves, discard the water. Copiously butter an earthenware baking dish having a tight cover; sprinkle freshly ground peppercorns all over the butter; place in the dish, a layer of blanched cabbage, then a layer of flaked pike; repeat this operation until the dish is nearly full, seasoning with salt, pepper, and nutmeg to taste each time. Cover the last layer with butter, dotting here and there, using three or four tablespoons. Adjust the cover tightly and set in a moderately hot oven (350°) for 30 minutes. Remove the cover and add ½ cup of strained fish stock made from the trimmings, to which has been added a generous tablespoon of kneaded butter (*see* Compounded Butters). Cover again tightly and cook for 10 minutes longer. Rectify the seasoning and serve right from the baking dish with a side dish of green salad with French dressing.

BAKED FILLET OF PIKE LOUISIANA

Select a large pike of about 3 lbs. Split open from the back, wash, fillet (*see* Meaning of the Word "Fillet" in Cookery), wipe dry, and rub with salt and pepper to taste, using pepper from the mill or crushed peppercorns. Place first, 3 slices in a well-buttered baking dish covered with peeled slices (rather thick) of tomatoes; sprinkle over a teaspoon of finely chopped shallot and a teaspoon of finely chopped parsley, then sprinkle with salt and pepper and lay the 3 remaining fillets over this; season again with salt and pepper and pour over all ½ cup of stock made from the trimmings of the fish. Dot here and there with 3 tablespoons of butter, cover with a buttered paper and set in a moderately hot oven (375°) for 20 to 25 minutes. Remove the paper and rectify the seasoning and serve right from the baking dish with a side dish of plain boiled potato balls.

BAKED FILLET OF PIKE GRAND'MÈRE

Fillet a 3-lb. pike, sponge, season with salt and pepper, and spread each fillet with finely chopped cooked shrimps, blended with 1 whole egg and well seasoned with salt, pepper, and a few grains of Cayenne pepper. Place side by side in a well-buttered baking dish, pour over ½ cup of strained stock, made from the trimmings of the fish and sprinkle with a teaspoon of finely chopped shallot and the same amount of finely chopped parsley; then pour over ½ glass of dry white wine, cover with a buttered paper, set in a moderately hot oven (375°) and cook for 15 minutes. Remove the paper, add a tablespoon of kneaded butter and cook 10 minutes longer, basting often. Dress on a hot platter after rectifying the seasoning, garnish each fillet with a large mushroom cooked in butter and well drained and cover with the following sauce:

Grand'mère Sauce

Pour the cooking liquor in a saucepan and bring to a boil, add ½ cup of thick cream, previously scalded, and boil once. Finish off the fire with 3 egg yolks added one at a time, while stirring continuously. Rectify the seasoning again and pour over the fish. Garnish the edge of the platter with fresh parsley, quartered lemon, interspersed with small triangles of bread fried in butter and sprinkle over the sauce a little finely chopped parsley.

BOILED PIKE AU BLEU

Clean a 3-lb. pike through the gills, wash and sponge well. Place in a fish kettle and pour over a cupful of boiling tarragon vinegar. Let stand a while; then cover the fish with plain salt water and cook as indicated under How To Boil Fish. Drain, skin, dress on a hot platter covered with a napkin and remove the skin carefully without damaging the fish; decorate with bits of curled parsley, garnish with plain boiled potatoes and quartered lemon and serve with a side dish of Drawn Butter Sauce, page 38, and a side dish of cucumber salad with French dressing.

BAKED PIKE GARNI VAUCOULEURS

Author's Note

This delicious recipe will delight the most sophisticated epicure, gourmet, or gastronome. It is a succulent dish for those connoisseurs who appreciate something that is not commonplace. It is the creation of the well-known French author, poet, and gastronome, Edmond Richardin, prepared for the first time at his country house "La Follie," in Lorraine, in September, 1883. Trout, perch, carp, or any other delicate white-fleshed fish may be prepared in the same way.

Clean, wash, trim, and sponge well a very large pike of 3 to 3½ lbs. and place in a fish kettle. Cover with white wine court bouillon (see How To Boil Fish) and cook for 30 minutes. Lift out the fish, drain, and place in a well-buttered large baking dish. Keep hot, while cooking 2 dozen crayfish in the same court bouillon in which the pike was cooked. Lift out the crayfish, shell, pound the inside of the crayfish in a mortar, moistening, little by little, with good white wine so as to form a paste, and add the yolk of an egg. Season to taste with salt, pepper, and a few grains of nutmeg and place this paste all over the pike. Set the baking dish in a moderately hot oven (400°) for 15 minutes, covered with a buttered paper; remove from the oven, add the tails of the crayfish (set aside and kept hot), and serve with a side dish of WHITE BUTTER SAUCE, page 48. A side dish of freshly made small French fried potatoes will not be amiss.

BOILED PIKE PERIGORD

Pound in a mortar 2 or 3 small cloves of garlic with a tablespoon each of finely chopped parsley, shallot, and chervil. Season with salt and pepper and moisten with a scant cup of white wine and a generous cup of stock made from the trimmings of the fish. Place a cleaned, trimmed, washed, and well-sponged 3- to 3½-lb. pike in a fish kettle and cover with the mixture, adding a generous tablespoon of kneaded butter. Cook as indicated under How To Boil Fish, for 25 minutes. Lift out the fish carefully, drain, and dress on a hot platter; remove the skin and keep hot. Reduce the cooking liquor to half volume over a hot fire and add 2 tablespoons of sweet butter and 2 egg yolks, alternately, off the fire, while stirring constantly. Rectify the seasoning and pour over the fish. Garnish with small triangles of bread fried in butter, alternated with quartered lemon. Sprinkle over the fish a teaspoon of truffle, finely chopped, and serve with a side dish of small potato balls cooked in butter and a side dish of your favorite green salad with French dressing.

BOILED MARINATED PIKE TOURAINE

AUTHOR'S NOTE

Eel, perch, carp, brook trout, pickerel, and almost all the fish having a fine, firm, white flesh may be prepared in this delicious way, which had its origin in Tours, Touraine, France, a district well known to Americans for its outstanding cuisine and natural beauty, where one may not only regale himself with ordinary dishes such as "guogues" and bouilletures, but also with highly specialized preparations confined to this delightful region.

Along the banks of the Loire River, in France, are scattered right and left princely châteaux, interspersed here and there with little "hôtelleries," where the food is always good; and beside each is a well-kept vineyard; in fact vineyards are everywhere, which produce such delicious and seldom-exported wines as "Saint Avertin," "Membrolle," and many others, proving once more that wine and food were made for each other, both coming from Mother Earth, and consequently inseparable.

Select a large pike of 3½ to 4 lbs., clean, trim, wash, and sponge and marinate for 2 hours in 4 tablespoons of olive oil, to which is added a small pony glass of brandy. Turn and baste often. Place the fish in a fish kettle, dripping with the marinade, and cover with a red wine court bouillon, adding a small clove of crushed garlic. Cook as indicated under How To Boil Fish, for 25 minutes. Lift out the fish, drain well, place on a hot platter and keep hot. Reduce the strained cooking liquor to a generous cupful. Meanwhile, melt 4 tablespoons of butter and, when hot, pour over a drained small can of mushrooms (fresh mushrooms are preferable) and add 3 generous tablespoons of thick fresh cream. Boil once or twice, add the reduced cooking liquor, rectify the seasoning, and let simmer gently for 5 minutes. Dress the pike, skinned, on a very hot platter over freshly-made toast, dipped in melted butter; skin the fish carefully to prevent damage, and pour over the sauce. Garnish with small triangles of bread fried in butter, slices of lemon, one half dipped in chopped parsley and the other half in cinnamon, and serve immediately.

DAUBED PIKE IN RED WINE

Author's Note

Its rustic title is indicative; this is not a dish of great and famous restaurants, but a healthful and delicious farmer's dish. It is indeed the traditional fish dish of the northeast of France; during the season of the pike, this preparation will be found on many a farmer's table all along the eastern frontier of France and especially in the Haute Marne Department.

It is the bouillabaïsse of the northeast of France as it includes several fish, but pike is predominant.

Take 1½ lbs. of pike and 1 lb. each of eel and carp; clean, wash, sponge, then cut in service pieces, and cook in a red wine court bouillon as described under How To Boil Fish. Lift out the pieces of fish when done (in about 30 minutes) and dress on a hot platter and keep hot.

Prepare a roux (blended butter and flour) well browned with 3 tablespoons of butter and 2 of flour in a skillet over a hot fire. When well blended and browned, moisten with the cooking liquor reduced to a cupful, after being strained through a fine sieve. Add a cupful of fresh cream and boil 10 minutes. Finish the sauce with a tablespoon of butter, alternating with 2 or 3 egg yolks and stirring all the while. Place the fish in the sauce and let stand on the side of the fire a while to mellow, but do not let boil. Serve on a hot, deep, round platter and serve with toasted French bread. Also serve with a side dish of plain boiled potatoes.

FRICASSEE OF PIKE PARISIENNE

Clean a 3½-lb. pike or 2 pike equaling 3½ lbs. or thereabouts, trim, wash, and sponge, then cut in 3-inch pieces. Brown lightly in 4 tablespoons of butter over a low fire, turning the pieces of fish often; sprinkle a tablespoon of flour over, stir, and pour over a large can of tomatoes. Add a small can of mushrooms (drained), a teaspoon each of shallot, and finely chopped parsley, a bit of bay leaf, and a few thyme leaves. Season with salt, pepper, and a few grains of Cayenne pepper and add a scant half cup of small dices of cooked ham. Cover, bring to a boil, reduce the heat, and allow to simmer very gently for 25 to 30 minutes. Rectify the seasoning, dress on a hot, deep, round platter; garnish with small triangles of bread fried in butter, and serve with a side dish of plain boiled small potato balls.

FRICASSEE OF PIKE CREOLE

Prepare a 3- to 3½-lb. pike as indicated above. Roll the pieces in salted, peppered flour and brown in 4 tablespoons of bacon drippings and a teaspoon each of finely chopped onion and parsley. Lift out the fish, drain well, and place in another saucepan. Cover with a cupful of fish stock and add a small can of drained mushrooms, one large green pepper, cut julienne-like, and a small can of tomatoes, drained. Add a bit of bay leaf, 1 clove, and a few thyme leaves. Season with salt, pepper, and a little paprika to taste, bring to a rapid boil and set immediately into a moderately hot oven (375°), tightly covered, for 25 minutes. Dress, after rectifying the seasoning, on a hot platter; garnish with parsley, slices of lemon, and serve piping hot.

ROAST PIKE IN WHITE WINE

Clean a 3- to 3½-lb. pike, trim, sponge well, and rub with salt, pepper, and a little nutmeg. Place in a buttered earthenware baking dish and add a bouquet garni, a few thyme leaves, a very tiny blade of garlic, a teaspoon of finely chopped shallot, and a tablespoon of finely chopped gherkins; pour over a generous tablespoon of olive oil, a generous tablespoon of fish stock, and a scant wineglass of white wine (lemon juice may be substituted, in which case use a tablespoonful). Cover with a buttered paper and set in a hot oven (400°) for 15 minutes, basting frequently. Remove the paper and continue cooking for 15 minutes or until the fish is done, basting often. Remove the fish to a service platter; strain the sauce over a saucepan; bring to a rapid boil and add a cupful of CREAM SAUCE I, page 36. Boil 10 minutes, strain, rectify the seasoning, and finish with a tablespoon of butter. Pour over the fish, sprinkle a little paprika over, garnish with potatoes rissolé in deep fat, parsley, and quartered lemon.

SAUTÉED FILLET OF PIKE ON SPINACH

Roll 6 fillets of pike in salted, peppered flour and sauté in plenty of butter, turning often to prevent scorching and to ensure browning on both sides. Dress in center of a hot round platter bordered with plain cooked spinach, generously buttered. Pour the butter from the pan over the fish, sprinkle over finely chopped parsley and garnish with 3 quartered hard-boiled eggs, interspersed with quartered lemon. Serve very hot.

SAUTÉED FILLET OF PIKE
FINLAND STYLE

Fillet a 3½-lb. pike in the usual way and divide each fillet in two equal parts, crosswise; season with salt, pepper, and a little paprika to taste; dip in melted butter and sear rapidly under the flame of the broiling oven. Turn immediately into a frying pan containing 3 tablespoons of hot butter and 1 tablespoon of finely chopped parsley. Sauté rapidly over a hot fire, turning often. Dress on a hot platter, covered lightly with DUTCH BUTTER SAUCE, page 38; garnish with baked stuffed cucumber (using for stuffing any kind of left-over cooked fish), quartered lemon, and fresh parsley. Serve the remainder of the Dutch Butter Sauce aside.

POMPANO

In addition to the following recipes, the various methods of preparing flat fish such as carp, sole, sturgeon, flounders, and the like, may be adapted to the pompano.

BAKED POMPANO CREOLE

Clean, trim, wash a large pompano of 2½ to 3 lbs. and gash all along the back. Rub with lemon juice, then with salt and pepper and a little nutmeg to taste. Place in a well-buttered earthenware baking dish, brush with butter and set in a hot oven (400°) for 15 minutes, basting often with melted butter. Remove from the oven and turn the fish, pouring in the dish, a generous cupful of CREOLE SAUCE, page 37. Dot here and there with 2 tablespoons of butter, sprinkle over a teaspoon of very finely chopped shallot, rectify the seasoning and cover with buttered crumbs. Set covered with a buttered paper in a moderately hot oven for 20 minutes; remove the paper and cook 10 minutes longer, or until the crumbs are well browned. Serve right from the baking dish with a side dish of cucumber salad with French dressing.

BAKED POMPANO BOURGEOISE

Prepare 2 pompanos weighing 1½ lbs. each as indicated above. Place in a well-buttered earthenware baking dish; sprinkle over a teaspoon each of parsley, chives, shallots, all finely chopped, and add a pinch of tarragon herbs, also finely chopped and well mixed; season with salt and pepper to taste, dot here and there with 2 tablespoons of butter, and pour over ½ wineglass of white wine. Cover with a buttered paper and set in a hot oven (400°) for 20 minutes, basting frequently. Remove the paper, lift out the fish, dress on a hot platter, keep hot. Pour the cooking liquor into a saucepan and add a cupful of fish stock made from the trimmings, reduce to a scant cup in volume over a hot fire and add ½ cup of thick fresh cream. Boil once and let simmer very gently for 10 minutes; skim, strain through a very fine sieve, and finish with a tablespoon of butter and ⅓ cup of sweet gherkins, finely chopped. Pour over the fish, garnish with fresh parsley and small triangles of bread fried in butter, and serve with a side dish of plain boiled small potato balls.

BAKED POMPANO SPANISH STYLE

Clean, wash, trim, sponge well, and lard with matchlike strips of salt pork, the top of 2 pompanos of 1½ lbs. each. Sprinkle with peppercorns, freshly crushed, and a very little salt, and place in a buttered baking dish on the bottom of which are laid 6 strips of bacon; sprinkle over 2 generous tablespoons of finely chopped raw mushrooms and place over 6 more strips of lean bacon, sprinkle with a generous teaspoon of finely chopped parsley; dot here and there with a tablespoon of kneaded butter and pour over a generous half cup of stock made from the trimmings and to which is added half a wineglass of white wine, or a generous tablespoon of strained lemon juice, and 2 tablespoons of tomato purée. Cover with a buttered paper and set in a hot oven (400°) for 20 minutes, basting once in a while. Remove the paper and cook 5 minutes longer. Take from the oven, rectify the seasoning, and serve right from the baking dish with a side dish of cucumber salad with French dressing.

BAKED POMPANO MIAMI

Clean and split completely open from the back, remove the large bone of 3 pompanos weighing 1 lb. each, cut into 6 large fillets, trim the edges, split in two, lengthwise. On 6 slices, spread a thin layer of fresh crab meat, seasoned highly, blended with a whole egg; cover with the remaining fillets, pressing slightly, sandwich-like. Dip each sandwich in melted butter and wrap in oiled paper, individually, place in a lavishly buttered baking dish, and set in a hot oven (400°), basting frequently over the paper with melted butter, for 20 to 25 minutes. Remove from oven, unwrap; dress on a hot platter, cover with MORNAY SAUCE, page 43, and glaze rapidly under the hot flame of the broiling oven. Garnish with 6 triangles of golden browned puff paste, stuffed with a large oyster, previously parboiled in fish stock and rolled in melted shallot butter, interspersed with small quarters of lemon, one half dipped in finely chopped parsley and the other half in paprika. Serve with a side dish of shoestring potatoes.

BAKED POMPANO J. B. MARTIN

Prepare 3 pompanos weighing 1 lb. each as indicated above, leaving the fillet whole. Sauté lightly in butter for 5 minutes and add a scant ⅔ cup of small dices of cooked ham and a teaspoon of finely chopped shallot and turn, butter included, into a buttered baking dish. Place over 3 fillets of pompano, salted and peppered with crushed peppercorns or pepper from the mill and pour over a small can of mushrooms, well drained; arrange over the mushrooms, the 3 remaining fillets, sprinkle with a scant teaspoon of finely chopped chives and 2 or 3 leaves of tarragon herbs, dot here and there with 2 tablespoons of butter and pour over the whole a generous half cup of thick cream, previously scalded. Cover with a buttered paper and set in a very hot oven (450°) for 10 minutes. Lift out the paper and pour over a generous tablespoon of good sherry wine, cook 10 minutes longer, and serve right from the baking dish after rectifying the seasoning. Serve with a side dish of small potato balls, cooked in butter, then rolled in finely chopped parsley.

BAKED POMPANO KNICKERBOCKER

Prepare 3 pompanos each 1 lb. in weight as indicated for above recipe, rub with lemon juice, then with salt, pepper, and a few grains of nutmeg. Set in a copiously buttered baking pan and barely cover with strained stock made from the trimmings of the fish. Dot here and there with a tablespoon of butter and another of kneaded butter and put in 3 or 4 slices of seeded lemon. Set covered with a buttered paper in a hot oven (400°) for 15 minutes. Lift out the fish, dress on a hot platter, and keep hot. Pour the cooking liquor into a saucepan and reduce to nearly 2 tablespoons over a hot fire. Incorporate, bit by bit, sufficient butter to make a thick foamy sauce, beating constantly meanwhile. Finish with 3 tablespoons of coarsely chopped green olives and a tablespoon of sweet gherkins. Pour over the fish and pour over the whole a teaspoon of extract of meat, slightly melted, and set under the flame of the broiling oven to glaze slightly. Garnish with small triangles of bread fried in butter and quartered lemon. Serve at once.

BROILED POMPANO EVERGLADES

Clean, trim, and split from the back 3 pompanos of 1 lb. each, remove the large bone, wash, and sponge well. Marinate for 30 minutes in 4 tablespoons of olive oil, salted and peppered, and add a teaspoon of lemon juice. Drain well and place on a well-greased double broiler and set on the rack of the broiling oven, flesh side up. Turn and brown, basting frequently with melted butter. When half done, turn into a baking pan, pour over a little melted butter, sprinkle over a little finely chopped parsley and continue cooking, basting often. Remove to heated service platter and garnish with quartered lemon, fresh parsley, and 6 large mushrooms cooked in butter. Pour over the butter from the baking pan and serve with a side dish of HOLLANDAISE SAUCE, page 40, and a side dish of freshly made French fried potatoes.

BROILED POMPANO WITH FRICASSEE
OF CLAMS

Clean 3 pompanos of 1 lb. each, split open from the back, remove the large bone, wash, and sponge well. Rub with lemon juice and then with salt, pepper, and a few grains of Cayenne pepper. Place on a double broiler and set on the rack of the broiling oven. Broil under a hot flame, turning and basting frequently with melted butter. When half done, turn into a lavishly buttered baking pan and sprinkle over a little finely chopped parsley and a teaspoon of finely chopped shallot, sautéed in butter. Continue cooking in a moderately hot oven (350°) basting often. Place on a hot platter or an oak plank, bordered with 2 rows of mashed potatoes, 1 inch apart, forced through a pastry bag with a fancy tube. Arrange 10 halves of clamshells between the potato borders, at equal distances; fill spaces between the shells with broiled small tomatoes. Keep hot in oven with door open while preparing the following:

FRICASSEE OF CLAMS

Clean 1 pint of clams, finely chop the hard portions, and reserve the soft. Melt 2 tablespoons of butter, add the chopped clams, sprinkle over 2 tablespoons of flour, and pour on gradually, ⅓ cup of scalded thick cream; strain, add soft parts of clams, cook 1 minute, and stir in, off the fire, 2 egg yolks, well beaten. Season with salt, pepper, and a few grains each of Cayenne pepper and nutmeg, then fill the clamshells on the platter. Sprinkle a little paprika over and serve.

BROILED POMPANO BENNETT TOUSLEY

Clean, split clear from the back, remove the large bone, trim, wash, and sponge well 3 pompanos of 1 lb. each. Rub with a little tarragon vinegar and then with salt and pepper. Dip in olive oil; place on a double broiler, well greased, set on the rack of the broiling oven and broil under a hot flame, turning and basting often with olive oil. When half done, turn into a lavishly buttered baking pan and pour over 2 tablespoons of melted anchovy butter (*see* COMPOUNDED BUTTERS). Continue cooking in a moderately hot oven (350°), basting frequently. Dress on a hot platter; pour over the butter from the baking pan and garnish the fish, alternately with a large broiled mushroom and a fillet of anchovy, well sponged, dipped in BATTER IV (*see* BATTER FOR FRYING FISH) and fried in boiling deep fat, having, in all, 6 mushrooms and 6 fillets of anchovy. Garnish the edges of the platter with small baked tomatoes stuffed with creamed crab meat, alternating with small triangles of bread fried in butter. Place a large bunch of green curled parsley at the head of the fish, and quartered lemon. Serve very hot.

PLANKED POMPANO FLORIDA

Select a large pompano of 3 lbs. Split open from the back, remove the large bone but do not separate, wash, sponge, rub with a tablespoon of lemon, then with salt, pepper, and a little nutmeg well mixed. Dip in olive oil and place skin down on a buttered oak plank, a little longer and wider than the fish. Set in a hot oven (400°) covered with a buttered paper for 25 minutes, basting very often and turning once or twice; remove the paper and cook 5 minutes longer. Take from the oven and edge the plank with mashed potatoes, forced through a pastry bag having a fancy tube, sprinkle with butter and set in the oven to brown slightly or, better, under the flame of the broiling oven. Remove to the side of the range and garnish the space between the fish and the potatoes as follows: a little mound of very small glazed white onions, a mound of string beans, cut julienne-like, peas, glazed small carrot balls, asparagus tips, small beet balls, sprig of cauliflower, brocolli covered with HOLLANDAISE SAUCE, page 40, small tomatoes broiled and rolled in finely chopped parsley, and in fact any vegetables desired and available, not forgetting small mushroom buttons, cooked in butter and well drained. Heat under the flame or in a hot oven. Set the plank on a plank holder, or on a platter covered with a napkin, and serve with a side dish of DRAWN BUTTER, page 38.

STEWED POMPANO À LA POULETTE

Prepare, cook, dress, garnish, and serve as indicated in recipe for PERCH À LA POULETTE, page 147, substituting pompano for perch.

RED SNAPPER

The red snapper is an important food fish related to the sea bass and found on rocky banks in the warm seas. It reaches a length of about two feet. The species found from the Gulf Coast up to New Jersey are deep-water fish and include the mangrove, or grey snapper, also called Pensacola snapper, which, like the red snapper, is a very delicate morsel.

The various methods employed in the preparation of bass, herring, pickerel, pompano, and whitefish may be adapted to this excellent fish.

SALMON

The large salmon and slices of salmon, called *"darnes"* in culinary terms, and "steak" in common cookery, except when the latter (slices) are broiled, baked, or short fried or sautéed, are generally boiled in a vinegar court bouillon (*see* How To Boil Fish), covered with a towel, and brought slowly and gradually to the boiling point. The types of sauces which usually accompany boiled salmon, suitable for this popular and delicious as well as nourishing fish, are: Anchovy, Brown Butter, Caper, Egg Sauce, Genevoise, Hollandaise, Lobster, Oyster, Louisa, Mousseline, Ravigote, and Venetian. The traditional cucumber salad with French dressing is its side dish.

When salmon is prepared to be served cold, at luncheon or supper, for instance, it is preferable to have the fish boiled whole and allowed to cool in its broth. In this way the flavor and quality are entirely preserved. When boiled in slices, the meat has a tendency to dry up and lose flavor. In either instance, hot or cold, the skin is removed when lukewarm and before dressing on the service platter, to facilitate decoration and garnishing.

The decoration of cold salmon is ordinarily made of slices of cucumber cut in fancy shapes, fillets of anchovy, capers, slices of tomatoes (not too ripe), or tomato bijou, sprigs of parsley, slices or strips of gherkins, sweet or sour, or slices of hard-boiled eggs.

Any one of the cold fish sauces may be served with cold salmon, as well as any kind of green or vegetable salad, including the cucumber.

The garnishings best suited to cold salmon are small tomatoes, peeled, scooped, and filled with a vegetable salad; hard-boiled eggs, quartered or sliced in either of two ways: the hard yolk removed and replaced by any kind of filling, such as chopped olives and gherkins mixed with mayonnaise or a sour cream dressing; or left-over fish meat, such as crab, lobster, shrimps, or any other kind of fish, crustaceans, or hard-shelled crabs, chopped fine or passed through the meat chopper and moistened with mayonnaise, sour cream dressing, catsup, French dressing, etc., sprinkled with paprika and topped with a small slice of red beet, or black olive, or radishes, a caper, or a truffle. Or a small cucumber cut in fancy shape, then scooped and garnished with coral lobster, roe of fish, etc.; or it may be a small cooked red beet, scooped and filled with a mixture to taste, or a ring of anchovy with an olive in the center, a few slices of lemon, dipped half in paprika and half in finely chopped parsley, or half in paprika and half in ground nutmeg, or three tints may be used—red, brown, and green, etc. All of which is left to the ingenuity and taste of the cook.

In addition to the following recipes, the various methods employed in the preparation of pompano, pike, muskallonge, turbot, and the like may be adapted to this universally popular and nourishing fish.

BAKED SALMON IN CREAM

Wipe dry 3 large cuts of salmon, cut in two, season with salt and pepper to taste, place in a buttered baking pan and barely cover with thin fresh cream, to which add a bit of bay leaf, 1 clove, 3 thin slices of onion, a sprig of parsley, and a few thyme leaves. Set in a very hot oven (400°) for 25 minutes, basting once in a while to prevent drying on the top. Lift out the fish and dress on a hot platter. Keep hot while making a CREAM SAUCE I or II, page 36, using part of the cooking cream. Pour over the fish, sprinkle with finely chopped parsley, border with slices of lemon, interspersed with quartered hard-boiled eggs. Serve with a side dish of plain boiled potatoes.

BAKED SALMON BAYONNE

Select 3 slices of fresh salmon from the middle of the fish, weighing 1 lb. each, and wipe dry. Season with salt and pepper and a little nutmeg to taste. Place in a well-buttered earthenware baking dish, one-half a cup of sliced raw mushrooms and spread over a scant teaspoon each of finely chopped parsley and shallots, add a bit of garlic, a bit of bay leaf, a pinch of basilic, 4 or 5 thyme leaves, and a small clove. Place the fish over this and cover with 12 slices of lean bacon, pour over ½ wineglass of dry white wine and 2 or 3 tablespoons of fish stock. Cover tightly and set in a hot oven (400°) for 20 minutes; remove the cover and continue cooking 10 minutes longer in oven reduced to moderate; add more stock if too dry, rectify the seasoning, and serve right from the baking dish with a side dish of plain boiled potato balls.

BAKED SALMON VERT GALLANT

Place in a deep baking dish in the order named the following ingredients: a thin slice of very lean raw ham 2½ inches in diameter, top with a thin slice of very lean veal of the same size as the ham, then a slice of fresh salmon of the same dimensions, and cover with a thin slice of larding pork of similar size. Repeat this operation making 3 sets of the layers. There should be 6 slices each of ham, veal, fish, and larding pork. Add a small bouquet garni, a tablespoon of very finely chopped chives, a crushed clove, and 6 bruised peppercorns. Place the baking dish on the range, add a tablespoon of butter, season to taste with salt and a few grains of Cayenne pepper and nutmeg and cook very slowly for 15 minutes; then add a wineglass of dry white wine, and ¾ cup of fish stock. Cover tightly and set in a hot oven (400°) for 30 minutes. Remove the cover and cook 10 minutes longer, basting frequently. Lift out the meat and fish carefully so as not to disarrange the shape and place the 3 loaf-like layers on a very hot platter. Keep hot.

Place the baking pan over a hot fire and reduce the cooking liquor to nearly nothing, then add a full cup of scalded thick cream. Bring to a boil, let simmer for 5 minutes, strain through a fine sieve, add, off the fire, 2 egg yolks, separately, stirring constantly, and finish with a generous tablespoon of sweet butter. Rectify the seasoning and strain half the sauce over the fish and the remainder into a sauceboat. Serve with a side dish of green salad with French dressing.

BAKED SALMON IN RHINE WINE

Wipe dry a 4-lb. piece of salmon taken from the middle, rub with salt and pepper from the mill and place in a well-buttered baking dish. Spread over a tablespoon of finely chopped onion, a teaspoon of finely chopped parsley, a few thyme leaves, a bit of bay leaf, and a sprig of parsley. Cover with a generous wineglass of Rhine wine and ½ cup of strained fish stock and dot here and there with a generous tablespoon of kneaded butter. Set, covered with a buttered paper, in a hot oven (400°) and cook for 35 minutes, basting frequently. Remove the paper and cook 10 minutes longer. Lift out the fish, place on a hot platter. Keep hot. Strain the cooking liquor through a very fine sieve over a saucepan and add another wineglass of Rhine wine and ½ cup of fish stock. Reduce to a generous cupful over a hot fire; add gradually, while stirring constantly, 5 tablespoons of butter so as to obtain a foamy, rich, thick sauce. Rectify the seasoning and pour half the sauce over the fish and serve the remainder in a sauceboat with a side dish of plain boiled small potato balls. Garnish with fresh parsley and slices of lemon, interspersed with small triangles of bread fried in butter.

BAKED SALMON PARISIENNE

Sponge 3 slices of fresh salmon, weighing 1 lb. each, with a damp cloth; rub with a tablespoon of lemon juice, then with salt, pepper, and a little nutmeg. Place in a buttered baking dish and sprinkle over a tablespoon each of finely chopped shallot, parsley, and mushrooms, add a bit of garlic, a small piece of bay leaf, a small clove, a few thyme leaves, and ½ cup of small dices of cooked ham. Pour over the whole, a small can of tomatoes, a tablespoon of lemon, and dot here and there with 2 tablespoons of butter. Cover tightly, set in a very hot oven (450°) for 20 minutes, remove the cover, add a tablespoon of kneaded butter, and cook 10 minutes longer. Rectify the seasoning and serve right from the baking dish with a side dish of cucumber salad with French dressing.

BOILED SALMON

IMPORTANT: The method of preparation, cooking, and dressing for salmon when boiled is invariably the same (*see* How To Boil Fish), and variety in the dish is furnished through the numerous sauces applicable.

The garnishing of boiled salmon, or any other fish, is dependent upon availability, and in this matter the ingenuity of the cook is given free play. Although it is customary to serve a side dish of plain boiled potatoes with boiled salmon, any other kind may be served according to taste.

BOILED SALMON AMERICAN SAUCE
(*Master Recipe*)

Sponge a 3½-lb. piece of fresh salmon, rub with salt and pepper and place in a fish kettle. Pour over a cold vinegar court bouillon (or white wine court bouillon may be used according to taste) and cook as indicated under How To Boil Fish. Lift out the fish. Dress on a hot platter, garnish with fresh parsley and slices of lemon, and serve with a side dish of AMERICAN SAUCE, page 33, or EGG SAUCE I or II, page 38. Prepared in this method, you may substitute any other kind of sauce according to taste.

BRAISED SLICE OF SALMON RICHARD

Sponge with a damp cloth 3 slices of fresh salmon, weighing 1 lb. each. Marinate for 30 minutes in a little white wine and aromatic herbs. Place in a braising kettle, ½ cup of sliced white part of leeks, a teaspoon of finely chopped shallots, and a teaspoon of finely chopped parsley. Put the three slices of fish on this, side by side; pour over the marinade, herbs, and liquid, and empty over a small can of small mushrooms. Dot here and there with a generous tablespoon of kneaded butter and another tablespoon of butter, season with salt, pepper, and a few grains of nutmeg, cover tightly and set in a hot oven (400°) for 30 minutes. Remove the cover and cook 5 minutes longer, after adding 3 tablespoons of thick tomato purée. Lift out the fish carefully, dress on a hot platter, and, after rectifying the seasoning and adding a tablespoon of sweet butter, pour over the fish. Border the platter with small triangles of bread fried in butter, alternating with slices of lemon, each topped with a large caper.

BRAISED SLICE OF SALMON ROYAL

Wipe dry 3 slices of fresh salmon of 1 lb. each. Lay in a braising kettle and season with salt, pepper, and a few grains each of Cayenne pepper and nutmeg; then add a teaspoon each of shallots, parsley, chives, and onions, all finely chopped and mixed with 2 tablespoons of finely chopped fresh mushrooms; add a small bouquet garni, a small crushed clove, and a few thyme leaves; dot here and there with a generous tablespoon of butter and pour over a wineglass of Sauternes wine. Cover tightly and set in a hot oven (400°) for 30 minutes; remove the cover and add a cupful of coarsely chopped artichoke bottoms and cook 5 minutes longer. Dress on a hot platter, rectify the seasoning of the sauce and pour over the fish. Garnish rapidly with the following ingredients, dressed in small mounds: 6 crayfish cooked in white wine court bouillon (*see* How To Boil Fish), 6 medium mushrooms cooked in anchovy butter and well drained, 6 small truffles shaped in olive form and sautéed in butter (optional), about 2 dozen small white onions (glazed), and 2 dozen small potato balls cooked in butter. A dish of Normande Sauce, page 44, may be served aside.

BROILED SALMON

Important: The one-dish meal is the culmination of years of planning and economizing on the part of the hostess. A one-dish meal is not a success unless it furnishes the essential combination of nutritive properties and saves time and labor. In the following recipes, as in the preceding ones, you will notice the different garnishing for each and every recipe. These garnishings are merely suggestions. They are interchangeable or may be combined according to fancy and availability. The slices of one pound each are halved only when presented on the table, thus apportioning eight ounces of fish to each guest.

BROILED SALMON STEAK
MAÎTRE D'HÔTEL
(*Master Recipe*)

Wipe dry 3 slices of fresh salmon of 1 lb. each and marinate for 15 minutes in either oil or melted butter, to which is added salt, pepper, and paprika to taste. Place dripping on a well-greased double broiler, place on the rack of the broiling oven, and broil, turning and basting frequently with the marinade. When the fish is done to the desired point, dress on a hot platter, surrounding with small potato balls, cooked in butter over a gentle fire and rolled in finely chopped parsley. Garnish with fresh, crisp watercress and quartered lemon and place on each slice of fish a generous teaspoon of MAÎTRE D'HÔTEL BUTTER, page 57.

Prepared in this way, you may substitute any other kind of sauce according to taste.

PÂTÉ DE SAUMON À LA FRANÇAISE
(*Salmon Loaf French Style*)

AUTHOR'S NOTE

During Lent, as well as during the summer, for cold supper or impromptu or formal luncheon these seemingly complicated but, in reality, easily prepared and economical dishes are very much appreciated in England and on the Continent.

They may be made with a flaky crust or in an earthenware terrine, similar to the oval one containing the famous PÂTÉ DE FOIE GRAS (Goose Liver Pâté), so much appreciated by Americans traveling abroad, and which may be found in first-class groceries and delicatessen stores.

Flounder, halibut, muskallonge, turbot, and in fact all the white-fleshed fish may be prepared in the same way.

DIRECTIONS FOR FIRST OPERATION—PREPARATION OF THE FISH

Prepare a pie dough. Let stand in a cool place until wanted. Skin and bone thoroughly and carefully a 3-lb. piece of fresh salmon, cut in 4 slices, and each slice in ½-inch strips. Marinate in 1½ cups olive oil, to which add the following ingredients: 1 scant teaspoon of finely chopped shallot, 2 medium-sized peeled mushrooms, finely chopped, 1 tablespoon of *very, very finely chopped* parsley, 3 washed, sponged fillets of anchovy, finely diced, salt and a few grains of Cayenne pepper to taste.

SECOND OPERATION—COOKING THE FISH

Melt 3 tablespoons of clarified butter in a flat saucepan and, when beginning to smoke, put in the fish well drained and sponged, and cook 3 or 4 minutes, turning frequently; then turn fish with butter into a large bowl.

THIRD OPERATION—PREPARING THE STUFFING

Skin and bone thoroughly enough raw whiting or pickerel (whiting is more delicate) to obtain 2 lbs. of flesh and pass through the meat chopper, adding alternately a generous ½ cup of soft bread crumbs, moistened with milk, then squeezed through a cloth and tossed a little to loosen. To this mixture, add 1 lb. of sweet butter, the size of a small walnut of anchovy paste, a teaspoon of *very, very finely chopped* shallot, a tablespoon of very finely chopped parsley, and 1 whole egg. Mix thoroughly, then pass through the meat chopper again to ensure homogeneity and smoothness, adding this time, little by little, a tablespoon of thick fresh cream.

FOURTH OPERATION—FILLING THE MOLD

Butter a bread tin, place on a buttered baking tin and line the inside with a sheet of pie dough as for a pie, leaving ½ inch of dough overlapping the edge for joining with the top. Spread the inside with the stuffing an inch thick, then spread a layer of salmon, then a layer of stuffing, and so on until fish and stuffing are exhausted, seeing to it that the top is of stuffing and well rounded in the middle. Cover with a sheet of dough and solder well on the edge with the overlapping dough, brushing with white of egg to facilitate fusion; then brush all over with white of egg, and, if there is any dough left, decorate the top with small squares, round, oval or fancy shapes by means of cutter. Brush then with egg yolk to golden glaze. You may also twist, gimlet-like a long narrow strip of dough and attach to the edge with water or white of egg. Surround the edge with a strip of buttered paper 2 inches wide, securing with a string, and set in a moderately hot oven (375°). When the top begins to brown, cover with a buttered paper. Reduce the temperature to 325° and cook for nearly 2 hours, again reducing the heat to 300° after 1 hour, and removing the buttered paper on the top after 1½ hours of cooking. Remove and cool.

If this delicious preparation is not to be eaten at once, but kept for several days, the following day lift the top crust carefully and introduce a little fish gelatine made from the trimmings reduced to the gelatine point over a hot fire, then cooled, but not entirely settled, to which you may also add a little finely chopped truffles.

The PÂTÉ IN TERRINE (loaf in earthenware) is prepared in the same way. It is cooked in a pan containing hot water for 2 hours, and the top is covered with a crust. If not to be eaten as soon as cold, the next day lift off the crust carefully and fill the hollow with clarified butter, nearly cooled.

Both pâtés (loaves) keep two weeks in a refrigerator. The pâté is served in slices and usually with a green salad with French dressing and a side dish of freshly made French fried potatoes.

SALMON MOUSSE

Skin and bone carefully enough fresh raw salmon (piece from the tail) to obtain a generous pound of flesh and pass through the meat chopper twice with a tablespoon of butter, added bit by bit, and the white of an egg, added in same way. Set for an hour in the refrigerator. Place in a large bowl and work with a wooden spoon, adding bit by bit, 3 tablespoons (more if necessary) of thick fresh cream, stirring constantly and seasoning with salt and white pepper to taste, until light and creamy and volume is increased one third.

Try a teaspoonful of the mixture in rapidly boiling salted water and taste. It must be delicate and should not break. If too firm, add a little more cream, and if it is too soft, breaks, and does not hold, add a little more egg white. Butter a large ring mold, decorate the bottom and sides with small strips of lobster, hard-boiled egg white, slices of olive, strips of gherkin, etc., to your fancy. Pack the mold with the mixture, pressing a little to fill the hollow up to ¼ of an inch from the edge, cover with a buttered paper; place in a pan containing hot water and set in a moderately hot oven (350°) for 35 minutes. Remove, turn the mold upside down, let stand a few minutes and unmold. Cover with a MORNAY SAUCE, page 43; glaze under the hot flame of the broiling oven or in a very hot oven a few seconds and decorate rapidly the border of the platter with small fresh sardines fried in butter and here and there small mounds of small squares of French fried potatoes.

A side dish of cucumber salad with French dressing will not be amiss.

SHAD

"My mitre for a shad!" exclaimed a Bishop, as widely renowned for his connoisseur's knowledge of fine dishes as he was for his diplomacy in spiritual matters.

"Shad is one of the sheer delights of the table, especially during Lent," commented the Marquis de Cussy, ". . . and sorrel seems to grow especially and for the sole purpose of accompanying shad. Both are like the Siamese twins, inseparable, they are born for each other. . . ."

"Shad," declared Grimmod de la Reyniere, one of the greatest epicures known to history, "is a fish extremely delicate and generous, which ascends the rivers to charm the palates of the gourmets and connoisseurs. . . ."

Formerly, shad was the traditional fish during fast days and was always to be found on the aristocratic tables of the Faubourg Saint Germain, in Paris, and under the forks of the pious nobles.

Shad, which is found only in the Atlantic Ocean, the Caspian Sea, and the Mediterranean, to be really in its prime, should be caught in the spring, when it leaves the ocean to ascend the rivers to cultivate gently and leisurely in appropriate waters the plumpness of its fine flesh for gourmets.

Shad is a plain-mannered fish and likes particularly *au Bleu*. À la meunière, it is a delight, braised in a bath of red Burgundy wine, its goodness surpasses description; in matelotte (stew) sauce it is a delicacy for a queen, but grilled with or without its succulent *roe,* after being marinated in virgin oil, it is a morsel that melts in the mouth. It should be basted very often when the meat crackles on the grill, then laid gently into a tender purée of delicate sorrel. The shad loves sorrel as the goose loves chestnuts; the turkey, truffles; the sole, white wine; the thrush, juniper; fried fish, parsley and lemon; lobster, mayonnaise.

Roasted, when heavy and plump, previously bathed in melted

butter, sweet it must be and flavored with lots of spices, and plainly dressed on a white napkin, necklaced with green, crisp, young watercress, *Shad Is Then in Its Full Glory.*

And its *roe,* its tender *roe,* so artistically and symmetrically arranged, like a pearl necklace, is not it a morsel for the most sophisticated? Notwithstanding all its goodness *Shad Is Not Perfect.* It has its flaw, even as the queen of the flowers: as there is no rose without its thorn, there is no shad without its sharp bones. Head, body, and tail are as full of bones as a porcupine is full of quills—not a single spot without a bone, except the roe, of course.

In addition to the following recipes, the various methods of preparation of mackerel, herring, bluefish, and the like, may be adapted to this popular and delicious fish.

BOILED SHAD IN WHITE WINE

Clean a 3-lb. shad, wash, sponge, and rub with a tablespoon of lemon. Place in a fish kettle and pour over a rapidly boiling white wine court bouillon (*see* How To Boil Fish). Dress on a hot platter covered with a napkin, remove the skin, garnish with crisp green parsley and slices of lemon, and serve with a side dish of White Wine Sauce, page 46, using part of the cooking broth for its preparation, and a side dish of plain boiled small potatoes.

BOILED SHAD BURGUNDY WINE

Follow the directions as indicated for recipe above, using red wine court bouillon made with red Burgundy wine. Dress as indicated, garnish with small perch, fried in deep fat, one for each person, fresh parsley and slices of lemon, and serve with a side dish of Red Wine Sauce, page 46, using part of the cooking broth for its preparation, and a side dish of small French fried potatoes.

BROILED SHAD MAÎTRE D'HÔTEL

(*Master Recipe*)

Clean, wash, and sponge a 3-lb. shad. Split open from the back and remove the large bone, season with salt and pepper and roll in melted butter, place on a double broiler, skin down, set on the rack of the broiling oven. Broil, turning and basting frequently until half done; turn into a buttered baking pan, pour over 3 tablespoons of melted butter and finish cooking in a hot oven, basting very often. Dress on a hot platter, garnish with fresh parsley and quartered lemon, and place on each half of the fish a generous tablespoon of MAÎTRE D'HÔTEL BUTTER, page 57. Serve with a side dish of cucumber salad with French dressing. Any other kind of sauce may be substituted, if desired.

BROILED SHAD GAULOISE

Select a large shad of 3½ to 4 lbs., having a soft roe. Remove the gills and clean through the opening, taking care not to bruise the soft roe, which set aside. Remove the reddish fibers from the soft roe and place in strongly salted water with 6 carp soft roe. Trim the fish, wash and sponge well, and with a sharp-pointed knife make 6 superficial slashes on each side. Rub the fish with salt and pepper to taste and place in a deep platter, pour over a cupful of olive oil, a small onion sliced thin, a teaspoon of finely chopped parsley, a bit of bay leaf and 5 or 6 thyme leaves, and let stand for 2 hours, rubbing the fish once in a while with the oil.

An hour before serving, drain and stuff the fish through the gills with a stuffing made of 1 cup of raw eel flesh carefully boned and passed through the meat chopper, ½ cup (more or less) of freshly made soft bread crumbs, salt, pepper, and a few grains of Cayenne pepper, the whole blended with a little CREAM SAUCE I, page 36, to which is added a tablespoon of onion juice. Sew up the opening carefully. Rub a double broiler with oil or bacon skin, place the fish on it, set on the rack of the broiling oven and broil first under a hot flame, then under a very low one, turning and basting frequently with olive oil. Dress on a long hot platter and cover the fish with the following sauce:

Sauce Française

Take a small amount of fish trimmings, add 5 slices of carrot, 5 slices of onion, a generous sprig of parsley, a few top leaves of green celery, all finely chopped, a tiny bay leaf, 5 or 6 thyme leaves, 5 crushed peppercorns, salt to taste, and moisten with 2 generous cups of dry white wine to make a fish stock. Bring to a boil and let reduce very gently to half volume; strain through a fine sieve and add a generous tablespoon of thick tomato purée (thickened with a little flour if too thin); boil once or twice again and set aside on the range, then add gradually, while beating constantly with a wire whisk, 3 tablespoons of butter and 1 tablespoon of crayfish butter (*see* Compounded Butters). Finish with a few drops of strained lemon juice and strain over the fish. Garnish with 6 large mushrooms cooked in butter, 6 large shrimps cooked in fish stock, then rolled in melted butter, 6 small oysters cooked in fish stock and rolled in melted butter, and the 6 carp roe and the shad roe cooked in fish stock and rolled in melted crayfish butter, placing the shad soft roe on top of the fish. Decorate with small sprigs of green curled parsley and quartered lemon, and serve with a side dish of small potato balls cooked in butter and well browned.

BROILED SHAD AND ROE ANNA HELD

Prepare, cook, and dress a 3-lb. shad and 3 shad roe as indicated for master recipe, Broiled Shad Maître d'Hôtel, page 181. Garnish with 6 poached eggs, each placed on a round piece of toast the size of the egg, slightly buttered with anchovy butter (*see* Compounded Butters), interspersed with half a roe, also broiled and brushed with melted Maître d'Hôtel Butter, page 57, fresh parsley, and quartered lemon. Serve with a side dish of Normande Sauce, page 44, and a side dish of small French fried potatoes.

BROILED SHAD GEORGE CLARETIE

Prepare, cook, and dress a 3-lb. shad as indicated for master recipe, BROILED SHAD MAÎTRE D'HÔTEL, page 181. Garnish with 6 medium-sized baked stuffed tomatoes made as follows:

BAKED STUFFED TOMATOES GEORGE CLARETIE

Chop and mix together 2 hard-boiled eggs, 4 tablespoons of tuna fish (canned), 2 fillets of anchovy, 8 green olives, 2 tablespoons of well-washed capers, 1 medium-sized sweet gherkin, a scant teaspoon finely chopped shallots (first sautéed in a little butter), the butter from the shallots, and 1 generous tablespoon of melted butter. Season to taste with salt, pepper, and a little nutmeg and a few grains of Cayenne pepper. Place in a saucepan, heat thoroughly, and fill the scooped parboiled tomatoes. Cover with fine buttered crumbs mixed with grated Swiss cheese and brown in a hot oven (400°) or under the hot flame of the broiling oven. Garnish also with fresh parsley and quartered lemon placed between each tomato and serve with a side dish of RIALTO SAUCE, page 46.

FILLET OF SHAD GOURMET

Have 6 fillets of shad well trimmed and wiped dry. Place in a deep skillet and cover with a generous cupful of strained stock, made from the trimmings of the fish, 2 tablespoons of olive oil, and add a small bouquet garni, a crushed clove, a few tarragon leaves, 6 thyme leaves, 1 teaspoon of finely chopped shallots, 6 crushed peppercorns, and salt to taste and cook over a gentle flame for 15 to 20 minutes, reducing the heat after the first boil and letting simmer very gently until done. Lift out the fish, drain, and place on a hot platter. Keep hot. Melt 2 tablespoons of butter, add salt, pepper, and a few grains of nutmeg to taste, 6 slices of lemon, and moisten with the strained cooking liquor, reduced to a cup. Stir once in a while, while boiling a few minutes, and strain through a fine sieve over another saucepan; rectify the seasoning and add, off the fire, 3 egg yolks, alternating with 1 tablespoon of anchovy butter (*see* COM-POUNDED BUTTERS), added bit by bit, stirring gently. Pour over the fish; garnish the top of each fillet with 2 large mushrooms, cooked in butter and stuffed with creamed crab meat, fresh parsley, and small triangles of golden browned puff paste, stuffed with an oyster, alternating with quartered lemon. Serve with a side dish of Brussels sprouts, first boiled in salt water, drained, sautéed in butter, and sprinkled with finely chopped parsley.

PANNED SHAD ROE CREOLE

Parboil 3 shad roe in salted, slightly acidulated (lemon or vinegar) water for 10 minutes, remove the reddish fibers and cut each roe into quarters. Sprinkle with freshly ground peppercorns to taste, then with lemon juice; roll in bread crumbs, then in well-beaten eggs, and again in bread crumbs. Sauté in butter, turning carefully frequently, and dress on a hot round platter, covered with CREOLE SAUCE III, page 37. Surround the edge of the platter with slices of lemon, interspersed with small triangles of bread fried in butter, and fresh curled parsley, and serve with a side dish of melted butter, to which add the size of a hazelnut of extract of meat (Liebig, Oxo, etc.), and a side dish of French fried potatoes.

PANNED SHAD ROE ON SPINACH

Parboil 3 shad roe in salted, acidulated (lemon or vinegar) water for 15 minutes, plunge in cold water, remove the membrane, and cut in two. Melt 4 tablespoons of butter and add the size of a hazelnut of anchovy paste; sauté, turning carefully frequently, and cook until golden browned on both sides. Lift out the roe and dress on a hot platter, covered with plain boiled spinach, copiously buttered. Surround the edge of the platter with quartered hard-boiled eggs, interspersed with quartered lemon, and place a small bunch of green parsley in center of platter. Serve with a side dish of OLIVE SAUCE, page 44, and another side dish of plain boiled potato balls.

PLANKED SHAD EPICURE

Prepare a 3-lb. shad as for broiling. Rub with salt and pepper and brush with plenty of butter, place skin down on a buttered oak plank 1 inch thick and a little longer and wider than the fish, leaving space of about 1½ inches for garnishing. Set the plank in a hot oven (400°) and bake for 20 to 25 minutes, basting very often with melted butter; remove the plank from the oven and surround the border with mashed potatoes forced through a pastry bag having a fancy tube; sprinkle with melted butter and brown rapidly under the flame of the broiling oven or in a very hot oven, sprinkling the fish with butter to prevent burning or scorching or, better, spreading a buttered paper over the fish.

Garnish as follows: 6 oysters, fried in Batter III, page 16; 6 slices of tomatoes fried in butter, 6 large mushrooms broiled under the flame of the broiling oven and dipped in melted anchovy butter, 6 small fillets of anchovy, sponged thoroughly and dipped in melted butter and placed at equal intervals over the fish. Sprinkle with finely chopped parsley and serve with a side dish of Gooseberry Sauce, page 40, and a side dish of French fried potatoes.

PLANKED SHAD WITH CREAMED ROE

Prepare, cook, and dress a 3-lb. shad as indicated above. Meanwhile, parboil a shad roe in salted, acidulated water for 15 minutes; lift out, plunge in cold water, drain, remove the membrane, and mash. Melt 3 tablespoons of butter, add 1 teaspoon of very finely chopped shallot and cook 4 or 5 minutes; add the mashed roe, sprinkle with a generous tablespoon of flour, and pour on gradually 5 tablespoons of fresh cream, stirring meanwhile. Let simmer very gently for 10 minutes, adding more cream if getting too thick; remove from the fire and add 2 egg yolks, one by one and stirring all the while. Season highly with salt, freshly crushed peppercorns or pepper from the mill (just one turn), and a few drops of lemon juice. Remove the fish from the oven; spread thinly with the roe mixture; cover with freshly made buttered soft bread crumbs and surround with a border of mashed potatoes forced through a pastry bag with a fancy tube and sprinkled with melted butter. Return the fish to the oven to brown. Garnish with small glazed white onions, small potato balls cooked in butter and well drained, 6 large broiled mushrooms, a small mound of cooked peas, well buttered, same amount of string beans, cut julienne-like and well buttered, and a small mound of artichoke bottoms, sautéed in butter and sprinkled with finely chopped parsley. Cross the fish with 6 slices of broiled bacon and serve with a side dish of melted butter.

SHAD ROE À LA MEUNIÈRE

(Serves Two)

Parboil three shad roe as indicated in recipe for PANNED SHAD ROE ON SPINACH, page 184. Plunge in cold water and remove the membrane. Split in two and fry in hot butter. Dress on a hot platter, placing a slice of toast under each half; sprinkle finely chopped parsley over the roe, a little lemon juice, and a few well-washed capers and when ready to serve, but not before, pour over 3 or 4 tablespoons of very hot brown butter. Garnish with fresh curled parsley and quartered lemon and serve with a side dish of hashed creamed potatoes.

SHAD ROE BONNE FEMME

Parboil and prepare 3 shad roe as indicated in recipe for PANNED SHAD ROE ON SPINACH, page 184, and, after removing the membrane, cut in dices ½ an inch square. Sprinkle on the bottom of a well-buttered earthenware baking dish 2 or 3 tablespoons of sliced cooked mushrooms in butter, a teaspoon of finely chopped shallots, first sautéed in butter and well drained and as much finely chopped parsley; lay on the pieces of roe and add ½ cup of white wine, 1 generous tablespoon of kneaded butter, and 3 tablespoons of thick cream.

Cover with a buttered paper and set in a hot oven (400°) for 15 minutes, remove the paper, season with salt, pepper, and a few grains of Cayenne pepper and continue cooking for 5 minutes. Serve right from the baking dish with a side dish of plain boiled small potato balls, rolled in finely chopped parsley, and a side dish of cucumber salad with French dressing.

SHEEPSHEAD

The sheepshead of the porgy family, a very popular fish among Americans, is found along the Atlantic Coast from Cape Cod to Texas. The name is derived from the shape of the head and the prominent incisor teeth.

It grows to a length of about thirty inches and weighs on an average from six to seven pounds, although specimens have been found weighing twenty pounds. The body is deep and marked by seven or eight dark transverse bands, most evident in the young.

Except during the spawning season from March to June, the sheepshead is gregarious in habit. It feeds on small crustaceans and shellfish, which it detaches from the sea bottom by means of its incisors, and also on seaweed.

The same name is given in the West to the "drum," a fresh-water fish of silvery grey hue with obscure oblique streaks on the sides, which in Texas and Louisiana is very popular but in the North is not eaten. This fish reaches sometimes a weight of fifty to sixty pounds.

In certain parts of the United States, the sheepshead is known under the name "gaspergou croaker," and in others "white perch."

In addition to the following recipes, the various methods of preparation of catfish, porgy, and smelts may be adapted to this fine fish.

BAKED SHEEPSHEAD HOME STYLE

Sponge with a damp cloth 6 slices of sheepshead totaling about 3 lbs. Roll in salted, peppered flour and place in a well-buttered earthenware baking dish, cover with a scant tablespoon of finely chopped parsley, 1 tablespoon of finely chopped sweet gherkins, 1 scant teaspoon of finely chopped onion, a very tiny bit of garlic, and a small bouquet garni, all chopped very fine and well mixed. Moisten with ½ cup of strained fish stock and pour over a drained small can of tomatoes; dot here and there with a tablespoon of butter and a tablespoon of kneaded butter, set in a moderately hot oven (375°), covered with a buttered paper, and cook for 20 minutes; remove the paper, add a scant teaspoon of lemon juice and cook for 5 minutes longer uncovered. Rectify the seasoning and serve right from the baking dish with a side dish of plain boiled potatoes.

BAKED SHEEPSHEAD SPENCER METHOD

Cut 3 lbs. of sheepshead into serving pieces. Dip in salted milk, using one tablespoon of salt for each cup of milk (evaporated milk may be used). Dip in finely ground or rolled cornflake crumbs. Arrange on well-oiled baking pan and sprinkle liberally with good oil. Bake in a very hot oven (450°) for about 15 minutes. Dress on a hot platter, garnish with fresh parsley and slices of lemon, and serve with a side dish of melted butter and a side dish of plain boiled potatoes.

BAKED SHEEPSHEAD CREOLE STYLE

Rub with a damp cloth 6 slices of sheepshead weighing 8 ozs. each. Rub with a tablespoon of lemon juice, then with salt and pepper and a little nutmeg to taste. Place the fish in a buttered baking dish, the bottom of which is covered with a cupful of CREOLE SAUCE III, page 37, and over the fish place another cup of the same. Dot here and there with a generous tablespoon of butter, sprinkle with finely chopped parsley, and set, covered with a buttered paper, in a moderately hot oven (375°) for 20 minutes. Remove the paper and add a generous tablespoon of sherry wine, a teaspoon of kneaded butter, and cook 10 minutes longer. Rectify the seasoning and serve right from the baking dish with a side dish of plain boiled potatoes and a side dish of cucumber salad with French dressing, to which has been added 1 generous tablespoon of coarsely chopped hard-boiled egg.

BAKED SHEEPSHEAD SPANISH STYLE

Wipe dry 6 slices of sheepshead, weighing 8 ozs. each, season with salt, pepper, and a few grains each of Cayenne pepper and nutmeg and place in a well-oiled (using olive oil preferably) earthenware baking dish, the bottom of which is spread with a large onion, thinly sliced, and a tablespoon of coarsely chopped green pepper. Place over each slice a sponged, washed, and rolled in melted butter fillet of anchovy, then cover with 6 slices of peeled tomatoes and sprinkle with a teaspoon of finely chopped chives and a scant cup of thinly sliced raw mushrooms. Pour over, a wineglass of white wine or 2 tablespoons of strained lemon juice and add 3 tablespoons of water. Dot here and there with 2 tablespoons of butter and a teaspoon of kneaded butter, cover tightly and set in a very hot oven (450°) for 25 minutes. Remove the cover, sprinkle over well-buttered bread crumbs and continue cooking until well browned. Serve right in the baking dish with a side dish of your favorite green salad with French dressing.

BAKED SHEEPSHEAD WITH SPINACH

Chop coarsely 2 lbs. of well-washed raw spinach and parboil in a saucepan without any water. Place in a bowl and add a teaspoon each of finely chopped shallot and parsley and cover with a cupful of thin CREAM SAUCE I, page 36. Place half the spinach in a well-buttered baking dish and lay the fish on it; cover with the remaining spinach, pour over another half cup of same sauce, season with salt, pepper, and a little nutmeg to taste, and dot here and there with a tablespoon of butter. Set, covered tightly, in a very hot oven (450°) for 20 minutes, remove the cover and cook 5 minutes longer. Correct the seasoning and serve right from the baking dish with a side dish of small potato balls cooked in butter and a side dish of egg sauce.

BOILED SHEEPSHEAD HOLLANDAISE SAUCE
(*Master Recipe*)

Rub with a damp cloth, 3 lbs. of sheepshead and place in a fish kettle over a hot fire. Pour over a white wine court bouillon (*see* How To Boil Fish) and cook for 20 short minutes, reducing the heat after the first boil. Lift out the fish, drain well, skin, and dress on a hot platter. Garnish with plain boiled small potato balls, slices of lemon, and a bunch of fresh parsley (or watercress) and serve with a side dish of Hollandaise Sauce I, page 40. Any other kind of sauce may be substituted if desired.

SKATE

Unlike other fish, the skate is much better when cooked one or two days after it has been caught. However, it should not be of a sourish taste. The liver of the skate is delicious to eat, and one should always save it, as it may be prepared in all the different methods adapted for chicken liver, shad roe, and in fact every method applied to beef, veal, pork, and lamb livers.

The skate may be prepared in countless ways, one more appetizing than another, but its preparation reaches the apex of glory when the fish is served in black butter, after being cooked in a court bouillon (*see* How To Boil Fish), and when the black butter is poured over sizzling hot, just before serving. When cooking skate, if only the fins are used, they may be cooked just as they are, but if the dorsal part be used, it should always be parboiled in salted water, to which may be added a little lemon juice.

BAKED SKATE WITH SWISS CHEESE

Place in a deep skillet, 2 fins of skate, rubbed with lemon juice, then sprinkled with a little salt and generously with coarse black pepper. Pour over one cup of milk and add 1 small clove, 1 bouquet garni, a scant teaspoon of finely chopped shallot or onion, and a very tiny bit of garlic (may be omitted). Cover, bring to a rapid boil, and set aside to simmer very gently for 15 minutes. Butter an earthenware baking dish, sprinkle with 3 tablespoons of grated Swiss cheese and place the fish over it. Prepare with the milk from the skillet Cream Sauce I, page 36, and pour over the fish; sprinkle again with 2 tablespoons of butter and set 10 minutes in a hot oven (400°) or until well browned. Serve right from the baking dish with a side dish of green salad with French dressing.

BOILED SKATE BLACK BUTTER

Boil 2 skate fins in a vinegar court bouillon as indicated under

How To Boil Fish. At the first boil, reduce the heat and let simmer very gently for 10 minutes; lift out, drain, place on a hot service platter, sprinkle a little coarse black pepper over, and set at the entrance of the oven to dry a little. Pour over a black butter made as follows: heat over a hot fire, 3 or 4 tablespoons of butter and let brown. Pour, holding the pan as far as possible from you so as not to be burned, a tablespoon of tarragon vinegar into the butter. Boil once and pour rapidly over the fish, generously sprinkled with finely chopped parsley. Garnish with fresh parsley and quartered lemon and serve with a side dish of small French fried potatoes and a side dish of cucumber salad with French dressing. This delicious dish should be served at once and sizzling hot.

BOILED SKATE PARISIAN STYLE

Boil a cleaned, sponged skate of 3½ to 4 lbs. in a vinegar court bouillon as indicated under How To Boil Fish. At the first boil, set aside and let simmer very gently for 20 minutes. Lift out carefully, drain, place on a hot platter, and remove the skin and replace in the broth if not ready to serve, otherwise the fish will turn black. Dress on a hot service platter, garnish with fresh parsley and plain boiled small potato balls and pour over a cupful of Caper Sauce, page 36. Serve at once with a side dish of your favorite green salad with French dressing.

FRIED SKATE

Prepare and cook a 3½- to 4-lb. skate as indicated for above recipe. Lift out carefully, drain well, and cut in 3-inch pieces; roll in flour and fry in plenty of butter, turning frequently until golden brown. Dress on a hot platter, garnish with 4 small mounds of glazed turnips mixed with small glazed white onions, fried parsley, and quartered lemon and serve with a side dish of Lemon Butter, page 42, and a side dish of young crisp watercress salad with sliced red beet and French dressing.

FRIED SKATE IN DEEP FAT
BOHEMIAN SAUCE

Use only the fins; there should be 3½ lbs. Skin, cut in 2½-inch pieces and marinate for 2 hours in 1½ cups of oil, 3 tablespoons of lemon juice, 12 slices of medium-sized onions, 6 thyme leaves, a bit of bay leaf, and 3 stems of fresh parsley, stirring once in a while. Lift out, drain, and sponge well; place the fish 5 minutes in BATTER III (*see* BATTER FOR FRYING FISH) and, when ready to serve, place in a wire basket and plunge in boiling deep fat until golden brown; lift out and drain. Dress on a hot round platter covered with a napkin and garnish as follows: 1 bunch of fried curled parsley, 1 mound of the onions from the marinade, strained, rolled in flour and fried in deep fat, 1 mound of glazed carrots, and 1 mound of 6 quarters of lemon. Serve with a side dish of BOHEMIAN SAUCE, page 50.

SKATE À LA SAINTE MENEHOULD

Place in a saucepan, 2 tablespoons of kneaded butter and blend well over a hot fire, moisten by adding, gradually, 2 cups of scalded milk, stirring meanwhile, add also 3 medium-sized onions thinly sliced, a bouquet garni, 1 small clove, a very tiny bit of garlic and, when beginning to boil, set aside and let simmer very gently for 10 minutes. Meanwhile cut 4 lbs. of skate as indicated for above recipe using only the fins, place in the cream sauce and cook 10 minutes over a low fire. Lift out the fish and place in a pan containing strained fish broth. Drain and roll in bread crumbs, then in melted butter and again in bread crumbs. Place on a well-greased double broiler, set on the rack of the broiling oven, and broil, turning and basting frequently under a low flame. Dress on a hot platter; garnish with fried curled parsley, strips of gherkins, and quartered lemon. Serve with a side dish of RIALTO SAUCE, page 46.

SKATE À LA MEUNIÈRE

Select, preferably, a "Buckled Skate," thick in proportion to length. Cut the fins, open the coffer by cutting the skin in the middle to clean and remove the liver without breaking; then cut the body in 3 pieces. Wash thoroughly in several waters and fillet body and fins. Place in fish kettle and barely cover with boiling vinegar court bouillon made as indicated under How To Boil Fish. Remove aside and let simmer very gently 10 minutes without cooking further. Lift out, drain, sponge gently but thoroughly. Melt 5 tablespoons of butter and place the salted, peppered, and rolled fish into the butter and brown rapidly on both sides. Lift out; dress on a hot platter; keep hot while straining the butter so as to have about 5 tablespoons. Heat up well. Sprinkle a little black pepper from the mill over the fish, then squeeze over two small lemons and sprinkle with a little finely chopped parsley and 2 tablespoons of well-washed capers. Pour the boiling hot brown butter over the fish rapidly, garnish with fresh parsley and quartered lemon, and serve immediately with a side dish of French fried potatoes and a side dish of cucumber salad with French dressing.

SHELL OF SKATE LIVER AU GRATIN

Marinate 5 skate livers in salt water for 15 minutes, slice in small scallops or pieces 1 inch square, and roll in salt and pepper. Fill 6 scallop shells, the edges of which are bordered with smooth mashed potatoes, forced through a pastry bag having a small fancy tube, with the slices or small scallops or pieces of skate liver, half cooked in butter; cover with a little Mornay Sauce, page 43, add a small layer of thinly sliced fresh mushrooms, cooked in butter and sprinkled with very finely chopped parsley, then another layer of skate liver and a little more sauce. Cover with well-buttered fine bread crumbs and set, covered with a buttered paper, in a hot oven (450°) for 5 long minutes; remove the paper and let cook longer to brown the top. Dress the shells on a hot platter, covered with a napkin; garnish with fresh parsley or watercress and quartered lemons and serve with a side dish of shoestring potatoes.

SMELTS

Owing to their small size, smelts, which are really delicious, do not lend themselves to many variations in cookery. When very small, they may be fried, "En Brochette," that is, threaded on a skewer three or four at a time and plunged into deep boiling fat, then dressed bushlike, similar to the whitebait or fresh anchovy, on a platter with a napkin, while the usual fried green parsley and quartered lemon are the only garnishing. A tartare sauce may be served separately or any of the other tangy cold sauces usually served with fried fish.

In addition to the following recipes, the various methods of preparation of anchovy, sardines, and whitebait may be adapted to this small fish.

BAKED STUFFED SMELTS CRYSTAL PALACE

Prepare 3 dozen smelts as indicated for recipe SMELTS À LA REINE, page 198, using the same stuffing.

Place the fish in a well-buttered earthenware baking dish, the bottom of which is sprinkled with 2 tablespoons of finely chopped olives mixed with 2 tablespoons of finely chopped fresh raw mushrooms and a teaspoon of finely chopped chervil. Pour over ½ cup of white wine and dot here and there with a teaspoon of kneaded butter and 1 generous tablespoon of anchovy butter. Place over each fish a strip of well-sponged anchovy, and sprinkle over a tablespoon of finely chopped parsley. Cover with a buttered paper and set in a very hot oven (450°) for 10 minutes; remove the paper and cook 5 short minutes longer. Lift out the fish carefully and dress on a hot platter crownlike. Garnish the center with creamed oysters, cover the whole with MORNAY SAUCE, page 43, and set under the hot flame of the broiling oven to glaze. Garnish rapidly with slices of lemon and sprigs of fresh parsley and serve with a side dish of small squares of French fried potatoes.

BREADED BROILED SMELTS MAÎTRE D'HÔTEL
(*Master Recipe*)

Split from the back and remove the large bone of 2½ dozen large smelts. Season to taste with salt and pepper, roll in fine bread crumbs, then in beaten eggs and again in bread crumbs; place on a well-greased double broiler, set on the rack of the broiling oven; broil, turning and basting frequently with melted butter. Dress on a hot platter; garnish with fresh parsley, quartered lemon, and sticks of sweet gherkins and serve with a side dish of MAÎTRE D'HÔTEL BUTTER, page 57, and a side dish of hashed brown potatoes. You may substitute any other cold, tangy sauce if desired.

FRIED SMELTS EN BROCHETTE
(*On Skewers*)

Remove the gills, sponge carefully and gently, dip in milk, and roll in salted, white-peppered flour. Thread through the gills on skewers, ½ dozen smelts for a serving, taking care to have them of the same size. When ready to serve, and only then, place in a wire basket and plunge into boiling deep fat until golden brown and crisp. Drain, dress on a hot platter covered with a fancy folded napkin; garnish with fried parsley and quartered lemon and serve with a side dish of LEMON BUTTER SAUCE, page 42, and a side dish of cucumber salad with sour-cream dressing.

FRIED STUFFED SMELTS PARISIAN STYLE

Prepare, stuff as indicated in recipe for SMELTS À LA REINE, page 198, 2½ dozen smelts of the same size, roll in bread crumbs, then in beaten eggs and again in bread crumbs and, when ready to serve, place in a wire basket and plunge in boiling deep frying fat. Drain, dress on a hot platter covered with a folded napkin, and sprinkle over French fried onions. Garnish with fresh parsley and quartered lemon and serve with a side dish of mayonnaise, to which is added a scant teaspoon of prepared mustard and a tablespoon of coarsely chopped sour gherkins.

FRENCH FRIED ONIONS

Slice 3 very large onions, freeing each ring. Dip in milk, seasoned with salt and white pepper, then in flour, and plunge in boiling deep frying fat. Drain well.

FRIED SMELTS GOURMET

Clean 3 dozen small smelts, remove the heads and tails, roll in salted and white-peppered flour, and fry in olive oil over a hot fire, turning the fish frequently and carefully to brown both sides. Drain, dress on a hot platter, and sprinkle over, ½ a cup of blanched large almonds, cut in strips and mixed with finely chopped parsley. Garnish with potato curls and serve with a side dish of RUSSIAN SAUCE, page 52.

POTATO CURLS

Wash and pare large, long potatoes. Shape with a potato curler, soak 1 hour in ice-cold water; drain, dry between towels, and fry in boiling deep frying fat. Drain and sprinkle with salt.

SMELTS À LA REINE

Skin and bone enough raw flounder to obtain a cupful of flesh and pass through the meat chopper, adding alternately ½ cup of soft bread crumbs, moistened with fish stock, then squeezed through a cloth and tossed a little to loosen. To this mixture, add ½ cup of raw mushrooms, peeled and passed through the meat chopper with a teaspoon of finely chopped shallot, a scant teaspoon of finely chopped parsley, and a whole fresh egg, salt, pepper, and a few grains of nutmeg to taste. Place in a large bowl and mix thoroughly, then pass through the meat chopper again, adding 2 tablespoons of thick fresh cream and 2 egg yolks. Mix with a generous half cup of CREAM SAUCE I, page 36, and place in a saucepan to heat thoroughly, stirring constantly and not letting boil. Meanwhile, remove the heads and tails of 2 dozen large smelts, split open from the back and remove the large bone, sprinkle with lemon juice, then with salt and white pepper. Roll in flour and sauté 5 minutes in very hot butter. Place a third of the stuffing in a buttered earthenware baking dish, lay on this a third of the fish, cover with another third of the stuffing, then with fish, and so on. Sprinkle the top with buttered bread crumbs and brown in a hot oven (400°) for 5 minutes or longer. Serve right from the baking dish with a side dish of cucumber salad with French dressing.

SMELTS IN CREAM AU GRATIN

Remove the heads and tails of 2½ dozen small smelts, split from the back and remove the large bone. Place in a deep saucepan and pour over salted and white-peppered milk, barely covering the fish; bring to a rapid boil, remove immediately aside and let simmer 5 short minutes. Lift out the fish, carefully, place in a buttered baking dish and keep hot. Make a CREAM SAUCE I, page 36, using part of the cooking milk or all if necessary, cover the fish, dot here and there with 2 tablespoons of butter and 1 tablespoon of kneaded butter with a few grains of Cayenne pepper and nutmeg to taste; sprinkle with buttered bread crumbs and set in a hot oven (400°) to brown. Serve right from the baking dish with a side dish of Potato and Spinach Croquettes.

POTATO AND SPINACH CROQUETTES

Force hot boiled potatoes through a potato ricer; there should be 2 cupfuls. Add 2 tablespoons of butter, 2 egg yolks, slightly beaten, and a scant half cup of finely chopped cooked spinach, season with salt and pepper and a little nutmeg to taste. Cool. Shape in regular croquettes, or in pear shape, or in ball, according to fancy, dip in bread crumbs, then in beaten eggs, and again in bread crumbs and fry in boiling deep frying fat. Drain and serve. If in pear shape, stick a frill on the top to resemble the stem of a pear, or a small sprig of green parsley.

SHIRRED SMELTS PARISIAN STYLE

(*Smelts sur le Plat*)

Split open from the back, remove the large bone, heads, and tails of 2½ dozen small smelts. Place 4 fillets in an individual shirred egg dish, copiously buttered; pour over a generous tablespoon of stock, made from the trimmings of the fish; squeeze a few drops of lemon juice over and set in a moderately hot oven (375°), basting frequently until the liquid is reduced to almost nothing. Remove from the oven and cover the fish with MORNAY SAUCE, page 43, glaze rapidly under the flame of the broiling oven and serve with a side dish of small square French fried onions, or a side dish of Sweet Potato au Gratin.

SWEET POTATO AU GRATIN

Cut 5 medium-sized, cold, boiled, sweet potatoes in slices, place a layer in a copiously buttered baking dish, sprinkle with salt and pepper and 3 tablespoons of brown sugar; dot with 1 generous tablespoon of butter. Repeat. Cover with buttered cracker crumbs, and bake in a moderately hot oven until the crumbs are golden brown.

STEWED SMELTS NORWEGIAN STYLE

Remove the heads and tails of 2½ dozen smelts; cut in two, crosswise and proceed as indicated in recipe for STEWED PICKEREL BOURGEOISE, page 152.

STEWED SMELTS PARISIENNE

Prepare the fish as indicated in recipe for STEWED PICKEREL BOUR-GEOISE, page 152. Roll in salted, white-peppered flour and sauté in plenty of butter 4 or 5 minutes over a low fire. Lift out and place in a saucepan, pour over a heated large can of tomatoes, a drained small can of mushroom buttons; add the butter of the frying pan, a tablespoon of very, very finely chopped parsley, a tiny bit of garlic, and a small bouquet garni. Season to taste with salt and pepper, taking into consideration that the fish have been already salted and peppered. Cover, bring to a rapid boil, and set aside the range to simmer a few minutes. Dress in a hot round deep platter, garnish the edge with small triangles of bread fried in butter and serve with a side dish of plain boiled small potato balls and a green salad of your choice with French dressing.

STEWED SMELTS ENGLISH STYLE

Remove the heads and tails of 2½ dozen large smelts and cut in two, crosswise. Place in a saucepan and cover with boiling fish stock; add a cupful of cooked shrimps, 3 hard-boiled eggs, finely chopped, and a tablespoon of kneaded butter. Season to taste with salt, pepper, a few grains of Cayenne pepper, and a scant half teaspoon of Worcestershire sauce. Bring to a rapid boil and let simmer very gently on the side of the range for 4 or 5 minutes. Rectify the seasoning, add a scant teaspoon of lemon juice, and dress on a hot, round, deep platter; sprinkle over a tablespoon of finely chopped parsley and serve with a side dish of plain boiled potatoes.

SKIPJACK—SKIP-MACKEREL—SNAPPERS

In certain sections of the country, bluefish are known under the name of skipjack, while in others as skip-mackerel. Snappers are young bluefish known in certain parts of the country under that name. Either of the three may be prepared in all the methods used for bluefish.

SPANISH MACKEREL

All the different methods of preparation of the mackerel, herring, and bluefish, as well as all the fish having the fat distributed throughout the body, may be adapted to this fine fish, which is nothing but a mackerel, pure and simple.

SOLE

The author deems it necessary to call the attention of the hostesses and cooks to the fact that genuine sole is rarely to be found in our markets, being imported from Europe at prohibitive prices. The fillets sold under the name "sole" are usually those of flounder, or of some other white-fleshed fish. It is essential to stress this important fact for the sake of accuracy of quotation in general, for it must be emphasized that there is a great difference in flavor, texture, and flexibility between genuine sole and its various substitutes. Consequently, the author has eliminated this fish, so as not to mislead.

STURGEON

Sturgeon may be eaten in the fresh state, dried, smoked, or canned. It is from the eggs of the sturgeon that real caviar is prepared and from the spinal-marrow is prepared a sort of fish gelatine called "Vesiga," frequently used in Russian cookery.

The caviar, the genuine caviar, made from the sturgeon's roe, with large transparent grains and of clear and brilliant color, which promotes appetite and digestion and prevents flatulence, is usually served as an appetizer or as a garnishing for certain fish and other cooking preparations.

The practice of serving finely chopped onion with this unsurpassed delicacy is absolutely wrong according to food authorities. It is wrong because the perfect and unrivaled flavor of this tidbit *does not* require any enhancement. The use of onion may be advisable with the cheap imitations.

Returning to sturgeon, in addition to the following recipes, the various methods of preparation of the tuna may be adapted to this excellent fish, which, because of its large size, is usually cut either in slices, or in pieces of three to four pounds each. However, small sturgeons of four pounds, or thereabouts, may be found in the markets and these are as a rule cooked whole.

BOILED STURGEON METROPOLE

Select a 3½- to 4½-lb. young sturgeon and superficially slash the sides along the spine with a sharp knife to prevent deformation while cooking. Clean, wash, and sponge thoroughly, place in a fish kettle and cover with white wine court bouillon (*see* How To Boil Fish). At the first boil, remove aside and let simmer very gently for 35 minutes. Lift out, skin, and place on a hot platter. Reduce the strained cooking liquor over a hot fire so as to obtain a generous cupful; add, off the fire, 3 egg yolks, one by one, stirring constantly. Rectify the seasoning and finish off the fire with a generous tablespoon of sweet butter. Pour over the fish and glaze rapidly under the flame of the broiling oven. Garnish around the fish 6 large broiled mushrooms, interspersed with small baked stuffed tomatoes, using leftover cooked fish to fill the tomatoes. Serve with a side dish of Swedish Potatoes made as follows:

SWEDISH POTATOES

Slice one and a half plain boiled long potatoes, cooked in their skins and peeled, in small rings; butter an earthenware or Pyrex baking dish and place in it a layer of potatoes, then half a dozen fillets of anchovy, cut in thin strips, lengthwise, over this a layer of sliced hard-boiled eggs, sprinkling each layer with salt, pepper, and a little finely chopped parsley, and half a cup of CREAM SAUCE I, page 36. Repeat; dust the top with crushed peppercorns to taste and squeeze over the juice of a medium-sized lemon. Sprinkle with freshly made buttered soft bread crumbs and set in a hot oven until golden brown on top. Serve right from the baking dish.

BOILED STURGEON IN WHITE WINE

Prepare a 4-lb. sturgeon or thereabouts as indicated in recipe above, leaving the skin on; place in a fish kettle, and cover with a white wine court bouillon as indicated under How To Boil Fish. After the first boil remove aside the range and let simmer very gently for 35 minutes. Lift out carefully, place on a hot platter, and skin. Keep hot. With a reduced cupful of cooking liquor, prepare a WHITE WINE SAUCE, page 49, pour a little over the fish, serving the remainder aside, and garnish with quartered lemon, fresh parsley, and plain boiled small potato balls. Serve also a side dish of cucumber salad with French dressing.

FRIED STURGEON CUTLET INDIAN STYLE

Cut 6 slices, a quarter of an inch thick, from a piece of sturgeon weighing 3 lbs.; rub with a damp cloth, season with salt and pepper and a little nutmeg to taste and roll in flour, then in beaten eggs, in bread crumbs mixed with a little finely chopped parsley, and fry in plenty of butter, turning frequently to golden brown both sides. Dress on a hot platter; garnish with Indian pickles, broiled slices of green tomatoes, fresh parsley, and quartered lemon, arranged symmetrically. Serve with a side dish of Sauce Piquante and a side dish of plain boiled rice.

SAUCE PIQUANTE (*For Fish*)

Blend a tablespoon of butter with one of flour and let brown slightly, moisten with a generous cup of fish stock, made from fish trimmings and cook for 15 minutes, removing aside after the first boil to simmer gently. Skim. Meanwhile chop fine a small shallot and place in a saucepan with a tablespoon of tarragon vinegar and reduce to half over a hot fire; add to the sauce with a tablespoon of finely chopped sour gherkins and one scant teaspoon of finely chopped capers. Finish with a tablespoon of butter. If the sauce is too thin, use a tablespoon of kneaded butter to finish instead of the fresh butter; boil once or twice, skin, and use the sauce.

ROAST STURGEON ENGLISH STYLE

Wrap slices of larding pork about a 3½-lb. piece of sturgeon, previously rubbed first with lemon juice then with salt and pepper, secure with string, and roast as you would a round piece of kernel of veal in a roasting pan with a cupful of rich beef stock, a small bouquet garni, 2 cloves (slightly crushed), a small carrot (sliced), a small sliced onion and a few thyme leaves, basting frequently. Dress on a hot platter and serve with a side dish of Sour Cream Sauce (described below) and the traditional cucumber salad with French dressing.

SOUR CREAM SAUCE

This fine sauce is very popular in the north of Europe and is usually served with boiled and roasted large fish. It is also used for asparagus, cauliflower, broccoli, and cooked plain cabbage.

Stir a tablespoon of flour with 4 egg yolks and 2 tablespoons of cold water, mixing well. Strain through a fine sieve over a saucepan and add a cupful of sour cream, stir constantly over a gentle fire until the sauce thickens, and finish with 2 generous tablespoons of butter added, bit by bit, beating meanwhile with a wire whisk.

STEAM ROAST STURGEON RUSSIAN STYLE

Lard a 3½- to 4-lb. piece of sturgeon with strips of larding pork, interspersed with strips of fillet of anchovy and strips of sweet gherkins, season to taste with salt (very little) and plenty of crushed peppercorns to taste and wrap slices of fat larding pork around, securing with string. Place in a braising kettle with all sorts of cut-up vegetables, a bouquet garni, a small crushed clove, and 6 thyme leaves; pour over a generous cup of equal parts of fish stock and white wine (lemon juice may be substituted for wine, in this case use a generous tablespoon). Cover tightly and set in a moderately hot oven (350°) for 2½ hours, basting frequently. Remove from the oven; place the fish on a hot platter, skin and keep hot. Remove the excess of fat from the cooking liquor and strain, pressing a little, through a fine sieve. Set the sauce over a hot fire, bring to a boil, add 12 black olives (stoned), 12 green olives, 12 large mushrooms, and let simmer gently for 15 minutes, adding a little more fish stock if the sauce is too thick. Rectify the seasoning and pour part of the sauce over the fish. Garnish with the olives and mushrooms, quartered lemon, and fresh parsley and serve the remainder of the sauce aside with a side dish of plain boiled small potato balls.

STURGEON FINLAND STYLE

Place 6 slices of sturgeon, ¼ of an inch thick, salted, peppered, and dusted with a few grains of nutmeg and Cayenne pepper in a buttered baking pan; barely cover with white wine fish stock and add a teaspoon each of finely chopped parsley, shallot, mushrooms, and chives. Cover with a buttered paper and set in a hot oven (400°)

for 20 long minutes, basting once in a while. Lift out the fish and place on a hot service platter. Keep hot. Place the cooking liquor in a saucepan and bring to a rapid boil; rectify the seasoning and add, off the fire, bit by bit, 4 tablespoons of butter, beating gently and thoroughly meanwhile. Pour over the fish and garnish with a dozen glazed small white onions, a dozen small glazed carrots, and 2 dozen or thereabouts small potato balls, cooked in butter and well drained. Garnish with a small bunch of parsley surrounded with 6 quarters of lemon and serve very hot.

SWORDFISH

Related to the mackerel, the swordfish is one of several fish having an elongated snout, forming a flattened sharp-edged sword. This weapon is about half as long as the body and becomes so strong that it may be driven far through the planking of a rowboat or even a sailing vessel.

The swordfish, which is an excellent food fish, reaches its largest size off the coast of New England, where in midsummer it comes near the shores in pursuit of schools of herring, mackerel, and other gregarious fish, upon which it mainly feeds.

The average length of the swordfish in the Atlantic Ocean is about seven feet and the weight reaches sometimes 250 pounds, but there are authentic records of fish more than twice this size.

Similar to the mackerel, the swordfish belongs to the category of rich food fish in that it is oily and the fat is distributed throughout the flesh. The various methods employed in the preparation of mackerel, bluefish, pompano, herring, and the like, may be adapted to this fish when sliced.

TROUT

Speak about trout and the epicure's imagination rises to heights of delight. Trout, the "queen" of lakes, rivers, and the sea, may be dressed in an endless variety of ways and with all manner of sauces, as a capricious coquette changes her gown to charm the eyes and disturb the heart. This most completely toothed of all fish belongs to the salmon family. In the lake trout both jaws are nearly equal, the mouth is wide and large with a pointed snout, the head rather small, the body elongated and the back thick and rounded. The sea trout has sides sprinkled with small crescent-shaped spots on a silvered base. Its flesh is of a yellowish-orange color, resembling that of the salmon, to which it may be compared in delicacy, hence its name "salmon trout." The brook trout, always caught in clear running brooks, is considered superior to the two varieties above mentioned. Its flesh is snow-white, it has brown spots on its back, and red spots outlined with a shadowy circle on the sides.

From the culinary point of view, trout may be divided into two distinct classes: the large and the small. The large are the salmon trout and sea trout; the small, the brook and lake trout. The various methods, garnishings, and sauces of salmon, hot or cold, may be adapted to the large trout.

BRAISED SALMON TROUT PARISIENNE

Wrap a cleaned, washed, trimmed, and sponged 3-lb. salmon trout with thin slices of larding pork, after rubbing it with salt, crushed peppercorns, and a little nutmeg to taste, place in a well-buttered baking dish, barely cover with pure white wine, and add a teaspoon each of finely chopped shallot, parsley, chives, and onion and 3 tablespoons of finely chopped raw mushrooms. Cover with a buttered paper, and cook in a moderately hot oven (350°) for 25 to 30 minutes, basting occasionally, remove the paper and cook 5 minutes longer, basting very often. Dress the fish on a hot platter; rectify the seasoning and add a generous tablespoon of thick tomato purée, 3 tablespoons of fresh cream, previously scalded, and boil 5 minutes. Finish with 2 tablespoons of sweet butter. Pour a little over the fish, garnish with quartered lemon and fresh parsley and serve a side dish of the remainder of the sauce with a side dish of plain boiled potatoes.

BRAISED SALMON TROUT DUTCH STYLE

Select a 3½-lb. salmon trout or 2 of 1½ lbs. each; split open from the back, remove the large bone, head, and tail; wash, trim, sponge well, and rub with lemon juice, then with salt, white pepper, and a few grains of nutmeg and place in an earthenware or Pyrex baking dish. Pour over 4 tablespoons of MAÎTRE D'HÔTEL BUTTER, page 57, and 2 tablespoons of fish stock, made from the trimmings; cover with a buttered paper, set in a moderately hot oven (350°), and bake 25 minutes, basting frequently; remove the paper and cook 5 minutes longer. Meanwhile, brown very lightly a tablespoon of very finely chopped onion in 1 tablespoon of olive oil and sprinkle with a scant tablespoon of flour, blend well, and moisten with a wineglass of white wine and the same quantity of salted hot water; pepper highly with crushed peppercorns and a few grains of Cayenne pepper and add a small can of thick tomato purée. Let come to a rapid boil and set aside to simmer very gently for 15 minutes. Skim, lift out the fish from the baking pan and place on a long hot platter. Rectify the seasoning in the sauce after skimming again thoroughly and pour over the fish. Garnish both ends of the platter with mixed glazed small white onions and small potato balls, cooked in butter to a golden brown, the sides with quartered lemon and fresh parsley and sprinkle all over the fish finely chopped parsley.

BRAISED SALMON TROUT
DUNKERQUOISE STYLE

Select a large salmon trout of 3½ to 4 lbs. or thereabouts; clean, wash, split on the side and stuff with STUFFING IV (*see* FISH FORCE-

MEAT AND FISH STUFFING), to which add a teaspoon of finely chopped truffles which play the major rôle with the wine in imparting the delicious flavor. The head is wrapped in a thin slice of fat larding pork, tied, and the opening sewed up to prevent any escape of the smooth stuffing. Place the fish thus prepared in a fish kettle and meanwhile prepare a Mirepoix as follows:

MIREPOIX

Sauté 1 carrot in plenty of butter, 1 onion, both finely sliced, and add a scant quarter of a pound of fresh pork diced, 1 tablespoon of diced small raw lean veal, a bouquet garni, a crushed clove, a very small clove of garlic, bruised, and salt and pepper to taste, until well browned. Pour over this mixture, called in cookery "Mirepoix," a bottle of white wine, one pony glass of good brandy, a cup of good beef consommé, salted and peppered highly, and add 6 whole peppercorns; strike a match, let the flame die out, then pour the mixture over the fish in the kettle. Cook very slowly for 35 to 40 minutes, gently simmering, no more, no less. Remove the fish, let cool a little and place in a well-buttered earthenware baking dish; pour over the strained wine broth, reduced to half, cover with a buttered paper and set in a moderately hot oven (375°) for 15 minutes. Remove the fish from the baking dish, place on a hot platter; keep hot. Again reduce the cooking liquor to half, correct the seasoning, add one generous tablespoon of sweet butter and a few drops of anchovy essence or extract or a pea size of anchovy paste. Boil once and strain over the fish. Garnish with crayfish, cooked in fish stock, slices of truffles, dipped in melted meat extract, and small (about a dozen) fish forcemeat balls, cooked in fish stock. Decorate with fresh parsley and slices of lemon, dipped in paprika, and serve with a side dish of small potato balls cooked in butter and well browned.

BRAISED SALMON TROUT
GERMAN STYLE

Proceed as indicated for above recipe, using a 3½- to 4-lb. salmon trout. Garnish with small baked tomatoes stuffed with creamed crab meat, topped with a little MORNAY SAUCE, page 43, glazed under the flame of the broiling oven, and serve with a side dish of coleslaw in mayonnaise dressing, to which has been added a teaspoon of prepared mustard and a little finely chopped parsley.

BOILED SALMON TROUT EPICURE

Clean a 3½-lb. salmon trout, wash, trim, sponge, rub with lemon juice, then with salt and pepper to taste, and cook in a white wine court bouillon as indicated under How To BOIL FISH. At the first boil, remove aside and let simmer very gently for 25 to 30 minutes. Remove the fish, dress on a hot platter, remove the skin, garnish all around with sprigs of fresh, crisp, curled parsley so as to form a kind of green necklace, interspersed with quartered lemon, and serve with a side dish of EPICUREAN SAUCE, page 39, a side dish of plain boiled small potato balls and a crisp young watercress salad with slices of hard-boiled eggs and French dressing.

BOILED SALMON TROUT TROCADERO

Prepare, cook, and dress a 3½-lb. salmon trout as indicated for above recipe. Garnish the top of the skinned fish with a line of cooked large shrimps and pour over a little OLIVE SAUCE, page 44, to which is added 1 tablespoon of shredded, blanched almonds, to which has been added a scant half cup of sliced mushrooms cooked in butter and well drained. Serve the remainder of the sauce with a side dish of Endives à la Mornay, made as follows:

ENDIVES À LA MORNAY

Cook 1 lb. of cleaned Belgian endives in salt water for 30 minutes, barely covering the vegetable. Drain; dress in a generously buttered earthenware baking dish; sprinkle with a little coarse pepper (pepper from the mill, preferably, and one turn or two) and cover with a cupful of CREAM SAUCE I, page 36, to which is added

½ cup of grated American cheese; sprinkle with plenty of melted butter and set in a hot oven (400°) until the top is golden brown and sizzling.

BROILED FILLET OF SEA TROUT

Split open from the back, remove the large bone, clean, wash, and fillet 3 sea trout of 1½ lbs. each; sponge well after washing again, rub with lemon juice, then with salt and pepper, and place in hot butter for a few minutes. Lay dripping from the butter on a double broiler, set on the rack of the broiling oven and broil, turning and basting very often with melted butter. Dress the 6 fillets on a hot platter. Cover with Diplomate Sauce, page 37, and serve with a side dish of Celery Remoulade (see below), after garnishing with quartered lemon and fresh parsley, and a side dish of plain boiled potatoes.

Celery Remoulade (*Cold*)

Cut the white part of three stalks of celery, julienne-like, as small as possible. Wash and drain well, marinate for an hour in French dressing; drain, pressing a little and mix with remoulade dressing. Dress individual portion in a cup of crisp lettuce leaves, sprinkling finely chopped parsley over. A little finely chopped chives enhances the flavor.

BROILED FILLET OF SEA TROUT ENGLISH STYLE

Prepare the fish as indicated for above recipe, dip in beaten egg, then in bread crumbs, and place on a well-greased double broiler, set on the rack of the broiling oven, broil, turning very often and basting frequently with melted butter. Dress on a hot platter; garnish with quartered lemon and fresh parsley, serve with a side dish of Drawn Butter Sauce, page 38, and a side dish of cucumber salad with French dressing.

LAKE TROUT

BAKED LAKE TROUT AURORA

Clean, split open from the back, remove the large bone, head, fins, and tail of a 3-lb. lake trout or two of 1½ lbs. each, roll in salted, peppered flour and place in a baking pan, the bottom of which is thinly covered with a scant half cup of fish stock. Add a tablespoon of Worcestershire sauce and place 6 slices of bacon, coarsely chopped, on the sides of the fish and a small lemon cut in 6 slices. Cover the baking pan and set in a moderately hot oven to start, raising the heat 15 minutes after and cooking 15 minutes longer uncovered and basting frequently. Dress the fish on a hot platter and garnish with 6 slices of grilled green tomatoes, alternating with stuffed small green peppers and quartered lemon. Serve with a side dish of ANNA SAUCE, page 33, and a side dish of plain boiled small potato balls.

BAKED LAKE TROUT NORWEGIAN STYLE

Place a 3½-lb. lake trout, cleaned, washed, trimmed, and sponged in a buttered baking dish, after rubbing with salt and pepper. Pour over a scant cup of fish stock made from the trimmings, adding 3 slices of lemon, seeds removed, and 2 tablespoons of butter. Set, covered with a buttered paper in a hot oven (400°) for 25 to 30 minutes. Lift out; place on a hot platter and pour over a little DIPLOMATE SAUCE, page 37, serving the remainder in a sauceboat; garnish with quartered lemon, quartered hard-boiled eggs, slices of sweet gherkins, and fresh parsley, with a side dish of plain boiled potato balls.

BAKED LAKE TROUT HUSSARD

Select 6 small lake trout of ¾ lb. each or thereabouts, split open from the back, remove the large bone, head, fins, and tail, wash and sponge well. Fill the opening with FISH STUFFING I (*see* FISH FORCE-

MEAT AND FISH STUFFING) in which the onion previously browned in butter and well drained predominates. Lay the fish in a baking dish, copiously buttered, the bottom of which is strewn with 2 small onions thinly sliced and half cooked in butter; add a small bouquet garni and pour over a wineglass of white Burgundy wine (Chablis). Set, covered with a buttered paper, in a moderately hot oven (375°) for 15 to 20 minutes, basting frequently. Dress the fish on a hot platter; keep hot. Strain the cooking liquor through a fine sieve, pressing a little to obtain as much of the onion as possible; thicken with a half cup of reduced fish stock made from the trimmings and to which has been added a generous tablespoon of kneaded butter; rectify the seasoning and add gradually, bit by bit, 4 or 5 tablespoons of butter, stirring meanwhile until the sauce is fluffy and foamy. Pour a little over the fish and serve the remainder aside with a side dish of fried eggplant. Garnish with quartered lemon, fresh parsley, and small triangles of bread fried in butter.

BAKED LAKE TROUT MANTOUE

Fillet 6 small lake trout of ¾ lb. each or thereabouts, wash and sponge well and spread one half of the fillets (there should be 12) lightly with a little FISH STUFFING I (see FISH FORCEMEAT AND FISH STUFFING), mixed with a little finely chopped truffles, covering with the plain ones, sandwich-like; secure with string and place in a buttered baking dish lined with a teaspoon each of shallot, parsley, onion, all finely chopped and well mixed; add a few leaves of tarragon herbs, season with salt and pepper to taste and pour over ⅔ cup of white wine. Set, covered with a buttered paper, in a moderately hot oven (375°), basting often, and cook 20 to 25 minutes. Dress on a hot platter and pour over the sauce, thickened with a little kneaded butter and the seasoning rectified. Garnish with fresh parsley and quartered lemon and serve with a side dish of small square French fried potatoes and a side dish of cucumber salad with sour cream dressing.

BOILED LAKE TROUT AU BLEU

Have ready and boiling rapidly a strong vinegar court bouillon, prepared as indicated under How To Boil Fish, and plunge in quickly 2 lake trout of 2 lbs. each, cleaned, washed, and sponged. Set aside and let simmer very gently for 15 to 20 minutes. Dress on a hot platter and surround the fish with sprigs of fresh curled parsley, quartered lemon, and plain boiled potato balls. Serve with a side dish of Hollandaise Sauce I, page 40, and a side dish of your favorite green salad with French dressing.

GRILLED LAKE TROUT MAÎTRE D'HÔTEL

(*Master Recipe*)

Fillet 3 lake trout of 1½ lbs. each and marinate ½ an hour in a little white wine with aromatic herbs and a teaspoon of strained lemon juice, salt and pepper to taste. Lift out and roll dripping in freshly made soft bread crumbs, then in beaten eggs, and again in bread crumbs. Place on a double broiler, set on the rack of the broiling oven, broil under a low flame, basting and turning often. Dress on a hot platter and place on each fillet the size of a small walnut of Maître d'Hôtel Butter, page 57. Surround the fish with freshly made shoestring potatoes and garnish with quartered lemon and fresh parsley.

GRILLED LAKE TROUT BEARNAISE

Operate exactly as indicated for above recipe, substituting Bearnaise Sauce, page 34, for Maître d'Hôtel Butter, and garnishing with four small mounds of O'Brien potatoes, fresh parsley, and quartered lemon.

BROOK TROUT

In addition to the following recipes the various methods of preparation of perch, pickerel, and sardines, as well as small whiting, may be adapted to this delicious little fish.

BAKED BROOK TROUT MONTBARRY

Clean, wash, and sponge well 6 brook trout of the same size, season with salt and pepper to taste, using pepper from the mill, and lay in a well-buttered baking dish, the bottom of which is spread with a teaspoon each of parsley, onion, chives, and chervil, finely chopped, a few leaves of tarragon herbs, and 3 generous tablespoons of finely chopped raw mushrooms, all well mixed. Pour over the fish 2 tablespoons of slightly melted butter and set, covered with a buttered paper, in a hot oven (400°) for 10 minutes. Open and pour over the fish a mixture of 4 fresh eggs yolks beaten with a scant pony glass of brandy; sprinkle over 5 tablespoons of grated Swiss cheese, mixed with equal parts of freshly made soft bread crumbs and a little paprika. Cook until the crumbs are golden brown in a very hot oven. Serve right from the baking dish with a side dish of grilled large onions and large mushrooms (6 of each) set on slices of green tomatoes, also grilled.

BOILED BROOK TROUT SWISS STYLE
(*Cold*)

Clean, wash, trim, and sponge well 6 brook trout of similar size; place in the bottom of a fish kettle and pour over a white wine court bouillon as indicated under How To Boil Fish. At the first boil, remove aside and let simmer 15 minutes very gently; lift out, cool, and dress on a cold platter over a napkin covered with a large layer of crisp green curled sprigs of parsley. Garnish with quartered lemon, quartered hard-boiled eggs, and serve with a side dish of the following sauce:

SAUCE

⅔ of thick tomato purée to ⅓ of stiff mayonnaise, to which is added a few grains of Cayenne pepper, the juice of a small lemon, and a teaspoon of finely chopped lemon rind, salt and pepper to taste.

BOILED BROOK TROUT GAVARNIE

Clean, wash, trim, and sponge well 6 brook trout of the same size; place in a fish kettle and cover with a red wine court bouillon as indicated under How To Boil Fish. At the first boil, remove aside and let simmer very gently for 15 minutes. Lift out the fish and place on a hot platter; keep hot. Reduce the strained court bouillon so as to have one generous cup, rectify the seasoning, and add 1 tablespoon of kneaded butter; boil once, add the fish, and let stand a few minutes. Dress the fish on a hot platter, pour the sauce over, sprinkle over a little finely chopped parsley; garnish with crisp green curled parsley and slices of lemon dipped in paprika and serve with a side dish of plain boiled small potato balls and a side dish of cucumber salad with French dressing.

BREADED FRIED BROOK TROUT HÔTELIÈRE

Clean, wash, trim, and sponge well 6 brook trout of the same size, dip in beaten eggs, then in freshly made soft bread crumbs, again in beaten eggs and in bread crumbs, and fry in plenty of butter, turning often. Dress on a hot platter, the bottom of which is spread with softened MAÎTRE D'HÔTEL BUTTER, page 57, mixed with a generous tablespoon of tomato purée. Garnish with fresh parsley and quartered lemon and serve with a side dish of small green peppers stuffed with creamed crab meat, topped with MORNAY SAUCE, page 43, glazed under the flame of the broiling oven.

BROILED STUFFED BROOK TROUT DIPLOMATE

Clean, wash, trim, and sponge well 6 brook trout of the same size and slit the sides, filling with STUFFING I (*see* FISH FORCEMEAT AND FISH STUFFING), highly seasoned; roll in salt and pepper, then wrap in oiled paper. Place on a double broiler, set on the rack of the broiling oven, and broil under a low flame, turning and basting very often with melted butter. Unwrap; dress on a hot platter; garnish with quartered lemon, fresh parsley, and small mounds of freshly made, very crisp shoestring potatoes. Serve also a side dish of DIPLOMATE SAUCE, page 37; a side dish of cucumber salad with French dressing would not be amiss.

BROOK TROUT À LA MEUNIÈRE

Clean, trim, wash, and sponge well 6 brook trout and proceed as indicated in recipe for SHAD ROE À LA MEUNIÈRE, page 186. Serve with a side dish of freshly made French fried potatoes.

MARINATED BROOK TROUT TOURAINE

Proceed exactly as indicated in recipe for BOILED MARINATED PIKE TOURAINE, page 157, using 6 small brook trout.

SAUTÉED BROOK TROUT NORMANDE STYLE

Clean 6 brook trout of the same size, wash, trim, sponge well, roll in peppered and salted flour and sauté in plenty of butter, turning frequently to prevent scorching and ensure cooking and browning on both sides. Dress on a hot platter and pour over a cupful of the following sauce:

SAUCE

Mix ½ cup of brown butter with ½ cup of thick cream heated to the scalding point, season to taste with salt and pepper; sprinkle over a teaspoon of finely chopped parsley with a few leaves of finely chopped tarragon herbs and a scant ½ teaspoon of finely chopped shallot. Finish with a few drops of strained lemon juice. Serve with a side dish of French fried potatoes.

BROOK SALMON TROUT IN RED WINE

Clean 6 small salmon brook trout, wash, trim, and sponge well, and cook in a red wine court bouillon or short broth as indicated under How To Boil Fish. At the first boil, remove aside the range and let simmer very gently for 15 minutes. Lift out the fish, dress on a hot platter; keep hot. Strain the cooking liquor, reduce to half volume so as to obtain a generous cupful, boil once; rectify the seasoning and add off the fire one or two egg yolks, stirring meanwhile and alternating with a tablespoon of sweet butter. Pour over the fish; garnish with quartered lemon, fresh parsley, and small triangles of bread fried in butter, after being rubbed very lightly with garlic (optional), and serve with a side dish of French fried potatoes in butter.

SAUTÉED BROOK TROUT AU BEURRE NOIR

(Black Butter)

Clean, trim, wash, and sponge well 6 brook trout of the same size; roll in salted and peppered flour and sauté in plenty of butter, turning frequently. Dress on a hot platter. Heat the butter from the pan, adding more if necessary, so as to obtain about 5 tablespoonfuls and brown well. Pour over 1½ tablespoons of tarragon vinegar, holding the pan as far as possible from the face. Sprinkle finely chopped parsley over the fish and pour the butter over. Garnish with quartered lemon, fresh parsley, and triangles of bread fried in anchovy butter. Serve with a side dish of macaroni au gratin.

SAUTÉED BROOK TROUT FLEMISH METHOD

Prepare and cook 6 brook trout of the same size as indicated for above recipe. Dress on a hot platter, covered with plain boiled spinach, generously buttered and mixed with 3 hard-boiled eggs, finely chopped. Garnish the edge of the platter with quartered hard-boiled eggs, dipped in melted anchovy butter and interspersed with quartered lemon. Serve with a side dish of LEMON BUTTER SAUCE, page 42, and a side dish of small French fried potatoes.

TUNA

The flesh of this popular fish is a treat in flavor and texture resembling veal, while the flesh over the stomach is still more delicate. The tuna fish may be salted, preserved in oil, or cooked in the fresh state.

In addition to the following recipes, the various methods of preparation of sturgeon may be adapted to the tuna, which should always be well washed, using if necessary a hard brush to remove the coating of mud which sometimes has accumulated on the surface of this fine fish.

BAKED FRESH TUNA STEAK
ENGLISH STYLE

Select 3 slices of fresh tuna of 1 lb. each, and cut lengthwise so as to obtain 6 portions of 8 ozs. each. Lay 3 pieces in a well-buttered baking dish, the bottom of which is covered with a tablespoon each of finely chopped chives, small dices of fresh pork (bacon may be used advantageously), and 1 tablespoon of finely chopped parsley. Season highly with salt and coarse black pepper. Repeat with the 3 other pieces. Cover the top with thin slices of bacon, pour over ⅓ cup of fish stock, cover tightly, and set in a hot oven (400°) for 25 minutes; remove the cover and continue cooking for 5 minutes. Rectify the seasoning, remove the excess of fat, and dress on a hot platter, fish and sauce. Garnish with plain boiled small potatoes, slices of lemon, and fresh parsley.

BAKED FRESH TUNA STEAK
DANISH STYLE

Place 6 small slices of fresh tuna, salted, peppered, and sprinkled with a few grains of nutmeg in a copiously buttered baking pan, barely cover with fish stock, and set, covered with a buttered paper, in a moderately hot oven (375°) for 30 minutes, basting often. Remove the paper and cook 5 minutes longer. Dress on a hot platter; keep hot. Reduce the cooking liquor so as to obtain a generous cupful and boil once or twice, remove aside the fire and add, gradually, 4 or 5 tablespoons of butter, alternating with 4 teaspoons of thick purée of tomato. Rectify the seasoning, squeeze the juice of a small lemon over, and pour over the fish. Garnish with fresh parsley and plain boiled small potato balls and serve with a side dish of string beans in butter.

BRAISED TUNA INDIAN STYLE

Lard a 3-lb. piece of fresh tuna with 1 dozen matchlike strips of well-sponged anchovy, using a larding needle, and marinate in a wineglass of white wine to which add a cupful of cold strained fish stock, the juice of a large lemon, 2 whole cloves, a bouquet garni, 2 or 3 thin slices of onion, and same amount of thinly sliced carrot; season highly with pepper and a little salt and let stand for an hour. Meanwhile, brown 1 cup of finely cut-up vegetables (mirepoix) in 3 tablespoons of butter, adding ½ teaspoon of saffron and a teaspoon of curry powder, moistened with a little of the strained marinade. Place the larded fish on this bed of vegetables, cover and set in a hot oven (400°) for an hour and a half. Dress the fish on a hot service platter; keep hot while straining the cooking liquor through a fine sieve, pressing a little and removing the excess of fat. Heat to the boiling point; rectify the seasoning and finish with 2 tablespoons of tomato purée and 2 tablespoons of butter added bit by bit, while stirring, and a few drops of lemon juice. Pour ½ the sauce over the fish and the remainder in a sauceboat. Serve with a side dish of plain boiled rice.

BRAISED TUNA ITALIAN STYLE

Marinate a 3-lb. piece of fresh tuna for an hour in olive oil and add the juice of a lemon, a small bouquet garni, a few thyme leaves, and salt, pepper, and a few grains of Cayenne pepper. Drain and sponge well. Heat 3 tablespoons of olive oil and fry in it a large sliced onion, 3 finely chopped shallots, and ¼ lb. of sliced mushrooms until light brown; then add the fish, cover with the marinade, and set tightly covered on top of the range for 20 minutes over a low fire. Lift the cover and add a wineglass of dry white wine. Cover tightly and set in a moderately hot oven (350°) for an hour, turning the fish carefully once in a while. Dress on a hot platter; keep hot. Pour the cooking liquor into a saucepan, removing the bouquet garni, heat up, remove from the fire, and finish with a tablespoon of kneaded butter. Boil once or twice, rectify the seasoning and pour one half of the sauce over the fish and the remainder in a sauceboat. A side dish of glazed small white onions and plain boiled potato balls is the usual accompaniment.

CURRIED FRESH TUNA STEAK ORIENTAL

Place 6 slices of fresh tuna of 8 ozs. each, salted and highly peppered with coarse black pepper, in a well-buttered baking dish and barely cover with a vinegar court bouillon as indicated under How To Boil Fish; place on a hot fire and bring to a boil, remove aside and let simmer very gently for 25 minutes. Meanwhile, brown in a tablespoon of butter, a generous tablespoon of finely chopped onion, turn into a buttered earthenware baking dish and add the well-drained slices of fish, then 2 cloves, 1 teaspoon of curry powder, diluted in a scant cup of fish stock, a tablespoon each of finely chopped chives and parsley, a small bouquet garni, and 3 tablespoons of white wine. Cover tightly and set in a hot oven (400°) for 30 minutes. Dress the fish on a hot platter; keep hot. Strain the cooking liquor, forcing a little, and add gradually, beating with a wire whisk, 3 or 4 egg yolks, rectify the seasoning and finish with a tablespoon of butter and a few drops of lemon juice. Pour over the fish, garnish with small mounds of plain boiled rice, interspersed with quartered lemon, and serve as hot as possible.

GRILLED TUNA BERCY SAUCE
(*Master Recipe*)

Marinate 6 slices of fresh tuna of 8 ozs. each, in olive oil, lemon juice, salt and pepper, 3 slices of onion, and 1 crushed clove, for an hour. Roll, dripping in olive oil, place on a double broiler and set on the rack of the broiling oven; broil first under a very hot flame, turning and basting frequently with olive oil. Remove from the fire and place in a buttered baking pan, pour over ¼ (generous) cup of Maître d'Hôtel Butter, page 57, set in a moderately hot oven (350°), and continue cooking until done, turning often carefully. Dress on a hot platter; garnish with quartered lemon and fresh parsley and serve with a side dish of Bercy Sauce, page 35, and a side dish of small French fried potatoes in butter. A side dish of cucumber salad with French dressing makes also a good combination.

Any other kind of sauce may be substituted if desired.

TURBOT

In bygone days, at a festivity or family reunion, a large turbot was the traditional dish, especially during the Lenten period, and it was served with due ceremony, after careful and loving preparation, on a long porcelain dish, garnished with a lacelike necklace of green curled parsley, previously slightly moistened then dipped in paprika. This simple adornment accentuated, through the contrast of colors, the whiteness of the flesh of the fish and enhanced its beauty.

The turbot, that in America is frequently called halibut, although smaller and of much more delicate flavor, has a body of almost square proportions, which is "roughcast" on the left side.

The turbot inhabiting the rocky shores are much superior in flavor to those which inhabit the muddy shores, and have a firmer and more delicate flesh. This fish is in season from January to March.

Large turbot are usually boiled in a milk or cream court bouillon (short broth) and are dressed on a service platter covered with a napkin, the only garnishing being a crisp bunch of green parsley and slices of lemon. Just before serving, after the skin is removed, it is advised to brush the fish with melted butter to give it brilliancy and an appetizing appearance.

To prevent disfigurement of the fish before it is plunged into the cold liquid, both sides should be slightly slashed to permit the breaking of the collar bone, and also hasten cooking.

As explained in section How To Boil Fish, the liquid containing the fish should be brought slowly and gradually to ebullition, then immediately removed aside to simmer gently, very gently, so as to ensure uniform and thorough cooking. This is of great importance to the success of the dish and also to prevent indigestion, caused by insufficient cooking. The directions apply also to sliced fish, cooked by the same method.

Invariably, the accompaniment of boiled hot turbot, whole or in slices, is plain boiled potatoes and the most appropriate sauces are those indicated for boiled salmon.

Small and medium-sized turbot may be braised, but the ingredients should be prepared in advance (mirepoix), cooled, and then added to the fish, which is basted very frequently to ensure softness and uniform flavor.

The turbot, being a gelatinous fish, should not be boiled too long in advance when served cold, especially if in slices, as it may become tough, shrink, and the flavor be greatly impaired. The usual sauces for cold turbot are the same as for cold salmon.

LARGE PIECE OF TURBOT

In addition to the following recipes, the various methods of preparation of boiled, braised, and grilled salmon may be adapted to this fish when large.

BOILED TURBOT HOLLANDAISE

(Master Recipe)

Select a 3½- to 4-lb. piece of turbot; clean, wash, and sponge well. Place into a fish kettle and cover with a white wine court bouillon as indicated under How To Boil Fish. After the first boil, remove aside and let simmer very gently for 25 minutes; lift out the fish; drain and dress on a hot platter. Remove the skin carefully, brush the fish with melted butter, surround with plain boiled small potato balls, garnish with plenty of fresh parsley, quartered lemon, and serve with a side dish of Hollandaise Sauce I, page 40. A side dish of cucumber salad with French dressing may also be served.

Any other kind of sauce may be substituted if desired.

BRAISED TURBOT PARISIAN STYLE

Brown thoroughly in 3 tablespoons of butter, a small carrot, 1 medium-sized onion, a small stick of celery, all coarsely chopped, and add a small bouquet garni, a crushed clove, and a pinch of thyme leaves. Place a well-sponged 3½-lb. piece of fresh turbot in a braising kettle, pour over the vegetables, slightly cooled, a cupful of fish stock, and ½ cup of butter. Cover tightly and set in a hot oven (400°) for 35 minutes. Lift out the fish, dress on a hot platter, remove the skin, keep hot. Place the cooking liquor in a saucepan and bring to a boil; strain through a fine sieve and place over the fire again for a few minutes. Remove aside and add the size of a small pea of anchovy paste and 2 or 3 egg yolks, one by one, while stirring gently and constantly; rectify the seasoning and pour part of the sauce over the fish. Serve the remainder aside in a sauceboat with a side dish of plain boiled potatoes, not omitting the garnishing of fresh parsley and slices of lemon.

BRAISED TURBOT FISHERMAN

Brown thoroughly in 3 tablespoons of butter a mirepoix of vegetables as indicated for above recipe. Let this cool a little. Place a well-sponged 3½-lb. piece of fresh turbot in a braising kettle, then pour over the vegetables; season to taste with salt and pepper and pour over a cupful of fish stock, 2 tablespoons of lemon juice, and a scant cupful of butter. Cover tightly and set in a hot oven (400°) for 35 minutes, turning the piece of fish once. Lift out the fish, dress on a hot platter, remove the skin, and keep hot. Place the cooking liquor strained through a fine sieve, while pressing a little to extract all the vegetables possible, over a hot fire. Bring to a rapid boil and add the size of a small walnut of anchovy paste and 2 egg yolks, added separately, while stirring constantly; rectify the seasoning and pour the sauce over the fish. Serve with a side dish of plain boiled potato balls and a cucumber and lettuce salad with French dressing.

CREAMED TURBOT AU GRATIN
FRENCH STYLE
(You May Use Cooked Leftover Turbot)

Bone and skin carefully 2½ cups of cold cooked turbot and flake coarsely, place a layer in a buttered baking dish, cover with a layer of CREAM SAUCE I, page 36, season with salt and pepper to taste. Repeat until the dish is full to ¼ of an inch from the top, seasoning each time; dot here and there with a generous tablespoon of butter, and set, covered with a buttered paper, in a moderately hot oven (375°) for 15 minutes. Remove from the oven and surround the edge of the dish with a border of mashed potatoes, forced through a pastry bag with a fancy tube; sprinkle the center of the dish with equal parts of freshly made buttered bread crumbs and grated Swiss cheese and the potatoes with melted butter, and brown rapidly under the flame of the broiling oven. Serve right from the baking dish with a side dish of your favorite green salad with French dressing.

NOTE: By adding to the mixture small diced shrimps and cooked sliced mushrooms, you may garnish patty shells with this preparation. With the same ingredients, the fish may be diced instead of flaked, you may garnish small shells, individual ramekins, prepare small cutlets, croquettes, rissoles, or fritters, etc. This applies to any kind of cooked fish.

SHELL OF CREAMED TURBOT MORNAY

(*You May Use Leftover Cooked Turbot*)

Prepare the leftover fish as indicated for above recipe. Garnish 6 shells, pour over a little MORNAY SAUCE, page 43, instead of bread crumbs and set under the flame of the broiling oven to glaze.

GRILLED SLICES OF TURBOT
LOBSTER SAUCE

(*Master Recipe*)

Sponge with a damp cloth 6 slices of fresh turbot of 7 to 8 ozs. each; sprinkle with salt and pepper, dip in melted butter or in olive oil, place on a double broiler, set on the rack of the broiling oven; broil very slowly, turning and basting often with melted butter or olive oil. Dress on a hot platter; garnish with small mounds of small

French fried potatoes, quartered lemon, and fresh parsley and serve with a side dish of LOBSTER SAUCE, page 42, and a side dish of cucumber salad with French dressing.

You may substitute any other kind of sauce if desired.

SMALL TURBOT

In addition to the following recipes the various methods of preparation of halibut may be adapted to small turbot.

BAKED TURBOT NETHERLAND STYLE

Clean, wash, trim, and sponge well a 3½-lb. turbot and cook in plain salt water, following the directions under How To Boil Fish. Lift out the fish; drain and dress on a hot platter; remove the skin carefully and place the fish over a freshly boiled lobster, split open, the flesh removed, cut in small pieces, then replaced in the shell. Garnish with fresh parsley and quartered lemon and serve with a side dish of plain boiled potatoes and Egg Sauce I, page 38, after brushing the fish with melted butter.

BAKED TURBOT PARISIAN STYLE

Clean a 3½-lb. turbot, wash, trim, sponge well, and rub with salt and pepper. Place in a buttered baking dish and barely cover with equal parts of white wine and mushroom stock. Dot here and there with a generous tablespoon of butter, cover with a buttered paper and set in a very hot oven (450°) for 25 to 30 minutes. Lift out the fish, dress on a hot platter, and garnish the top with a dozen small mushrooms, sautéed in clarified butter, alternated with small blades of truffles (the latter may be omitted). Pour over White Wine Sauce, page 49, and garnish the platter with 6 large crayfish, cooked in fish stock, then rolled in melted butter, 6 quarters of lemon, and a bouquet of fresh curled parsley, dipped in paprika. Serve with a side dish of small potato croquettes and a side dish of cucumber salad with French dressing.

BOILED TURBOT BURGUNDY WINE SAUCE

Clean, trim, wash, and sponge a 3½-lb. turbot and boil in a white wine court bouillon as indicated under How To Boil Fish. Dress on a hot platter, remove the skin, brush with melted butter, garnish with plain boiled small potato balls, quartered lemon, and fresh parsley and serve with a side dish of Red Burgundy Wine Sauce, page 45. A dish of hearts of lettuce salad with Russian dressing may be served aside.

BOILED TURBOT HOME STYLE

Prepare and cook a 3½-lb. turbot as indicated for above recipe. Dress on a hot platter, remove the skin, brush with melted anchovy butter, and garnish with plain boiled potatoes, each topped with a teaspoon of Hollandaise Sauce I, page 40, quartered lemon, and fresh parsley and serve with a side dish of Creole Sauce, page 37, and a side dish of plain lettuce salad with French dressing.

BOILED TURBOT WITH OYSTERS

Clean, wash, trim, and sponge a 3½-lb. turbot and cook in a vinegar court bouillon as indicated under How To Boil Fish. Dress on a hot platter, remove the skin carefully, brush with melted anchovy butter, and place on the top 6 large or 18 small oysters, cooked in the same broth as that of the fish, then rolled in melted anchovy butter. Surround the fish with a ring of freshly made small French fried potatoes and garnish with quartered lemon and fresh parsley. Serve with a side dish of Egg Sauce IV, page 39.

BROILED TURBOT SHRIMP SAUCE

(*Master Recipe*)

Clean a 3½-lb. turbot, wash, and make a slight slash along the backbone to loosen the fillets a little and prevent shrinking; rub with salt and pepper, dip in olive oil, place on a double broiler, and set on the rack of the broiling oven. Broil first under a very hot flame to sear rapidly, reduce the flame and continue broiling slowly, turning and basting frequently with melted butter or olive oil. Dress on a hot platter and garnish the fish with a border of freshly cooked potatoes, cut in rings and golden browned in plenty of butter, quartered lemon, and fresh parsley and serve with a side dish of SHRIMP SAUCE, page 47.

Any other kind of sauce may be substituted if desired.

WEAKFISH

Commonly called "weakfish" because of its very tender mouth, in certain parts known as "deep water trout," this fish was originally called "squeteague" by the Indians.

The weakfish is found all along the eastern Atlantic seaboard, coming nearer the shores in May to spawn. The eggs after being laid are buoyed up by tiny oil drops and hatch in about two days.

This fish is of a pale-brownish color on the back with a greenish tinge, grading into silvery along the sides and belly, variegated with brown blotches, some of which form undulating lines running downward and forward. It has an average weight of from four to five pounds and is very often sold on the markets as sea trout, of which it has not the same delicacy.

The weakfish is a good food fish which may be prepared in hundreds of delicious ways. The various methods employed in the preparation of trout, smelts, and whiting may be adapted to this fish.

WHITEFISH

The whitefish, a fresh-water fish of which approximately fifteen species are known the world over under different names, ranks among the important fish of the smelt, whiting, and salmon family. The whitefish has an elongated and compressed body, the conical head has a projecting snout and a small toothless mouth, the teeth having been shed before maturity; the scales are larger than in the salmon, the caudal fin is deeply forked, and the dorsal fin is followed by an adipose dorsal. The fish is of a bluish-olive color on the back, silvery on the sides and belly.

This most important and popular of the fresh-water fish in America is found in enormous numbers throughout the Great Lakes and adjacent waters. While the average weight is from three to three and a half pounds, whitefish have been caught weighing fifteen and even twenty pounds.

The whitefish remain in deep water for the most part, but in autumn, which is the spawning season (and at certain other times for purposes which are not yet clear), they migrate to shallower water in great shoals, where they spawn.

A single fish will yield as many as seventy-five thousand eggs, never less than thirty-five thousand.

In addition to the following recipes, the various methods employed in the preparation of bass, flounder, pike, weakfish, and large whiting may be adapted to this popular fish.

BAKED WHITEFISH HOME STYLE

Mix together 1½ cups of freshly made soft bread crumbs, 2 generous tablespoons of minced bacon, 1 generous tablespoon of finely chopped green pepper, 1 medium-sized onion (finely chopped), a teaspoon of finely chopped parsley, and salt, pepper, and a few grains of nutmeg and a few thyme leaves, moistening with a little fish stock. Spread this mixture on a 3½- to 4-lb. whitefish, previously cleaned, trimmed, washed, and well sponged, laid on the bottom of a large earthenware baking dish, copiously buttered. Place over the mixture 6 slices of bacon and dot here and there with 2 tablespoons of butter. Place the baking dish in a very hot oven (450°) for 15 minutes, then reduce the fire to moderate (350°) and cook for 25 to 30 minutes or until done, basting frequently with the fat in the baking dish. Remove from the oven. Lift out the fish carefully and dress on a hot long platter. Garnish with slices of lemon and green parsley and serve with a side dish of OYSTER SAUCE, page 45, and a side dish of cucumber and lettuce salad with French dressing.

BAKED WHITEFISH CANADIAN STYLE

Clean, wash, and sponge well a 3½- to 4-lb. whitefish, rub with a tablespoon of lemon juice, place in a baking pan, well greased with bacon drippings, then sprinkled with a tablespoon each of parsley, onion, and lean pork all finely chopped and mixed together, pour over a large can of tomatoes, add 2 tablespoons of butter and 1 tablespoon of kneaded butter, season with salt, pepper, nutmeg, and a small sprig of thyme (or 6 thyme leaves) and set, covered, in a hot oven (400°) and cook for 30 minutes. Remove the cover, add a tablespoon of lemon juice and cook 10 minutes longer. Lift out the fish; dress on a hot platter; rectify the seasoning, and pour on both sides of the fish. Sprinkle a teaspoon of finely chopped parsley over the fish; garnish with quartered lemon and fresh parsley and serve with a side dish of plain boiled small potato balls. A side dish of green salad with French dressing is the usual accompaniment.

BAKED WHITEFISH WITH SPINACH

Clean a 3½-lb. whitefish, wash and sponge well, rub with salt and pepper to taste. Place in a lavishly buttered baking pan 2 lbs. of raw spinach, well washed in several waters and coarsely chopped, and dot here and there with ⅓ cup of butter; lay the fish on this, covering with thin slices of lean pork or bacon, and pour over 2 egg yolks, beaten in ½ cup of fish stock. Cover and set in a hot oven (400°) for 25 to 30 minutes, then remove the cover and cook 10 minutes longer. Lift out the fish and dress on a hot long platter and surround with a border of the cooked spinach. Garnish with quartered hard-boiled eggs, interspersed with quartered lemon and fresh parsley. Serve with a side dish of EGG SAUCE II, page 38, and a side dish of plain boiled small potato balls.

BROILED WHITEFISH LOBSTER SAUCE
(Master Recipe)

Split open from the back and remove the large bone of a 3½- to 4-lb. whitefish, clean, wash, and sponge well, roll in salted and peppered melted butter, to which is added a few grains of Cayenne pepper and a few grains of paprika, and place skin down on a well-greased double broiler, set on the rack of the broiling oven, and broil slowly under a low flame, turning and basting frequently with melted butter. Dress on a hot platter, the bottom of which is lightly spread with LOBSTER SAUCE, page 42; garnish with quartered lemon, fresh parsley, and 4 small mounds of freshly made shoestring potatoes. Serve with the remainder of the Lobster Sauce aside.

Any other sauce may be substituted if desired.

PLANKED WHITEFISH

Clean a 3½- to 4-lb. whitefish, split, remove the large bone, wash, sponge, and rub with salt and pepper, put skin side down on a buttered oak plank, 1 inch thick, a little longer and wider than the fish; brush copiously with melted butter and set in a hot oven (400°) for 25 minutes, basting frequently with melted butter. Remove the plank and fish from the oven and set 2 or 3 minutes under the flame of the broiling oven; remove and spread with MAÎTRE D'HÔTEL BUTTER, page 57, sprinkle over a little finely chopped parsley; garnish with a small bunch of green parsley and quartered lemon and send the plank and fish to the table on a plank holder, or placed on a long, large platter covered with a napkin, and serve with a side dish of Maître d'Hôtel Butter and a side dish of hashed-browned potatoes. A green salad with French dressing is a good accompaniment and completes the meal.

SAUTÉED FILLET OF WHITEFISH MEUNIÈRE

Fillet a 3½- to 4-lb. whitefish, as indicated under MEANING OF THE WORD "FILLET" IN COOKERY. Roll each fillet in salted and peppered flour and sauté in plenty of butter over a gentle fire. Finish as indicated in recipe for SKATE À LA MEUNIÈRE, page 194. Serve with a side dish of plain boiled small potato balls and a side dish of your favorite green salad with French dressing.

WHITEBAIT

The Atlantic and Pacific whitebait, truly analogous to the Mediterranean whitebait and the English specimen from the mouth of the Thames River, is a zoologic enigma. Assuming, as certain naturalists maintain, that whitebait is only a fry, it has never been clearly ascertained from what fish it is produced. Certain authorities claim it is from the herring, but their claims are not quite convincing.

The whitebait are known under different local and national names, such as: blanchaille, nonnats, fry, sand-eel, small fish, etc.

Whitebait is the component part of an incomparable fried dish, and these fish are sold in fabulous quantities throughout the world. Of a very fragile texture, this fish must be handled very carefully, especially when fried, as it breaks easily.

The whitebait, which does not adapt itself to many ways of preparation, is at its best when fried. The fish should be strictly fresh, as should be the frying fat. They are first washed in clear running cold water, sponged, then rolled in plenty of seasoned flour, the excess of which is eliminated by shaking the fish through a fine wire basket. The fish are then plunged into clear, clean, smoking, deep fat, a few at a time, lest they stick together, and for only a short minute, then lifted rapidly, drained, and dressed on a folded white napkin, placed on a hot platter, their only garnishing being fried green curled parsley and quartered lemon. They should be eaten piping hot.

In addition to the following recipes, the various methods of preparation of anchovy, small smelts, and sardines may be adapted to this delicate fish.

FRIED WHITEBAIT

Wash and sponge well 2½ to 3 lbs. of whitebait, dip in cold milk, then roll in salted and peppered flour. Only when ready to serve, place in a wire basket, shake a little to remove the excess of flour, and plunge rapidly in boiling deep frying fat, shaking immediately to prevent sticking and lift at once. Drain on paper, dress on a hot platter covered with a napkin, garnish with fried parsley and quartered lemon and serve with or without plain melted butter or TARTARE SAUCE, page 52. No side dish is needed with this fine little fish when prepared in this way.

SAUTÉED WHITEBAIT FRENCH STYLE

Heat on a hot fire, in a large frying pan, 6 tablespoons or more of olive oil and, when the oil is smoking, add 1½ lbs. of blanched spinach, coarsely chopped. Stir well so as to incorporate the oil throughout the spinach, taking care not to burn or scorch. Turn immediately into a heated bowl, put in 1 pound of whitebait blanched in fish stock for a short minute, and add 2 whole eggs, well beaten, salt and pepper to taste. Put this mixture into a well-buttered baking dish; spread the surface evenly, sprinkle with fine bread crumbs, then with olive oil here and there, and set in a moderately hot oven (375°) for 10 to 15 minutes. Serve right from the baking dish with a side dish of French fried potatoes and a side dish of cucumber salad with sour-cream dressing.

STEWED WHITEBAIT RHINELAND STYLE

Clean and sponge carefully 2 lbs. of whitebait. (To clean, make a small opening with a sharp knife just below the head and press between the blade of the knife and the thumb.) Place in a well-buttered baking dish, a tablespoon each of finely chopped parsley, chives, and a teaspoon of shallot. Mix well together, then add half a cup of finely chopped raw mushrooms and 2 or 3 leaves of tarragon herbs. Season with salt and pepper to taste and lay the tiny fish carefully over this scented bed. Sprinkle coarsely crushed peppercorns over the fish to taste, pour over a cupful of heated red wine, cover tightly, and bring to a rapid boil over a hot fire. Set aside immediately and let simmer very gently for 10 to 15 minutes on the side of the range until the liquid has reduced a little. Sprinkle over finely buttered bread crumbs, mixed with equal parts of grated American cheese, sprinkle over a little melted butter, and set under the flame of the broiling oven to brown. Serve sizzling hot with a side dish of coleslaw with thin mayonnaise dressing mixed with a little tomato paste to taste.

STEWED WHITEBAIT ITALIAN STYLE

Clean and wash carefully 2 lbs. of whitebait and sponge well, roll in salted and peppered flour, and place in a well-buttered baking dish, in which has been placed a large can of tomatoes. Sprinkle over a tablespoon each of finely chopped onion and parsley, dot here and there with 2 tablespoons of butter, and add a tablespoon of strained lemon juice. Cover and bring to a rapid boil over a hot fire. Remove aside immediately and let simmer very gently for 10 to 15 minutes. Rectify the seasoning and serve right from the baking dish with a side dish of plain boiled small potato balls.

WHITEBAIT OMELET

Prepare an omelet in the usual way and when ready to fold, add ½ pound of boned whitebait, fried in butter and well drained. Garnish with fresh parsley and a few whitebait, set aside and cooked in butter. Just before serving, brush the omelet with melted anchovy butter.

WHITING

The whiting is caught in great abundance on the eastern Atlantic seaboard, as are many other varieties resembling this fish, such as the "hake," also of the cod family, the "sandfish" or "deep-water whiting," the "hogfish" and the "harvest fish," and certain of the species of the whitefish, all of them unrelated to the whiting, but alike in the remarkable whiteness of their flesh or skin.

The whiting is indigenous to the Atlantic Ocean and Gulf of Mexico, being found from Chesapeake Bay and as far South as Brazil. It is closely related to the cod family, with which it is frequently found and caught. Among the differing characteristics is the absence of a barbel on the lower jaw of the whiting.

The average length of this most delicious fish is not quite a foot, the back is of dull silvery grey blending into a very light muddy-green color, while the rest of its body is of a brilliant silver. It is one of the most delicate of the sea fish, easily digested, and therefore well adapted to a weak stomach.

BAKED FILLET OF WHITING
DANISH STYLE

Split open from the back, remove the large bone, trim, wash, fillet, and sponge well 6 medium-sized whiting. Spread on one half of the fillets smooth STUFFING I (*see* FISH FORCEMEAT AND FISH STUFFING), highly seasoned, place over these the plain fillets, sandwich-like. Lay flat in a buttered baking dish and barely cover with stock, made from the trimmings of the fish, to which is added a scant wineglass of white wine and a tablespoon each of finely chopped parsley and fresh mushrooms. Season with salt and pepper and a few grains of nutmeg and set, covered with a buttered paper, in a hot oven (400°) for 15 to 20 minutes. Dress the fillets on a hot platter. Pour the cooking liquor in a saucepan and add, one by one, 3 or 4 egg yolks, stirring meanwhile. Finish with a tablespoon of sweet butter and a few drops of lemon juice. Rectify the seasoning and pour over the fish. Garnish with 6 large fried oysters, interspersed with 6 quarters of lemon and small triangles of bread fried in butter. Place a large bunch of fresh parsley at the head of the fish and serve with a side dish of scalloped tomatoes.

BAKED STUFFED FILLET OF WHITING AU GRATIN

Prepare and cook 6 small whiting as indicated for above recipe. Pour the cooling liquor into a saucepan and reduce to ⅔ its volume; add a cupful of CREAM SAUCE I, page 36, and bring to a rapid boil; rectify the seasoning and pour over the fish left in the baking dish; sprinkle with bread crumbs mixed with equal parts of grated American cheese, then with a little melted butter, and set in a hot oven (400°) to brown. Serve right from the baking dish.

BAKED WHITING LEMON BUTTER SAUCE

Clean, wash, trim, and sponge well 6 medium-sized whiting and rub with salt, pepper, and a little nutmeg; place in a buttered baking pan and barely cover with equal parts of white wine and mushroom stock. Set, covered with a buttered paper, in a hot oven (400°) for 15 to 20 minutes. Lift out the fish well drained; dress on a hot platter covered with a little LEMON BUTTER SAUCE, page 42; garnish with quartered lemon and fresh parsley and serve with the remainder of the Lemon Butter Sauce and a side dish of plain boiled small potato balls. A side dish of your favorite green salad with French dressing is a very good accompaniment.

BOILED WHITING EGG SAUCE

Clean, wash, trim, and sponge 3 large whiting of 1 lb. each, rub with a tablespoon of lemon juice and plunge in salted boiling water. Remove aside, immediately cover, and let simmer very gently for 15 minutes. Drain, dress on a hot platter; garnish with fresh parsley and quartered lemon and plain boiled potato balls. Serve with a side dish of EGG SAUCE II, page 38. A side dish of your preferred green salad with French dressing would not be amiss.

FRIED WHITING ORLY

Fillet 6 medium-sized whiting and sponge well. Dip in BATTER III (*see* BATTER FOR FRYING FISH) and, when ready to serve, place in a wire basket and plunge in a boiling deep frying fat. Drain, dress on a hot platter covered with a napkin; garnish with fried curled parsley and quarters of lemon and serve with a side dish of Tomato Sauce (*see* below). Serve also a side dish of French fried potatoes.

TOMATO SAUCE

Cut in small pieces 1 small carrot, 1 small onion, a small stalk of celery, a little parsley, a bit of bay leaf, 1 clove, salt and pepper to taste, and add a tablespoon of cooked ham trimmings. Brown slowly, over a low fire, turning frequently, in 2 tablespoons of butter. When well browned, add a large can of tomatoes and let simmer slowly for ½ hour; strain, forcing a little and pressing once in a while, through a fine sieve; set over the fire again and add the size of a walnut of meat extract and a few tablespoons of fish stock. Finish with a tablespoon of butter, stirring meanwhile. When the tomato sauce is prepared for a meat or vegetable dish, use beef stock instead of fish stock.

FRIED WHITING ENGLISH STYLE

Select 6 small whiting. Open the fish along the back to remove the large bone, wash and clean and sponge well; season with salt and pepper to taste, roll in flour, then in beaten egg and bread crumbs and fry in clarified butter over a moderately hot fire. Dress on a hot platter and cover each fish with a teaspoon of MAÎTRE D'HÔTEL BUTTER, page 57, slightly softened. Garnish with fresh parsley and quartered lemon and serve with a side dish of plain boiled small potato balls, rolled in finely chopped parsley.

FRIED BREADED WHITING
NORWEGIAN STYLE

Prepare, cook, dress, and garnish 6 medium-sized whiting as indicated for above recipe. Serve with a side dish of Egg Pudding (see below) and a side dish of cucumber salad with French dressing.

Egg Pudding (Agglada)

Beat 3 whole eggs thoroughly, adding gradually, ½ cup of rich milk or thin cream (the top of the milk will do), season with salt and a few grains of white pepper and finish, still beating, with 2 tablespoons of melted butter. Pour into a buttered baking dish and set in a moderately hot oven (350°) in a pan containing hot water. Cook until firm for about 25 minutes.

GRILLED WHITING DRAWN BUTTER SAUCE

Clean, wash, and sponge 6 small whiting, rub with a little tarragon vinegar, roll in oil, highly seasoned with pepper and salt, place on a well-heated and oiled double broiler, set on the rack of the broiling oven, broil slowly, turning frequently and basting with melted butter or olive oil. Dress on a hot service platter; garnish with strips of sour gherkins, fresh parsley, and quartered lemon and serve with a side dish of Drawn Butter Sauce, page 38, and a side dish of hashed-in-cream potatoes.

SAUTÉED WHITING RICHARD

Fillet 6 small whiting, wash and sponge well, rub with salted and peppered flour and fry in plenty of olive oil. Dress on a hot round platter, crownlike, place on each of the 12 small fillets, a broiled large mushroom and garnish in center with creamed cucumber and shrimps in equal parts. Serve with a side dish of Canotière Sauce, page 35, and a side dish of plain boiled small potato balls, rolled in finely chopped parsley.

WHITING AU GRATIN

Clean 12 small whiting and slash the back from head to tail very slightly to accelerate cooking and prevent breaking up, wash and sponge well; rub with salt and pepper and place in a well-buttered baking dish, the bottom of which is covered with 8 tablespoons of MORNAY SAUCE, page 43. Sprinkle over ⅔ cup of finely sliced raw mushrooms, moisten with ½ wineglass of white wine; you may substitute lemon juice for white wine (in that case use a generous tablespoonful); cover with more of the same sauce, sprinkle with well-buttered fine bread crumbs, and set in a moderately hot oven (400°) for 20 minutes, covered with a buttered paper. Remove the paper and continue cooking until the top is well browned; sprinkle a little finely chopped parsley over and a few drops of lemon juice and serve with a side dish of French fried potatoes.

WHITING SUR LE PLAT

(Shirred Whiting)

Prepare 12 small whiting as indicated for above recipe, lay in a generously buttered round baking dish, place over each fish the size of a large hazelnut of anchovy butter, sprinkle with a generous tablespoon of finely chopped parsley and set, covered with a buttered paper, in a moderately hot oven (375°) after heating for 2 or 3 minutes on top of the range over a hot fire and cook for 20 to 25 minutes, basting very often. Remove from the oven, squeeze the juice of a lemon over, dust with a little more very finely chopped parsley, and serve right from the baking dish with a side dish of String Beans Maître d'Hôtel.

NOTE: Usually this method of preparation is made in an individual dish of a round shape or boat shape, a piece of lemon being served aside with a side dish (individual) of String Beans Maître d'Hôtel made as follows:

STRING BEANS MAÎTRE D'HÔTEL

Clean, string, and wash a pound of string beans, cut in two, cross-wise, then in two, lengthwise (julienne-like). Drain and plunge in boiling salted water. Cook until tender (about 20 minutes). Drain, place in a saucepan 2 or 3 tablespoons of MAÎTRE D'HÔTEL BUTTER, page 57, into which is kneaded a tablespoon of finely chopped pars-ley, melt and add the strained string beans, sauté a few minutes, tossing in the pan, and dress on a hot platter. Sprinkle over a few drops of tarragon vinegar. Serve.

WHITING À LA MEUNIÈRE

Clean, wash, sponge, and rub with salt and pepper, 6 small whit-ing of equal size and proceed as indicated in recipe for SHAD ROE À LA MEUNIÈRE, page 186. Serve with a side dish of French fried potatoes and a side dish of cucumber salad with French dressing.

SHELLFISH

Fish, considering all species as a whole, are for the philosopher an inexhaustible source of surprise.

The varied forms of these strange animals, the senses of which they are deprived, and the limited character of those they have, their various modes of existence, the influence which is exercised over them by the difference of the medium wherein they are destined to live, breathe, and move, extend the range of our ideas and the indefinite modifications which may result from matter, motion, and life.

As for myself, I feel for these creatures a sentiment akin to respect, springing from a deep conviction that they are evidently antediluvian animals, because the great cataclysm which drowned our ancestors was for the fish nothing but a time of joy, conquest, and festivity.

BRILLAT-SAVARIN

CLAMS

The clam, which plows its way along sandy bottoms, standing erect upon the edge of its thin shell, is obtained wholly by raking in water from ten to forty feet in depth. It is still known in New England as "Quahog," the original name bestowed upon it by the Indians who used the purple margin of the shell for making their dark wampum, or money.

The common clam of the eastern markets abounds from Cape Cod to Florida and also around New Brunswick. The young species of the common clam, which are taken in great quantities from Long Island Sound near the town of Little Neck, are known under the name of this town.

The soft-shelled clams are of a very different character, having comparatively thin, smooth, elongated shells. They remain sunken in the sand of the shore, between tide marks, with their syphon mouth just at the surface, and, when disturbed, they eject a spurt of water as they withdraw to safer depths.

These clams are obtained by digging at low tide, and, with the hard clams and littleneck clams, they are cultivated on certain protected areas of sea beach, where they collect almost as thick as paving stones.

On the New England coast, two other large species of deep-water clams, in great demand, are known under the names of "beach," or "surf" clams.

The various methods employed in the preparation of oysters may be adapted to this delicious and healthful food fish, and their chemical composition is about the same as that of the oysters.

CLAM FRITTERS

Clean a pint of clams and drain thoroughly from their liquor. Beat 2 whole eggs together until very light, add ⅓ cup of milk, continue beating, interspersing with 1⅓ cups of flour sifted with 2 teaspoons of baking powder, salt and pepper to taste. Add the clams, chopped rather fine, and mix well so as to form a consistent liquid paste. Drop by tablespoonfuls into boiling deep frying fat. Drain and dress on a hot platter covered with a napkin. Garnish with green pepper, cut julienne-like, green parsley, and quartered lemon and serve with a side dish of TARTARE SAUCE, page 52, and a side dish of hashed-brown potatoes.

CLAM FRICASSEE

Clean 1½ pints of clams, finely chop the hard portions, and reserve the soft portions. Melt 2 generous tablespoons of butter and add the chopped clams, sprinkle over 2 tablespoons of flour and gradually pour on 1 cup of scalded fresh cream; strain the sauce and add the soft parts of the clams. Cook 1 minute; then season with salt and a few grains of Cayenne pepper and finish, off the fire, with 2 egg yolks, added separately while stirring constantly. Dress on a hot platter; sprinkle with finely chopped parsley and a little paprika and serve with a side dish of plain boiled small potato balls.

CLAM GRAND UNION

Clean and sponge 2 dozen selected large clams. Dip in BATTER III (*see* BATTER FOR FRYING FISH) and, when ready to serve, plunge in boiling deep frying fat. Drain, dress on pieces of toast, dipped in melted butter, seasoned with salt, celery salt, pepper, and Cayenne pepper to taste. Place on a hot platter. Garnish with fresh parsley and quartered lemon and serve a side dish of hot clarified butter and a side dish of French fried potatoes.

CLAM À LA NEWBURG

Clean 1½ pints of clams, remove the soft parts, and finely chop the hard parts. Melt 4 tablespoons of butter and, when well heated, add the chopped clams, season with salt and a few grains of Cayenne pepper, and stir well. Pour over 4 tablespoons of good sherry wine and cook 5 or 6 minutes, over a moderately hot fire, then add the soft parts of the clams and ⅔ cup of thick cream. Cook 2 or 3 minutes longer, add 4 egg yolks, slightly beaten and diluted, while stirring with a couple of tablespoons of the hot sauce. Dress either on a hot deep platter or in individual ramekins; sprinkle over a little paprika and serve with a side dish of shoestring potatoes and a side dish of cucumber salad with French dressing.

CLAM UNION LEAGUE

Scrape 30 clams and cook in a white wine court bouillon as indicated under How To Boil Fish until the clams open, remove from the shells, strain the cooking liquor and reduce to a generous cup over a hot fire. Melt 3 tablespoons of butter and add 2 tablespoons of flour, blend well and moisten gradually, stirring meanwhile, with the reduced liquor. Boil once. Remove aside and add one beaten egg yolk, stirring rapidly; then add the clams, season with salt and pepper to taste; refill the clam shells; sprinkle with finely chopped parsley and dress on a hot platter. Garnish with fresh parsley and quartered lemon. Place a small square of fried bacon over each clam and serve with a side dish of small potato balls, cooked in butter.

ROAST CLAM

This appetizing way of preparing large clams is popular at clambakes. The clams are washed in sea water, stones are heated by burning wood on them, the ashes removed and the stones sprinkled with thin layers of seaweed, and the clams are poured on the stones thus covered; they are in turn covered with a layer of seaweed and a piece of canvas is thrown over to retain the steam. Brown bread and butter sandwiches are a good accompaniment and potatoes may also be baked at the same time.

STEAMED CLAM

The clams should be large in the shell and alive, they should be well washed and scrubbed in several waters for this delicious method of preparation, which dates from the time of the Pilgrim fathers.

Put into a large kettle 4 quarts of clams, allowing ½ cup of hot water for each 4 quarts of clams; cover tightly and steam until the shells partially open, care being taken that the clams are not over-done, lest they become tough, stringy and rubber-like. Serve with individual dishes of melted butter, to which is added a few drops of lemon juice or tarragon vinegar, according to taste, and a little of the boiling cooking stock to maintain the heat of the butter by pro-tecting the surface. Saltine crackers or pilot crackers may be served as well as brown bread and butter sandwiches. A side dish of French dressing, or any one of the cold sauces found in the Book may be used.

STEAMED CLAM NEW ENGLAND AU GRATIN

Cover the bottom of a shallow baking pan with rock salt and arrange on it 3 quarts of large-sized soft-shelled clams. As soon as the shells begin to open, remove the clams rapidly and chop. Re-serve the liquor; strain and use in the preparation of CREAM SAUCE I, page 36, seasoned highly with lemon juice and Cayenne pepper. Pour the clams into the cream sauce and let stand a while, then refill the shells; sprinkle with grated young American cheese, then with fine cracker crumbs, sprinkle melted butter over and set under the flame of the broiling oven until golden brown. Serve the re-mainder of the sauce aside with a dish of cucumber salad with French dressing.

> In Virginny we goes clammin'—
> We goes clammin' ev'y night—
> An' de water lays dere still lak,
> Lawd, a mighty purty sight!

CLAMS

Clams an' oysters fo' de takin',
An' we gits 'em ev'y one:
Twell de sun comes up ashinin'
An' our clammin' she am done.
Ho! Clahmmmms!
Ho! Clahmmmmms!

Thus the clam man lifts his voice, the song dies out as trade languishes. So long as there are curb markets in Harlem, New Orleans, and Virginia, and a spirited, joyous race to buy at them, the pushcart men of these sections of our country undoubtedly will continue to contribute to the unique street cries of America.

CLAMBAKE ROAST

Make a circle of flat stones, the size of the circle, depending upon the size of the party. On this circle build a hot fire of wood. Let the fire burn two or three hours. Rake off the fire and cover the hot stones with fresh seaweed. On this lay fresh clams in their shells. Oysters, potatoes in the skins, corn in the husks, and so forth, even game birds, prepared as indicated in GAME COOK BOOK, may be added. Cover with a thick layer of seaweed and over all spread a large piece of sailcloth, weighting down the edges with heavy stones. Leave for 2 or 3 hours. Remove the sailcloth and top layer of seaweed and serve the roast in picnic style immediately.

CLAM VIRGINIA

Mince 2 large green peppers, removing the seeds and white ribs, and cook in 4 generous tablespoons of minced cooked ham, rather fat, with 1 generous tablespoon of finely chopped onions and 2 extra large fresh mushrooms, peeled, using caps and stems, and minced fine, stirring frequently, for 15 short minutes, over a gentle fire. Meanwhile, wash and pick over, 6 dozen soft clams, then mince, and add to the green-pepper mixture, stirring the while. Season to taste with salt, black pepper, a few grains of Cayenne, and pour over 1 scant cup of fresh cream. Stir and let simmer very gently for 10 long minutes, then add 4 or 5 ounces of good sherry wine. Just before serving, add, and off the fire, 3 egg yolks, beaten in 4 generous tablespoons of scalded, then cooled, fresh cream. Stir until the mixture thickens, and serve at once over freshly made toast, spread with a little anchovy butter. Garnish the platter with thin slices of lemon, dipped half in paprika, and the other half in finely minced parsley, interspersed with small triangles of bread fried in butter. You may prepare this delicious dish right on the table in a chafing dish if desired.

MUSSELS

The edible sea mussels, shellfish of the Mytilidae group, are gregarious and are found in great masses, closely crowded, adhering to rocks, sand, and one another by the very tough byssus, the entire beds being thus practically bound together. When young, the mussels move about, but they soon anchor themselves by the byssus and remain thus throughout life.

These delicious and nourishing shellfish are generally found in shallow water, and are often exposed at low tide. The shell, black on the outside and pearly blue inside, is oblong and generally about three inches long by one and a half inches wide, although some are found nearly double these dimensions.

Sea mussels are found in enormous quantities from New Brunswick as far south as North Carolina and are at their best from October till the end of April, after which they spawn and are rather indigestible.

HOW TO PREPARE AND COOK MUSSELS

Place the mussels in cold water and scrape with a knife, removing all the seaweed which may adhere and rinse in several waters, rejecting all mussels which are open. Place then in a large kettle with finely chopped onion, a small bunch of tied up parsley, thyme to taste, bay leaf, crushed peppercorns and moisten with a wineglass of white wine. Cover hermetically and set on a hot fire. One or two minutes are quite sufficient to open the shells. Remove the kettle aside, shell the mussels and place in a bowl, covering with the strained cooking liquor. By this method you may have always on hand mussels for garnishing or any other use.

FRIED MUSSELS

Select 3 dozen large mussels and cook as indicated above. Marinate for 15 minutes in oil, lemon, and finely chopped parsley. When ready to serve, dip in BATTER IV (*see* under BATTER FOR FRYING FISH), place in a wire basket and plunge in boiling deep frying fat. Drain, dress on a hot platter covered with a napkin, and garnish with fried curled parsley and quartered lemon. Serve with a side dish of small brown bread and butter sandwiches and a side dish of RAVIGOTE SAUCE, page 52. A side dish of your favorite green salad with French dressing will complete a delicious luncheon.

MUSSELS CATALANE

Cook 4 dozen large mussels as indicated under How To PREPARE AND COOK MUSSELS, above. Strain the the cooking liquor through a fine cloth and reduce to half volume over a hot fire; there should be ⅔ cup; incorporate gradually, bit by bit and stirring meanwhile, 3 tablespoons of butter and finish with a generous tablespoon of finely chopped onion light golden browned in butter and a few drops of lemon juice. Rectify the seasoning, dip each mussel in this foamy, unctuous sauce, replace in half shell, and glaze under the flame of the broiling oven. Serve with a side dish of French fried potatoes.

MUSSEL MARINIÈRE

Cook 3½ dozen mussels in the usual way, adding 1 cupful of fish stock and 2 tablespoons of freshly made soft bread crumbs. Serve as is, dressed on a deep hot platter, and sprinkled with finely chopped parsley. The mussels are usually taken in the hand and the liquor drunk from the shell. Small brown bread and butter sandwiches may be served at the same time, with quartered lemon and a side dish of freshly made small French fried potatoes.

MUSSEL PATTY

Cook 3½ to 4 dozen small mussels in the usual way, strain the cooking liquor through a fine cloth and prepare CREAM SAUCE II, page 36, using the liquor instead of milk. Finish the sauce with a tablespoon of sweet butter and a few drops of lemon juice, add ½ cup of sliced fresh mushrooms, cooked in butter and well drained, then the cooked mussels, and let stand a while. Fill 6 heated patty shells; dust with a little paprika and dress on a hot platter. Garnish with parsley between the patty shells and quartered lemon and serve with freshly made shoestring potatoes.

MUSSELS POULETTE
(*French Method*)

Scrape, wash, and sponge 3½ to 4 dozen small mussels, rejecting the opened ones as unfit to eat. Place in a large stock pot, containing nothing else, on a hot fire, so the heat will force open the shells. This accomplished, shell the mussels in a saucepan, taking care to remove the little oyster crabs which may be inside. Place the shelled mussels in a saucepan with half a pound of butter, 1 tablespoon of finely chopped parsley, 1 tablespoon of finely chopped chives, set on a low fire, stirring constantly, and when the butter begins to melt, sprinkle over the mussels a tablespoon of flour, pour in a cup each of white wine and fish stock, and let cook slowly for 20 minutes on a gentle fire. Meanwhile prepare a SAUCE POULETTE as indicated in recipe for PERCH À LA POULETTE, page 147, and place the mussels in it. Let stand a few minutes and dress on a hot, round deep platter. Garnish with small triangles of bread fried in butter and slices of lemon and serve with a side dish of plain boiled small potato balls.

SAUTÉED MUSSELS WITH RICE

Cook 3½ to 4 dozen small mussels in the usual way; drain the cooking liquor and strain through a fine cloth. Place in a saucepan (there should be 1 cup—if not, add a little fish stock), boil once, add, off the fire, 3 egg yolks, stirring meanwhile, and finish with a tablespoon of butter. Turn the mussels in the sauce and let stand a few minutes. Dress on a hot platter decorated with a border of plain boiled rice. Sprinkle a little finely chopped parsley over and serve with a side dish of cucumber and tomato salad with French dressing.

STEWED MUSSELS FISHERMAN

Prepare and cook 3½ to 4 dozen mussels in the usual way. Make a light thin cream sauce as indicated for CREAM SAUCE I, page 36, add the mussels with small plain boiled potato balls and pour over a drained small can of mushroom buttons. Let simmer very gently about 10 minutes. Dress in a deep round platter, sprinkle a little finely chopped parsley over, and serve with a side dish of plain lettuce salad with French dressing.

OYSTERS

The oyster, found in almost every sea, belongs to the Ostreidae family, and feeds on aquatic plants, diatoms, and, during the spawning season, on its eggs and fry. Those found on the eastern coast of the Atlantic are a valuable species of protean character.

Oysters are mollusks, having two shells, one on the right and one on the left, which are called right and left valves. That upon which the oyster rests, the left, grows faster and becomes deeper than the right. The valves are fastened by a sort of ligament which is elastic and permits the opening and closing of the shells.

The spawning season of the oysters is very variable and occurs according to locality: in Long Island Sound the spawning season occurs from May to August; in Chesapeake Bay, from April to October; in South Carolina, in March; and in Florida, as early as February. An average oyster will produce as many as sixteen million eggs and a very large one *sixty million*. During the spawning season, they are flabby and of a poor flavor, although, when fresh, they are perfectly wholesome.

From an economic standpoint, the oysters have been highly valued for many centuries, known to be an excellent and valuable food, and the presence of their shells in vast heaps among the relics of prehistoric man proves that oysters were quite well liked before the dawn of history. According to Pliny, it was Sergius Aurata who conceived the idea of cultivating oysters. He had constructed large fish ponds near Lucrin Bay, Rome, to fatten oysters for regal festivities.

Oysters are indeed one of the few living organisms that may be eaten either raw or cooked, although most epicures hold that a cooked oyster is a desecration of a good gift of Nature. Oysters constitute one of the most delicate and savory of foods and are excellent for invalids, as they are more readily digested than meat, in convalescence from fevers, and in many forms of gastric disorder.

The soft part of the oyster, like that of the majority of shellfish, is formed chiefly by the bulky liver, while the tough, harder portion is mainly the muscle which attaches the organism to its shell. This muscle is coagulated and rendered *tougher* by all forms of cooking; hence raw oysters are more tender and digestible than if stewed or broiled as is done in America.

In oysters, the liver is relatively larger and more nutritious than in clams. In recommending oysters to invalids, numerous medical authorities advise that only the soft parts be eaten, and when this advice is followed, the oysters may be cooked in a variety of ways such as stewing, broiling, roasting, or panning, and steaming. *They should never be fried for the sick.*

Oysters, like clams, are liked by most people and they add variety to the foods permissible in restricted diets. They impart an agreeable flavor to milk and broths. It is customary to forbid their use by diabetics, on the ground that their livers contain glycogen (animal starch).

America and France have the most important oyster industries in the world, and in the United States the industry is growing tremendously every year due to the increase in oyster beds on the coasts of the Atlantic and Pacific oceans. Oysters must be around five years old before they are suitable for eating.

Among the most popular oysters is the little plump blue point found at Blue Point, Long Island, and its popularity is increasing so rapidly that the supply is entirely inadequate, and many other small oysters from other points of the Atlantic seaboard are offered for sale by fish dealers under the name of blue point.

BAKED OYSTERS CASINO

Wash and open 3 dozen oysters. Over each oyster, put a few drops of lemon juice, 1 teaspoon of finely chopped green pepper and a square of bacon, sprinkle with pepper from the mill and salt to taste. Place in a tin pan and set in a hot oven (400°) for 10 minutes. Shallow fireproof dishes with the half shells embedded in rock salt are excellent for this purpose. Serve with melted butter. A side dish of cucumber salad with sour-cream dressing is a good accompaniment.

BAKED OYSTERS LOUISIANA

Clean and parboil 3 dozen loose oysters, reserve the liquor and add enough water (fish stock is much better) to make 1½ cups. Cook 3 tablespoons of butter with 2 of chopped red pepper and ½ tablespoon of finely chopped shallot 5 or 6 minutes. Add 2 tablespoons of flour and blend well, stirring meanwhile; then pour on the oyster liquor gradually, while stirring constantly. Bring to the boiling point; season with paprika and a few grains of Cayenne pepper. Dress the oysters in large buttered scalloped shells, pour over the sauce, sprinkle with grated young American cheese, and place around the edge a border of mashed potatoes, forced through a pastry bag with a small fancy tube. Set a few minutes under the flame of the broiling oven and serve with a side dish of your favorite green salad with French dressing.

BAKED OYSTERS NORFOLK

Lay on the bottom of a well-buttered baking dish a layer of freshly boiled rice (about ⅔ of a cup), cover the rice with 1½ dozen large oysters, pour over the oysters, ⅔ cup of CREAM SAUCE I, page 36, and dust with salt, pepper, and a few grains of Cayenne pepper. Repeat exactly. Cover with freshly made buttered soft bread crumbs and set in a hot oven (400°) for 15 minutes, sprinkling the crumbs once in a while with melted butter; if they brown too rapidly, place over a buttered paper. Serve with a side dish of small French fried potatoes.

BROILED OYSTERS MANHATTAN

Clean and sponge well 3 dozen large oysters, place in melted butter highly seasoned with salt and pepper from the mill or crushed peppercorns, then roll dripping in saltine cracker crumbs. Place on a well-buttered and heated wire broiler and set on the rack of the broiling oven and broil under a hot fire, turning and basting frequently with melted butter until the juices flow. Serve dressed on a hot platter, garnished with fresh parsley and quartered lemon, with a side dish of Maître d'Hôtel Butter, page 57, and a Hungarian Cucumber Salad made as follows:

Hungarian Cucumber Salad

Pare 2 large cucumbers and slice thin; sprinkle with salt generously and let stand for 2 or 3 hours; drain and sponge well between a towel. Prepare a dressing by mixing a cup of sour cream, a tablespoon of wine vinegar, and a scant tablespoon of ice-cold water. Put the sliced cucumber in a bowl, pour on this dressing, sprinkle copiously with paprika, and serve right from the bowl.

BROILED OYSTERS BROCHETTE
ENGLISH STYLE
(Also Called "Angel on Horse Back")

Author's Note

The original name of this delicious English preparation which may be served as an appetizer or an hors d'œuvre, being a savory, is "Angel on Horse Back." Clams may be prepared in the same way and, for variation, a cooked mushroom, or a square of lean cooked ham, or a small piece of sweetbread may be added.

Wash and sponge well 3 dozen oysters and wrap each oyster in a slice of very thin bacon, thread on a steel skewer; dip in melted butter highly seasoned with salt and Cayenne pepper and broil as indicated in recipe for Broiled Oysters Manhattan, above, until the juices flow. Dress on a long piece of toast the size of the brochette or skewer, sprinkle with very fine dry bread crumbs, and dust with a few grains of Cayenne pepper. Serve with a side dish of plain melted butter, to which may be added a few drops of onion juice or lemon juice.

CREAMED OYSTERS

Clean and cook 1 pint of oysters until plump and edges curl; drain, add 2 cups of CREAM SAUCE I, page 36, seasoned with celery salt and a few grains of Cayenne pepper. Dress on buttered toast, in timbale cases, patty shells, or vol-au-vent (large patty shell), or serve in shortcake style. If served in patty shells or vol-au-vent, ½ cup of sliced mushrooms, previously cooked in butter and well drained, should be added to the oysters.

VARIATION

You may mix half oysters and half shrimps, or lobster, scallops, crab meat, mussels, etc.

DEVILED OYSTERS ON HALF SHELLS

Wash and chop 1 pint of oysters. Melt 1 tablespoon of butter and cook 3 tablespoons of finely chopped shallots, then add 2 tablespoons of flour, stirring well until blended. Pour in gradually, and stirring meanwhile, ¾ cup of cream or half cream and half rich milk (top of the bottle), bring to the boiling point and add the chopped oysters, a few grains of Cayenne pepper, a generous half teaspoon of prepared mustard, ½ tablespoon of Worcestershire sauce, 2 tablespoons of finely chopped mushrooms, 1 teaspoon of finely chopped parsley, and let simmer very gently for 15 minutes. Finish with 2 slightly beaten egg yolks, added off the fire while stirring constantly, put the mixture in the deep, heated halves of oyster shells, cover with buttered bread crumbs, and set in a hot oven (400°) for 10 short minutes. Dress on a hot platter, garnish with parsley and quartered lemon and serve with a side dish of small French fried potatoes.

FANCY ROAST

Clean 1 pint of oysters and drain from their liquor, put in a saucepan and cook until plump and edges begin to curl, shaking the pan to prevent scorching. Season with salt and pepper and add 2 tablespoons of sweet butter, then pour the oysters over 6 small slices of toast. Dress on a deep hot platter and garnish with small triangles of freshly made toast, parsley, and quartered lemon. Serve with a side dish of Saratoga chips.

FRIED OYSTERS PHILADELPHIA

Parboil 3 dozen medium-sized oysters in their own liquor; lift out and sponge well; dip in BATTER I (*see* under BATTER FOR FRYING FISH) and let stand 15 minutes. When ready to serve, place in a wire basket and plunge in boiling deep frying fat until golden brown. Dress on a hot platter covered with a napkin; garnish with fried parsley, slices of gherkins, and quartered lemon and serve with a side dish of the following sauce:

PHILADELPHIA SAUCE

Mix together in order given: 2 cups of very finely shredded white cabbage, 2 medium-sized green peppers, finely chopped, 1 teaspoon of celery seed, 1 scant teaspoon of prepared mustard, 2 tablespoons of brown sugar, salt to taste and a few grains of Cayenne pepper and a generous ¼ cup of tarragon vinegar.

JACK'S OYSTER STEW

Parboil fresh honeycomb tripe and cut in ¾-inch pieces; there should be 1 cupful. Add an equal quantity of small boiled white onions and twice the quantity of raw oysters, previously cleaned. Melt 3 tablespoons of butter, add 4 tablespoons of flour, and blend well; pour on gradually, while stirring constantly, 1⅓ cups of thin cream (the top of the milk bottle may be used), previously scalded; bring to a boil and add tripe, onion, and oysters. When thoroughly heated, add the yolks of 3 fresh eggs, slightly beaten, stirring meanwhile and off the fire. Season highly with salt, black pepper from the mill or crushed peppercorns, and a little paprika to taste. Dress on pieces of freshly made toast placed on a hot platter; garnish with fresh parsley and quartered lemon and serve with a side dish of sliced tomatoes with mayonnaise, to which is added finely chopped blanched almonds.

OYSTERS FLORENTINE

Parboil 3 dozen oysters, well washed and cleaned; drain. Garnish the deep parts of the shells with plain boiled spinach, coarsely chopped and copiously buttered, and place an oyster on top. Cover with MORNAY SAUCE, page 43, and rapidly glaze under the flame of the broiling oven. Dress on a hot long platter; garnish with fresh parsley and quartered lemon and 4 small mounds of freshly made shoestring potatoes.

OYSTER FRICASSEE

Clean 3 dozen oysters; heat the liquor to the boiling point and strain through a fine cloth; add the oysters to the liquor and cook until plump and the edges curl. Remove the oysters with skimmer and add sufficient thick, scalded cream or, better, CREAM SAUCE II, page 36, to make 1½ cups. Season with salt and a few grains of Cayenne pepper and add, gradually and off the fire, 2 egg yolks separately, while stirring constantly. Finish with a tablespoon of finely chopped parsley and put the oysters in the sauce. Let stand awhile and dress on a freshly made piece of toast, lightly spread with anchovy paste, diluted with a little melted butter. Place on a hot platter, garnish with parsley and quartered lemon and serve with a side dish of Lyonnaise Potatoes.

LYONNAISE POTATOES (*Short Cut*)

Boil potatoes in the skin, peel, slice, and then sauté with fried slices of onion; ⅓ potatoes, ⅔ onions.

ORIGINAL METHOD

Slice cooked, peeled potatoes in rings and place in a saucepan containing 4 or 5 tablespoons of butter. Pour over a clear purée of onion in proportion of ⅔ onions; fry separately in butter 2 large onions, sliced thin, and, when golden brown, sprinkle over a teaspoon of flour; mix well, season with salt and crushed peppercorns and add ½ cup of beef stock or hot water and a teaspoon of tarragon vinegar. Let simmer for 15 minutes and mix with the potatoes.

Do not attempt to make this recipe with old potatoes, lest they form a paste.

OYSTERS AU GRATIN RUSSIAN STYLE

Clean and trim 3 dozen large oysters, parboiled, drain well, and return to the shell. Cover each oyster with CREAM SAUCE I, page 36, to which is added a tablespoon of caviar for each cup of sauce (more if desired rich); sprinkle with fine bread crumbs mixed with Swiss cheese, then with melted butter, to which has been added a little anchovy paste to taste and glaze rapidly under the flame of the broiling oven. Dress on a hot, long platter covered with a napkin; garnish with fresh parsley, quartered lemon, and quartered hard-boiled eggs dipped in melted anchovy butter. You may serve with a side dish of small French fried potatoes, or garnish the border of the platter with freshly made shoestring potatoes.

OYSTERS MORNAY

Open 3 dozen medium-sized oysters, wash, clean, and cook in their own liquor until plump and the edges curl. Put in each deep shell, a teaspoon of MORNAY SAUCE, page 43; sprinkle with freshly grated American cheese, then with melted butter, and glaze rapidly under the hot flame of the broiling oven. Dress on a hot platter covered with a napkin; garnish with fresh parsley and quartered lemon and serve with a side dish of your favorite green salad with French dressing.

OYSTER PATTY À LA RUSSE

Parboil in their own liquor, 3 dozen medium-sized freshly opened oysters, reserving the liquor; drain; there should be a generous ½ cup, if not, add a little fish stock. Prepare CREAM SAUCE I, page 36, using the oyster liquor instead of milk, and add to the sauce 3 egg yolks, one by one, stirring meanwhile and off the fire; then add to the sauce 1 tablespoon of strained lemon juice, 1 teaspoon of grated horseradish, and a generous tablespoon of well-washed capers. Season highly with salt, crushed peppercorns, and a few grains of Cayenne pepper and pour on gradually, stirring gently, ½ cup of thick cream, heated to the boiling point. Finally, add the oysters; let stand 5 minutes and fill heated patty shells. Dress on a hot platter, garnish with fresh curled parsley and quartered lemon, and serve with small sandwiches of caviar (may be omitted).

OYSTER UNION GRILL

This grill may be prepared right on the table in a chafing dish.

Clean 3 dozen oysters and drain off all the liquor possible, put the oysters in a chafing dish, and as the liquor flows from them remove rapidly with a spoon, and continue this until oysters are plump. Sprinkle with salt and pepper to taste, and add 2 or 3 tablespoons of butter. Serve on well-buttered toast.

OYSTER SOUFFLÉ

Open 2 dozen large oysters; drain and chop very fine, then pass through the meat chopper, adding very gradually while grinding, 2 egg whites. Force through a fine sieve, then incorporate gradually a scant cup of fresh cream and 1 egg yolk; season highly with salt and a few grains of Cayenne pepper. Place in the deeper side of oyster shells a generous teaspoon of this mixture; set over an oyster, parboiled until plump and dipped in CREAM SAUCE I, page 36; cover with more of the mixture, dressing until bulging in the middle, and surround the base with a line of fine dry bread crumbs. Place the shells thus stuffed in a pan containing hot water and set in a hot oven (400°) for 12 to 15 minutes. Dress on a long, hot platter and surround with plenty of fresh curled parsley and quartered lemon.

Serve with a side dish of small squares of French fried potatoes in butter mixed with finely chopped chives.

PANNED OYSTERS

Clean 3 dozen freshly opened oysters, place in a lightly buttered baking pan 6 large pieces of toast, and on each toast 6 oysters; sprinkle with salt, pepper, and a few grains of Cayenne pepper and bake in a moderately hot oven (375°) until oysters are plump. Dress on a hot, large platter; garnish with fresh parsley and quartered lemon, and serve with a side dish of Lemon Butter Sauce, page 42, and a side dish of hashed and browned potatoes in bacon drippings.

ROASTED OYSTERS

Wash thoroughly, scrubbing with a brush, 3 dozen large oysters, place in a shallow pan and set in a hot oven (400°) until they open. Sprinkle with salt and pepper and a few grains of Cayenne pepper and serve in the deep halves of the shells, dressed on a hot platter covered with a napkin. Garnish with fresh parsley and quartered lemon and serve with a side dish of Drawn Butter Sauce, page 38, or a side dish of Remoulade Sauce, page 52. A side dish of French fried potatoes is a good accompaniment.

SCALLOPED OYSTERS

Mix ½ cup of bread crumbs with 1 cup of cracker crumbs and stir in ½ cup melted butter. Put a thin layer of the mixture in the bottom of a well-buttered baking dish; cover with half a pint of cleaned oysters and sprinkle with salt, pepper, and a few grains of Cayenne pepper. Repeat and cover with the remaining crumbs. Set in a moderately hot oven (375°) and cook 15 to 20 minutes.

Author's Note

Never allow more than 2 layers of oysters for scalloped oysters; if three layers are used, only the bottom and top will be properly cooked; the middle layer will be underdone. A sprinkling of mace or grated nutmeg to each layer enhances the flavor. If the top browns too fast, cover with a buttered paper. Serve right from the baking dish with a side dish of cucumber and tomato salad with French dressing.

> ". . . Tom, whom today no noise stirs,
> Lies buried in these cloisters;
> If at the last trump
> He does not quickly jump
> Only cry OYSTERS . . ."
>
> EPITAPH ON A COLCHESTER MAN'S GRAVE.

SCALLOPS

The scallop is a bivalve of the Pectinidae family, of which two species appear along the eastern Atlantic seaboard: the "common scallop" and the larger and handsomer northern one frequently called "deep-sea scallop." The latter is found from Vineyard Sound northward, but more abundantly along the coasts of Maine and Nova Scotia and is twice the size of the common scallop.

The scallop, like the oyster, is hermaphroditic and the entire mass of eggs, probably more than a million, may be discharged in the course of an hour and a half or so. The breeding season is in June. The scallops spawn when one year old, and it is supposed that they die after two years.

The best scallops, according to epicures, are those found in Long Island Sound and Narragansett Bay.

The central muscle of the scallop forms the edible portion and is the only part found in the markets from October first to April first, the months when they are at their best.

The chemical composition of scallops is similar to that of the oysters.

DEVILED SCALLOPS AU GRATIN

Clean 3 dozen scallops, drain, and heat to the boiling point with the liquor; reserve the liquor. Cream ⅓ cup of butter, add a scant ½ teaspoon of prepared mustard, salt, and Cayenne pepper to taste, pour over ⅔ cup of the reserved liquor, and add the scallops, coarsely chopped. Let stand ½ hour to allow the liquid to penetrate into the meat. Put in a buttered baking dish, cover with bread crumbs, sprinkle with melted butter, and bake in a moderately hot oven (375°) 15 to 20 minutes.

VARIATION

You may add ½ cup of cooked sliced mushrooms and a tablespoon of finely chopped green pepper. Individual dishes may be served.

FRIED SCALLOPS DELMONICO

Clean 1 quart of scallops and add the juice of a lemon, 1 tablespoon of olive oil, ½ teaspoon of finely chopped parsley, salt and pepper to taste, and a few grains of Cayenne. Cover, let stand ½ hour and drain. Mix together 3 tablespoons of chopped cooked ham, 4 tablespoons of soft bread crumbs, 2 tablespoons of grated Parmesan cheese, and 1 tablespoon of chives, finely chopped. Dip the scallops in beaten eggs, roll in the mixture, and, when ready to serve and not before, place in a wire basket and plunge into boiling deep frying fat. Drain; sprinkle lightly with salt and pile up on a hot round platter; garnish by surrounding the scallops with quartered hard-boiled eggs, freshly cooked and hot, then dipped in melted anchovy butter, interspersed with quartered lemon and fried slices of small green tomato topped with a large mushroom cooked in butter and well drained. Serve with a side dish of Tartare Sauce, page 52.

FRIED SCALLOPS

Clean 1 quart of scallops, parboil 1 minute, drain, sponge between towels, season with salt and pepper, dip in beaten eggs and bread crumbs and, when ready to serve, place in a wire basket and plunge in boiling deep frying fat until brown. Drain, dress on a hot platter, garnish with fresh parsley and quartered lemon, and serve with a side dish of Tartare Sauce, page 52, or a side dish of Remoulade Sauce, page 52. A cucumber salad with French dressing is the usual accompaniment.

SCALLOPS CREOLE

Cook 3 tablespoons of finely sliced onion with 5 tablespoons of finely sliced green pepper in 4 tablespoons of butter, then add a small can of tomatoes (juice and pulp), a strained small can of mushrooms, and finally ½ cup of coarsely chopped green olives and cook 10 minutes over a hot fire, adding a bit of bay leaf, 6 thyme leaves, salt and pepper to taste. Prepare a cream sauce using the scallop liquor instead of milk (*see* CREAM SAUCE I, page 36); there should be a generous cup and the sauce should be a little thin, and add a generous tablespoon of sherry wine. Let this simmer very gently for 15 minutes. Meanwhile, clean 1 quart of scallops and drain well, parboil 2 minutes and drain again. Pour a layer of CREOLE SAUCE III, page 37, in a buttered baking dish, place over a layer of parboiled scallops; repeat and sprinkle buttered bread crumbs over the top. Set in a very hot oven (450°), covered with a buttered paper, for 15 minutes; remove the paper and cook 10 minutes longer or until the top is browned. Serve right in the baking dish with a side dish of cucumber salad with French dressing.

SCALLOPS NEW ENGLAND

Parboil 1 generous pint and a half of scallops in their own liquor; drain and cut in quarters. Melt 2 tablespoons of butter and add 2 tablespoons of flour; blend well, then pour on gradually, while stirring constantly, 1 cup of thin cream, bring to the boiling point and add ½ small can of well-drained tomatoes and a few grains of soda. Again bring to the boiling point, then add 1 cup of grated American cheese and, as soon as the cheese has melted, 2 whole eggs slightly beaten, put in the scallops and season with salt and Cayenne pepper to taste, as well as a scant teaspoon of prepared mustard. Dress on buttered toast placed on a hot platter; garnish with quartered lemon and fresh parsley and serve with a side dish of your favorite green salad with French dressing.

SCALLOPS NEWBURG

Put a generous pint of scallops in a frying pan and cook in their own liquor until beginning to shrivel; drain thoroughly, cut in halves, and cook in 3 tablespoons of butter for 5 short minutes, season with salt, Cayenne pepper to taste, and add a scant teaspoon of lemon juice. Simmer for 1 or 2 minutes. Melt 1 tablespoon of butter and blend well with a teaspoon of flour, stirring constantly; then pour on gradually, while stirring, ½ cup of thick cream. Bring to the boiling point, remove to the side of the range and add, one by one, slowly, 3 egg yolks, stirring meanwhile, then the scallops from the other pan and finish with 2 generous tablespoons of sherry wine. Serve in a chafing dish or in individual small casseroles or in ramekins, with a side dish of freshly made toast.

A side dish of your preferred salad will enhance this delicious preparation.

SCALLOP AND MUSHROOM PATTIES

Prepare and cook a pint of scallops as indicated for above recipe, adding a generous half cup of sliced mushrooms cooked in butter and well drained, or a small can of mushroom buttons, well drained. Fill heated individual patties and dress on a hot platter. Garnish with fresh parsley and quartered lemon and serve with a side dish of freshly made shoestring potatoes.

SCALLOPS À LA POULETTE

Parboil a quart of scallops in their own liquor and reserve the liquor. Melt 2 tablespoons of butter and add 2 tablespoons of flour, stirring until blended; moisten with the scallop liquor (there should be a generous cup, if not, add sufficient fish stock), stirring all the while. Let simmer very gently for 15 minutes on the side of the range; skim and finish with ½ cup of fish stock, heated to the boiling point. Boil once and add, off the fire, 3 egg yolks, separately, and stirring constantly. Squeeze over a medium-sized lemon, season with salt and pepper, a generous tablespoon of butter and a generous tablespoon of finely chopped parsley and put in the scallops. Let stand a few minutes and dress on a deep round platter or in individual dishes such as casseroles, ramekins, or patty shells, and if scallops are too large, use a pint only and cut in two.

SHELL OR RAMEKIN OF SCALLOP BELMONT

Parboil a pint of large scallops in their liquor; drain. Prepare 1 generous cup of MORNAY SAUCE, page 43, and place the scallops in it, adding ½ cup of finely sliced mushrooms cooked in butter and a teaspoon of finely chopped shallots. Let stand a few minutes. Fill shells or ramekins with the mixture, sprinkle with fine, buttered bread crumbs mixed with grated Swiss cheese in equal parts and brown under the flame of the broiling oven. Dress on individual plates covered with doilies and garnish each with a sprig of parsley and a small quarter of lemon.

SHELL OR RAMEKIN OF SCALLOP PARISIENNE

Parboil a pint and a half of large scallops, previously cut in two and well drained in white wine court bouillon as indicated under How To Boil Fish. Drain and reserve the cooking liquor. Make White Wine Sauce, page 49, using the cooking liquor, put in the scallops and let stand a few minutes. Fill shells or ramekins with the mixture, sprinkle well-buttered bread crumbs over and brown rapidly under the flame of the broiling oven. Serve on individual plates covered with doilies and garnish each with a sprig of parsley and a quarter of a small lemon. Serve with a side dish of romaine salad with French dressing.

SHELL OR RAMEKIN OF SCALLOP LOUISIANA

Cook for 5 minutes, 1½ pints of scallops, cut in two, in a white wine court bouillon as indicated under How To Boil Fish. Drain and chop. Cook a teaspoon of finely chopped onion in 2 tablespoons of butter for 5 minutes, stirring constantly, add a tablespoon of flour and stir until well blended and slightly brown. Pour on gradually, while stirring constantly, the strained cooking liquor of which there should be a cupful. Bring to the boiling point and add the scallops, ½ small clove of garlic finely chopped, 1 scant teaspoon of finely chopped parsley, 3 tablespoons of freshly made soft bread crumbs, salt, pepper, and a few grains each of Cayenne and nutmeg. Finish with 2 egg yolks, added separately while stirring gently and constantly, and fill the shells or ramekins with the mixture, spread with well-buttered bread crumbs, and brown rapidly under the flame of the broiling oven. Dress on individual plates covered with doilies, garnish each with a sprig of parsley and a quarter of a small lemon. Serve with a side dish of small potato balls, cooked in butter and well browned and a side dish of your favorite green salad with French dressing.

SCALLOP IN CASSOLETTE SUSIE

The following recipe, a creation of the Author, may seem long to prepare because of the elaborate explanation, but is very easy to make, and if you want to startle your guests, either for supper or even for a formal dinner or luncheon party, try this; and note that content and container are edible and really delicious.

The first operation consists in preparing the individual casserole or cassolette as follows:

2 lbs. boiled potatoes (hot)	3 tablespoons thin cream
2 whole eggs	Flour
4 tablespoons butter	Shredded Wheat crumbs
Salt, pepper, and nutmeg to taste	

Mash the potatoes very smooth, while still hot, using first a ricer, with the cream and butter (you may use undiluted evaporated milk). Add the eggs, one at a time, beating well after each addition.

Add seasonings. Stir vigorously over a low fire for 10 short minutes, then turn out onto a flat platter to cool, spreading the mixture flat. When cold and set, roll small balls the size of a billiard ball and flatten two sides so that they stand like sections of a cylinder. Incise the upper surface with a small pastry cutter, leaving a rim. Dip first in flour, then in beaten egg and crumbs, and leave them to dry a little.

Arrange the cassolette in a frying basket and fry in boiling fat to a rich golden color. Drain well, and remove the cut lids and the soft inner portions. Sprinkle with paprika. For added effect brush the fried cassolette with butter and sprinkle the outside with parsley, chives, nuts, etc., chopped fine.

Now for the scallops: Blanch 2 pints of scallops by boiling them 3 minutes in a cup of water and ½ cup of Sauternes wine (other wine may be used, but Sauternes gives a fine and delicate flavor). Drain and save the liquid. Sauté a minced medium-sized onion in 2 scant tablespoons of butter until it is tender but not browned. Add a tablespoon of kneaded butter, then the liquid from the scallops and ½ cup of undiluted evaporated milk, or rich milk, and mix all well over a low flame, stirring constantly till the sauce is smooth and thick; then add ¼ scant cup of more Sauternes wine, salt, pepper, and a few grains of nutmeg to taste—a dash of Cayenne will not be amiss. Put in the scallops, which should be halved or quartered if they are the large sea scallops, and 1 can of well-drained button mushrooms, heated first in their liquor, then thoroughly drained, and 1 generous teaspoon of finely minced chives, and 1 of parsley. Keep this mixture hot, over hot water, but do not allow to boil, keeping it at the scalding point, while you beat 4 egg yolks into ½ cup of cream. Stir the egg and cream very gently, very delicately, into the sauce and scallops and keep it simmering, not boiling, until the mixture thickens to a suitable consistency. Fill up the cassolette, which should have been heated, or kept hot, and dust each cassolette with a little black truffle, chopped fine. Serve immediately on individual plates, and garnish simply with a sprig of watercress. You may substitute a ring of cooked spinach for the cassolette, or a ring of homemade noodles, or rice mixed with a little curry powder if desired.

While one portion of SCALLOP IN CASSOLETTE SUSIE is all that one of good breeding should consume, it arouses regret that one has but one mouth.

CRUSTACEANS

CRABS

The One who formed the oceans and seas and their abysses has attended to the matter of sanitation of their shores and He has placed these shellfish as sentinels of the tributary streams of fresh water; to the lobsters, langoustes, crabs, and others generally has been assigned the task of keeping clean the immense areas of water.

The stomach of these scavengers is so perfectly equipped to receive all the refuse, to absorb and destroy it that it should be easy to recognize a Creator of these innumerable members of the Sea White Wings.

The crabs, of which there are more than one thousand species, are found all over the world and belong to the arthropod family. They supply food for edible fish, and are used as food for humans in various parts of the world.

From the water of Chesapeake Bay alone, where is found the delicious blue crab or common crab, hundreds of thousands are sent to the markets yearly, while hundreds of thousands are also canned every year. These shellfish are found all along the Atlantic seaboard down as far as Mexico.

Soft-shell crabs, also known as "shedders," are crabs which have just shed their shell and are covered only by a soft skin, such being regarded as the best by epicures.

The little "pea crabs," or "oyster crabs," frequently found in oysters and mussels are regarded as a luxury and are very numerous. They were known long before the days of Roman and Greek history.

The American Pacific coast from Alaska to Mexico also provides the markets with huge quantities of common and large crabs, these latter known under the name of "Morro crabs."

The "king crab," sometimes called "horseshoe crab," again "helmet crab," is found most plentifully at the mouths of the Kennebec and Penobscot rivers of Maine and along the Atlantic seaboard as far south as Mexico. In the southern states, it is called by the natives "casserole crab," because of its resemblance to a saucepan or casserole. The king crab is eaten only in the regions where found, and, not being widely popular, is seldom found in the markets.

The various methods employed in the preparation of the common crab may be adapted to these giant crabs.

BAKED CRAB MEAT NEW ORLEANS

(You May Use Canned Crab Meat)

Drain and pick a 1-lb. can, or 2 small cans, ½ lb. each, of crab meat and flake well. Prepare 2 cupfuls of CREOLE SAUCE, page 37, and arrange in nest in the bottom of a well-buttered baking dish. Mix the crab meat with a cup of CREAM SAUCE I, page 36, adding ½ cup of sliced fresh mushrooms cooked in butter and place in the nest of the baking dish. Sprinkle over well-buttered bread crumbs and set in a hot oven (400°) for 15 minutes or until crumbs are well browned. Serve with a side dish of small potato balls, cooked in butter and rolled in finely chopped parsley.

CRAB MEAT AU GRATIN PARISIAN STYLE

(You May Use Canned Crab Meat)

Drain and pick 2 small cans of crab meat, removing the bones carefully. Mix with the same amount (about a generous cup) of mashed potatoes and ½ cup of sliced mushrooms, coarsely chopped, cooked in butter, and well drained. Stir in 3 tablespoons of fresh cream, previously heated and seasoned with salt, pepper, and a few grains each of Cayenne pepper and nutmeg. Put this mixture in a well-buttered baking dish; cover with buttered bread crumbs mixed in equal parts with grated Swiss cheese and set in a hot oven (400°) for 15 minutes. Serve right from the baking dish with a side dish of cucumber salad with French dressing.

CRAB MEAT CANADIAN STYLE

Chop finely, a large green pepper and cook in butter for 5 minutes, add 1 lb. of fresh crab meat, well flaked and boned, and cook for 10 minutes, stirring once in a while, season to taste with salt, pepper, and a few grains of nutmeg. Place in a well-buttered baking dish, the bottom of which is lined with 6 slices of lean cooked ham and pour over the following sauce:

CANADIAN SAUCE

Melt 5 tablespoons of butter and add 2 tablespoons of flour; blend well and let simmer a few minutes on a low fire. Pour over a little milk, just enough to thicken slightly, and add 2 tablespoons of grated Parmesan cheese, salt, pepper, and paprika. Pour this sauce over the crab meat in the baking dish; sprinkle with a little Parmesan cheese and bake in a hot oven (400°) until brown. Serve right from the baking dish.

CRAB MEAT INDIAN STYLE

Cook a teaspoon of finely chopped onion in 2 tablespoons of butter, 3 to 4 minutes; do not brown. Add 3 tablespoons of flour, mixed with a scant tablespoon of curry powder; moisten with a cup of fish stock and ½ cup of chicken stock, in which dissolve ½ teaspoon of cornstarch; bring to a boil and add 2 cups of fresh crab meat, boned and shredded; season with salt and pepper to taste and finish with a tablespoon of butter. Dress on a hot round platter with a border of plain boiled rice; dust with a little finely chopped parsley and serve with a side dish of the following sauce:

CURRY SAUCE (*For Fish*)

Chop finely, a small white onion and a very small carrot, cook in 2 tablespoons of butter for 5 minutes, adding a sprig of parsley, and moisten with a cup of fish stock. Let simmer for 20 minutes on the side of the range, skim, strain through a fine sieve, add a scant teaspoon of cornstarch dissolved in 3 tablespoons of fresh thick cream, boil once or twice and add a tablespoon or less of curry powder, dissolved in a little cold fish stock, with the size of a small walnut of extract of meat (Liebig, Oxo, etc.). Boil once more and let simmer

5 long minutes; finish with a tablespoon of butter after rectifying the seasoning.

CRAB MEAT MORNAY

Melt 5 tablespoons of butter, add 3 tablespoons of flour and 2 tablespoons of cornstarch, salt and pepper to taste and stir until well blended; then pour on gradually, while stirring constantly, ¾ to 1 cup of fish stock. Bring to the boiling point and let boil 5 long minutes; then add gradually 1 scant cup of rich milk, again bring to the boiling point and add, off the fire, 3 egg yolks, one by one and stirring meanwhile. Finish with 2 tablespoons of grated American cheese. Butter 6 individual small casseroles or ramekins; line the bottom with crab meat, well boned and shredded (fresh or canned), cover with the sauce, sprinkle with grated American cheese and set under the flame of the broiling oven to brown. Dress on individual plates covered with doilies; garnish each with a sprig of parsley and a small quarter of lemon and serve with a side dish of French fried potatoes in butter.

CRAB MEAT AND MUSHROOM PATTY

Melt 3 tablespoons of butter, add 3 tablespoons of flour, and stir until well blended; then pour on gradually, while stirring constantly, 1 cup of rich fish stock (if not available use chicken stock) and ½ cup of cream. Bring to the boiling point and add 1½ cups of fresh crab meat, boned and flaked, and the caps from ½ lb. of small mushrooms (a small can of drained mushroom buttons may be used), cut in strips and sautéed in butter. As soon as thoroughly heated, add ½ cup of grated Parmesan cheese, 3 tablespoons of good sherry wine, salt, pepper, and a few grains of paprika to taste. Fill 6 patty shells, heated in a hot oven for a few minutes; adjust the cover and garnish with a sprig of crisp green parsley. Dress on individual plates with a small quarter of lemon and serve with a side dish of fried julienne potatoes.

CRAB MEAT RAVIGOTE

(*Cold*)

Season 1 lb. of fresh crab meat, well boned and shredded with a little salt and a few grains of Cayenne pepper and let stand, while mixing the following ingredients: 1 teaspoon of prepared mustard, 1 tablespoon of olive oil, ½ teaspoon of finely chopped parsley, 1 teaspoon of finely chopped chives, 1 hard-boiled egg, finely chopped, and 3 tablespoons of tarragon vinegar. After wiping well, add the crab meat to the seasoned mixture and fill 6 scallop shells, crab shells, or lettuce cups, spread evenly with ravigote mayonnaise, and garnish with a strip of fillet of anchovy and a few capers strewn over.

CRAB MEAT TERRAPIN STYLE

Cook a tablespoon of finely chopped onions in 4 tablespoons of butter until light golden; remove the onions, add 2½ cups of fresh crab meat and 4 tablespoons of good sherry wine; cook 5 minutes, then add 1 generous cup of heavy cream and fold in, while stirring constantly, 4 egg yolks. Season with salt and a few grains of Cayenne pepper and serve in individual casseroles or ramekins dusted over with a little paprika. Serve a side dish of small squares of potato fried in butter and a side dish of cucumber salad with French dressing.

CRAB MEAT DEWEY

(*You May Use Canned or Fresh Crab Meat*)

Take 2 cans or equivalent of fresh crab meat, bone thoroughly and set aside. In one frying pan, place the crab meat, 2 chopped shallots, and 2 wineglasses of white wine (about ½ pint). Simmer gently for 5 long minutes, stirring occasionally. In another pan, blend ½ lb. butter, 2 generous tablespoons of flour until very smooth and mixture begins to bubble, then add ½ lb. fresh mushrooms, peeled, then sliced finely, caps and stems. Brown this delicately, stirring occasionally from the bottom of the pan. Add the mushroom mixture to the crab mixture, adding 1 teaspoon of black truffles, chopped fine, and a generous ¼ cup of heavy cream, heated to the scalding point. Let this simmer very gently for 5 long minutes. Then set in a very hot oven (450°) or under the flame of the broiling oven. Serve immediately.

This may be prepared in individual casseroles, or served on freshly made toast.

CRAB IMPERIAL

Carefully pick the meat from a dozen boiled hard crabs. Simmer the flakes in 3 generous tablespoons of butter, in which has been cooked to a light brown, 1 large onion, minced fine, but not browned. Season to taste with salt and Cayenne pepper and add 1 quart of scalded thick cream, 1 teaspoon of Worcestershire sauce, 1 tablespoon of prepared mustard, and 1 tablespoon of chives, minced fine. Bring this to a boil, gradually and slowly, stirring occasionally. Then add 1 medium-sized green pepper, white seeds removed, and minced fine. Remove from the fire and bind with 4 or 5 egg yolks, beaten to a cream, gradually, while stirring all the while. Fill 6 of the shells with the mixture; spread over each shell a little French mustard, then 1 teaspoon of fine buttered bread crumbs. Set under the flame of the broiling oven to brown and serve at once.

The shells should be filled to the brim, domelike, as the mixture has a tendency to fall down under the heat.

CRAB MEAT TITA RUFFO

Melt 5 tablespoons of butter and add 4 tablespoons of flour, stirring until well blended; then pour on gradually, while stirring constantly, 1½ cups of fresh cream and ½ cup of milk mixed together. Bring to the boiling point; season with salt and a few grains of Cayenne pepper and add 1 lb. of fresh crab meat, boned and flaked, a drained small can of small button mushrooms or the equivalent of sliced fresh mushrooms sautéed in butter and well drained, 2 slices of pimento, cut in long, thin strips and a few drops of lemon. Finish with a tablespoon of sweet butter, stirring gently, and fill 6 Swedish timbales or patty shells, or one large patty shell (vol-au-vent). If individual (Swedish or patty shells), dress on individual plates covered with a fancy doily; if using a large shell or vol-au-vent, dress on a hot platter and garnish around with slices of lemon dipped in paprika, topped with a slice of hard-boiled egg in turn topped with a slice of stuffed olive. A side dish of cucumber salad with French dressing may be served.

CREAMED CRAB MEAT ON TOAST

Prepare 1½ cups of CREAM SAUCE I, page 36. Bone and flake 1 lb. of fresh crab meat and fold in the Cream Sauce. Heat well and dress on slices of freshly made toast, placed on a hot platter. Garnish with quartered lemon and fresh parsley and sprinkle over the fish, a little paprika and 1 hard-boiled egg yolk forced through a fine sieve. Serve with a side dish of lettuce and tomato salad with French dressing.

DEVILED CRAB MEAT I

Combine 2 cups of fresh crab meat (or canned crab meat) with 1½ cups of CREAM SAUCE I, page 36, highly seasoned, to which is added 1 tablespoon of Worcestershire sauce, 1 tablespoon of lemon juice, and a few grains of Cayenne pepper. Fill 6 individual shells, cover with buttered bread crumbs, and bake in a moderately hot oven (375°) until crumbs are brown. Dress on individual plates covered with doilies and garnish each with a sprig of parsley and a quarter of small lemon.

DEVILED CRAB MEAT II

Make a sauce with ¼ cup of butter, same amount of flour, and 1 cup of scalded milk and add gradually, while stirring constantly, 2 egg yolks, separately. Season with salt and a few grains of Cayenne pepper and add a teaspoon of Worcestershire sauce, a scant teaspoon of prepared mustard, 1 scant teaspoon of strained lemon juice, and, lastly, 2 cups of boned, flaked fresh crab meat (or canned crab meat). Combine well and put into a buttered baking dish. Cover with buttered cracker crumbs and set in a hot oven (400°) for 15 minutes or until crumbs are well browned. Squeeze over the juice of a small lemon and serve right from the baking dish.

OYSTER CRABS
FRIED OYSTER CRABS

Wash, drain, and sponge very carefully 3 dozen or more oyster crabs; roll in flour, salted and highly peppered with crushed peppercorns and a few grains of Cayenne pepper. When and *only when ready to serve,* place in a wire basket, shake to remove superfluous flour and plunge in boiling deep frying fat. Drain, dress on a hot platter covered with a napkin, and garnish with fried parsley and quartered lemon. Serve with a side dish of REMOULADE SAUCE, page 52, and a side dish of cucumber salad with French dressing.

OYSTER CRAB BEARNAISE

Wash and pick over 1½ pints of oyster crabs, put in a saucepan, place on the range, and add ½ cup sherry wine, 2 tablespoons of butter, salt, and paprika to taste. Light the sherry wine and let burn 2 or 3 minutes. Turn on serving platter and garnish with fresh parsley and quartered lemon. Serve with a side dish of BEARNAISE SAUCE, page 34, and a side dish of freshly made shoestring potatoes.

OYSTER CRAB POULETTE

Prepare and cook 1½ pints of oyster crabs, using brandy instead of sherry wine as indicated above, and letting burn 5 minutes, while stirring gently with a long fork. Dress on a hot platter, the bottom of which is lined with Poulette Sauce, made as indicated in recipe for MUSSEL POULETTE (*French Method*), page 257. Serve the remainder of the sauce aside with a side dish of O'Brien potatoes.

KING CRAB

The various methods of preparation of the common crab may be adapted to these giant crabs. On certain parts of the Pacific coast, they are boiled and picked right on the table, accompanied, if hot, by a dish of melted butter and, if cold, a side dish of either mayonnaise, to which may be added a little prepared mustard, or TARTARE SAUCE, page 52.

CRAYFISH

The crayfish is one of Nature's wonders. Very tiny when born, it is enveloped in a shell which seemingly would deprive it entirely of elasticity, and prevent it from moving. Growing up, it will change its dress. It lies on its back, on the bottom of the river, shakes its tiny tail protruding from under the stiff shield, rubs its little claws, moves its head, swings its feelers, flutters about, strives, inflates itself, and all this is done patiently and methodically.

Under these repeated exercises and efforts, the under part of its carapace splits open and the crayfish emerges gradually, the head first, then the eyes, its abdomen, its claws, its feelers, and the tail. The crayfish is thus practically nude, having on just a filmy coat as clear as cellophane. Now once more it depends upon its own efforts, and immediately from its pores a viscous secretion is exuded, weaving a new dress to its shape, and very soon this shellfish re-appears on the sand of the river with a brand-new and well-fitting garment, coquettishly choosing the spot where the sun shines, and any time that a crayfish wishes to don a new dress, it does so by the same process.

This shellfish is its own architect, its own builder, its own dress-maker, and its own physician—all at the same time. Nature has indeed attended to all the details marvelously.

The crayfish feeds on plants and animals. One of the simple water plants, Chara, furnishes it with lime for its skeleton. Crayfish seize food with their pincers and move it toward the mouth. Small food particles are also carried toward the mouth by currents of water produced by the mouth parts and the abdominal appendages.

The mouth of the crayfish is just back of the mandibles and connects with the stomach by a short esophagus. The stomach is divided into two sections, the front possessing a grinding structure known as the gastric mill, which serves to shred and crush the food and prepare it for digestion in the back part. The liver, or digestive gland, pours a fluid into the stomach, which prepares the food for absorption by the walls of the stomach and intestine. The intestine begins at the rear end of the stomach and extends to the last segment.

The crayfish obtains oxygen from the water by means of gills which are well covered by the overhanging skeleton of the head-thorax region, but are really outside of the body.

Crayfish have been used for centuries for food in Europe, while in France, crayfish breeding to increase the supply has been successfully practiced for many years.

CRAYFISH IN BUSH

(*Buisson d'Écrevisses*)

Prepare a white wine court bouillon as indicated under How To Boil Fish, using Chablis white wine instead of ordinary wine and, when boiling rapidly, add 4 dozen cleaned, washed, live crayfish with the greenish filament removed. Cook 3 to 4 minutes, set aside and let stand 3 or more minutes. Dress on a hot platter, garnish with fresh curled parsley and serve with a sauce made as follows:

Sauce

Reduce the cooking liquor to half over a hot fire, strain and add a tablespoon of kneaded butter, then 4 egg yolks added slowly, one by one, while beating constantly, with a wire whisk. Rectify the seasoning and finish with a pinch of saffron and serve aside with a dish of clarified butter.

CRAYFISH CREOLE

Prepare and cook 4 dozen selected crayfish as indicated above. Dress on a hot platter and serve with a side dish of Creole Sauce, page 37, highly seasoned with Cayenne pepper and a few drops of Angostura Bitters and a side dish of small French fried potatoes in butter.

CRAYFISH CZARINA

This delicate way of preparing the little crustaceans was the favorite dish of the late Czarina of Russia.

Place 4 dozen live crayfish in a terrine, trimmed and well washed and green filaments removed, pour over sufficient milk to cover, let stand in this simple marinade for 4 to 5 hours. When ready to serve, pour into a saucepan 1 bottle of dry white wine and add salt to taste —no pepper, no spices. When the wine is boiling violently, strain the crayfish from their milk bath and plunge into the boiling wine. Remove aside and let simmer 10 minutes. Strain and dress on a hot platter covered with a folded napkin and serve with a side dish of plain melted butter and a side dish of diced cucumber salad with French dressing.

CRAYFISH SOUFFLÉ FLORENTINE

Prepare a cheese soufflé in the ordinary way and, before adding the beaten egg whites, put in 6 tablespoons of creamed crayfish, mixing well. Cook as for an ordinary cheese soufflé, 25 minutes in a hot oven (400°). Serve right from the soufflé dish with a side dish of creamed spinach and a side dish of French fried potatoes.

CRAYFISH LIÉGEOISE

Prepare a mirepoix or braise, place over 3½ dozen cleaned crayfish, sprinkle with a few grains of Cayenne pepper, and moisten with a generous half cup of white wine or fish stock according to taste. Cover and cook very slowly for 15 minutes over a low fire. Dress the crayfish on a hot deep platter. Strain the cooking liquor, add a scant teaspoon of finely chopped parsley; correct the seasoning and serve aside with the crayfish garnished with fresh parsley and quartered lemon.

CRAYFISH MAGENTA

Prepare a mirepoix or braise, pour over ½ cup of olive oil, stir, and place on top 3½ dozen cleaned crayfish; let cook 2 or 3 minutes and add 3 large fresh tomatoes, peeled and coarsely chopped, 1 teaspoon of finely chopped parsley, and pour over a generous ½ cup of white wine. Cover and let simmer very gently for 15 minutes on the side of the range, shaking and tossing in the pan once in a while. Dress on a hot round platter and add to the cooking liquor 2 tablespoons of sweet butter, bit by bit, stirring gently, and a pinch of basilic. Pour over the crayfish and serve with a side dish of plain boiled potato balls, rolled in melted butter, mixed with finely chopped parsley.

CRAYFISH MARINIÈRE

Sauté in 3 generous tablespoons of butter 3½ dozen cleaned crayfish, over a hot fire, until quite red, tossing in the pan very often; season with a teaspoon of finely chopped shallots, 4 or 5 thyme leaves, salt and pepper to taste, and pour over 2 cups of white wine or 1 of white wine and 1 of fish stock. Cover and let simmer very gently for 15 minutes on the side of the range. Dress on a hot round platter; garnish with fresh parsley, quartered lemon, and quartered hard-boiled eggs. Serve with a side dish of clarified butter and a side dish of your favorite green salad with French dressing.

CREAMED CRAYFISH

Prepare a mirepoix or braise; moisten with a cup of hot water and season highly with a few grains of Cayenne pepper and crushed peppercorns to taste. Bring to a boil and add 3½ dozen cleaned crayfish. Cover hermetically and cook rapidly over a very hot fire for 6 or 7 minutes, shaking and rocking the pan frequently. To a cup of CREAM SAUCE III, page 37, add slowly, off the fire, 3 egg yolks, separately, stirring meanwhile, and pour in ½ cup of strained cooking liquor. Remove the tail and part of the shell of the crayfish; place in the Cream Sauce, to which has been added a tablespoon of sweet butter and seasoning rectified. Dress on a hot deep platter;

garnish with small triangles of bread fried in butter, slices of lemon dipped in finely chopped parsley, and serve with a side dish of heart of lettuce salad with French dressing.

SHELL OR RAMEKIN OF CRAYFISH NORMANDE

Border 6 scallop shells with a narrow edge of smooth mashed potatoes forced through a pastry bag with small tube; sprinkle with melted butter and brown under the flame of the broiling oven. Pour a generous teaspoon of NORMANDE SAUCE, page 44, in the bottom of each shell and place over ½ dozen or more, according to size of crayfish, tails cooked and shelled, a blade of truffle over each in the center, and cover the whole with Normande Sauce. Glaze rapidly under the flame of the broiling oven and serve with a side dish of shoestring potatoes.

LANGOUSTE

The langouste is very similar to the lobster in shape, flavor of the flesh, and in habits, and the various methods employed in the preparation of lobsters may be adapted to this crustacean.

LOBSTER

The lobsters head the list of the numerous shellfish belonging to the decapod family and, like the crabs, are scavengers of the ocean.

They are very active shellfish, and it is claimed that if transported several miles from their original habitat they will find their way back. The lobster is very similar to the langouste in shape, flavor of the flesh, and in habits.

Lobsters are found in most parts of the world and along our shores from Hendley Harbor in Labrador, southward to Delaware Bay, usually near the rocky shores in depths of from ten to twenty fathoms. Toward winter, they migrate into water from thirty-five to forty fathoms deep. They are bottom feeders, never rising more than a few feet above the bottom.

The breeding season is in July and August, though the eggs may be laid in the spring or autumn and even in winter, the number of eggs varying from five thousand to eighty thousand, according to age. The young, on hatching, are driven away by the fanning motion of the parent, and in May, June, and July they swim on the surface. During this time, and until the fourth stage (about twelve days) is reached, immense numbers are devoured by surface swimming fish and other animals, and it is estimated that a survival of two in every ten thousand larvae hatched would maintain the species.

Certain specimens have been found weighing from sixteen to twenty-five pounds, but such huge lobsters are apparently now extinct along our coasts. The average weight of a lobster is two pounds and the length from ten to fifteen inches.

Lobsters are largest and most abundant from June to September, but are obtainable all the year round. When taken from the water, the shells are of mottled dark-green color, except when the lobster is found on sandy bottoms, when the shell is quite red.

In the female lobster, sometimes called the "hen," is found, during the breeding season, the spawn known as coral. Lobsters shed their shells at irregular intervals, when old ones are outgrown like the crayfish and the new shells begin to form and take on distinctive characteristics before the old are discarded. The new shells after twenty-four hours' exposure to the sea water become quite hard.

Lobsters are caught chiefly by means of traps made of laths and stout cord into which they are beguiled by a bait of meat or fish.

How To Select a Lobster

Take the crustacean in the hand, and if heavy in proportion to its size, the lobster is fresh. Straighten the tail, and if it springs back into place, the lobster was alive (as it should have been) when put into the pot for boiling.

The cook should remember that there is a greater shrinkage in lobster than in any other fish.

How To Boil Lobster

Have ready a large fish kettle containing rapidly boiling salted water or any one of the liquids indicated under How To Boil Fish, according to recipe or formula. Plunge into the boiling liquid, tail end down, one at a time, having the liquid brought to the boiling point between each addition. Lobsters should be entirely immersed in the liquid. The time usually required for cooking lobster is about 15 to 20 minutes, according to size. After plunging the lobsters into the liquid, do not stop the rapid boiling as this will render the meat tough.

How To Open Cooked Lobster

Remove first, the large claws, then small claws and tail. (Tail meat may sometimes, after a little practice, be drawn out whole with a fork or a skewer, but more often it is necessary to cut the thin shell portion in under part of the tail, using a pair of kitchen scissors or a sharp can opener.) Divide the tail meat through the center and remove the small intestinal vein which runs along the entire length. Hold the body of the shell firmly in the left hand, and, with the first two fingers and thumb of right hand, draw out the body, leaving in the shell, the stomach, which is not edible, and also some of the liver (green part). Discard the lungs. Break the body through the middle and separate body bones, picking out the meat that lies between them, which is the sweetest and tenderest part of the lobster. Separate the claws at the joints.

How To Open Live Lobster

Live lobsters may be dressed for broiling at the fish store or may be done at home. Cross large claws and hold firmly with the left hand and with a sharp-pointed knife, held in the right hand, begin at the mouth and make a deep incision, and, with a sharp, rapid cut, draw the knife quickly through the body and entire length of tail. Open lobster, remove intestinal vein, liver, and stomach, and crack claw shells with a mallet or a cleaver.

BAKED STUFFED LOBSTER IN CREAM

Remove the meat from 6 small lobsters of 1 lb. each and cut in dices. Scald 1½ cups of milk with a bit of bay leaf, remove the bay leaf and make Cream Sauce II, page 36, using the milk and seasoning highly with a few grains of Cayenne pepper and using crushed peppercorns instead of ordinary pepper; add a teaspoon of finely chopped parsley, 3 egg yolks, one by one while stirring constantly, and a generous teaspoon of strained lemon juice. Put in the diced lobster meat, let stand a while and fill the cleaned shells. Cover with fine buttered bread crumbs and brown under the flame of the broiling oven. Dress on a hot platter; garnish with parsley, quartered lemon, and quartered hard-boiled eggs and serve with a side dish of shoestring potatoes.

BROILED LIVE LOBSTER

Prepare 3 large lobsters of 2 lbs. each as indicated under How To Open Live Lobster, above. Sprinkle generously with seasoned melted butter and broil under the flame of the broiling oven or in a pan placed in a hot oven (400°), basting frequently. (When placed in a baking pan and baked 15 to 20 minutes, lobsters taste practically the same as when broiled and the cooking process is simpler.) Dress on a hot platter, garnish with plenty of green parsley or, better, plenty of green watercress and quartered lemon and serve with a side dish of plain melted, clarified butter. A dish of cucumber salad with French dressing or tomatoes sliced and served with mayonnaise or French dressing is the usual side dish.

CREAMED LOBSTER

Proceed as indicated in recipe for CREAMED CRAYFISH, page 294, using the meat of 5 cooked small lobsters, cut in dices, instead of crayfish. Serve with a side dish of French fried potatoes.

FRICASSEE OF LOBSTER BELMONT

Remove the meat from 3 two-pound cooked lobsters, and cut in strips. Cook 1 cup of sliced fresh mushrooms in 3 tablespoons of butter for 4 minutes, adding a few drops of lemon juice and a few drops of Angostura Bitters to taste and sprinkle over 3 tablespoons of flour. Stir well to blend and pour on gradually, while stirring constantly, 1½ cups of thin cream (top of the milk will do). Season with salt, pepper from the mill, and a little nutmeg and add the lobster meat, slightly sprinkled with paprika. Stir gently and let simmer for 15 minutes; then add 2 generous tablespoons of sherry wine. Dress on a hot round platter; garnish with triangles of bread fried in melted anchovy butter, slices of lemon, and a small bunch of young, crisp watercress. Serve with a side dish of shoestring potatoes.

FRIED LOBSTER

Remove the meat from 3 large lobsters of 2 lbs. each, cut in large pieces, sprinkle with salt and pepper, with lemon juice, roll in butter, then in beaten eggs, and in fine cracker crumbs, again in eggs and in bread crumbs. When ready to serve, place in a wire basket and plunge into boiling deep frying fat until golden browned. Drain, dress on a hot platter, sprinkle over fried parsley and garnish with quartered lemon and a small bouquet of crisp young watercress, interspersed with slices of tomatoes seasoned, floured, and fried in plenty of butter.

LIVE LOBSTER EN BROCHETTE

Split in two 3 large live lobsters, remove the meat, and cut in pieces the size of a large walnut. Arrange on skewers, alternating the pieces with 1 square of bacon, 1 piece of lobster, and 1 mushroom cooked in butter, and so on, repeating until brochettes (skewers) contain 4 pieces each of ingredients. Dip in butter and place on a double broiler and set in a hot oven or under the flame of the broiling oven; if in oven, cook 10 short minutes, basting and turning frequently; if under the flame of the broiling oven cook 10 minutes turning and basting very often with melted butter. Dress on a hot platter, star shape, placing under each skewer a toasted buttered piece of bread the size of the brochette. Garnish the open space with small baked stuffed tomatoes and place in center a large bouquet of crisp watercress, surrounded with quartered lemon, and serve with a side dish of hot Tartare Sauce, page 52.

LOBSTER AMERICAN STYLE

Split 6 small lobsters of 1 lb. each and put in a large frying pan with 4 tablespoons or more of butter and a scant teaspoon of finely chopped onion. Season with a few grains of Cayenne pepper and cook 5 minutes. Pour over 3 cups of Tomato Sauce prepared as indicated for Fried Whiting Orly, page 242, and cook 4 or 5 minutes longer; then add a scant half cup or more, according to taste, of sherry wine, cover and set in a hot oven (400°) a good 5 minutes. To the liver of the lobsters, add 2 or 3 tablespoons of sherry wine, 5 or 6 tablespoons of tomato sauce, and 2 tablespoons of melted butter, and heat in the pan after the lobster has been removed. As soon as the sauce is heated, strain, forcing and pressing a little through a fine sieve and pour over the lobsters. Dress on a hot long platter, garnish with small triangles of bread fried in butter, quartered lemon, and serve with a side dish of Hungarian Cucumber Salad as indicated in recipe for BROILED OYSTERS MANHATTAN, page 261.

LOBSTER DELMONICO

Remove the meat from three 2-lb. cooked lobsters and cut in small cubes. Melt 4 tablespoons of butter and blend with a tablespoon of flour, let boil a couple of minutes and season with salt, pepper, and a few grains each of nutmeg and Cayenne pepper to taste. Pour over a generous scalded cup of heavy cream gradually, while stirring constantly; then add the lobster meat and, when well heated to the boiling point, remove aside and add gradually, one by one, while stirring constantly, 3 egg yolks slightly beaten before pouring. Finish with a tablespoon of sweet butter and 3 tablespoons of good sherry wine (more or less according to taste). Rectify the seasoning and dress on a hot round platter, surround with small triangles of bread fried in melted anchovy butter, interspersed with slices of lemon dipped in paprika, and serve with a side dish of small potato balls, boiled in fish stock, then rolled in butter and finely chopped parsley.

LOBSTER STEW ELSIE PULLIG

Cut 3 live lobsters of 2 lbs. each into serving pieces, leaving the shells on. Remove the intestinal vein, liver, and stomach and crack the large claws. Cook 1 generous tablespoon of finely chopped shallot, 1 scant tablespoon of finely chopped chives, 3 or 4 tarragon leaves, finely chopped, and 3 tablespoons of finely chopped raw mushrooms in 4 tablespoons of butter, 10 minutes over a moderately hot fire, stirring and tossing once in a while and adding 4 thyme leaves, a bit of bay leaf, and a few grains of Cayenne pepper, salt and 4 peppercorns crushed coarsely. Pour over a reduced 1½ cups of fish stock, a small can of tomatoes, well drained, and 4 tablespoons of good sherry wine; stir, bring to a boil, and add the lobster pieces.

Cover and cook 15 to 20 minutes over a very gentle fire. Lift out the lobster pieces with a strainer and place on a hot, deep, round platter. Boil the sauce to reduce a little and finish with 2 tablespoons of sweet butter and a tablespoon of good brandy; pour over the lobster after rectifying seasoning and sprinkle with a little finely chopped parsley. Garnish the edge of the platter with small triangles of bread fried in butter, interspersed with slices of lemon dipped in paprika, and serve with a side dish of plain boiled small potato balls.

LOBSTER FRENCH STYLE

Cut into serving pieces 3 live lobsters of 2 lbs. each and sauté in half cup of piping hot butter, to which add salt, pepper, and a few grains of nutmeg. When the lobster pieces are poppy-red, pour over a generous cup of white wine and a pony glass of brandy, and add 4 tablespoons of onion, cut julienne-like, and 4 tablespoons of carrot also cut julienne-like (small strips), 1 tablespoon of finely chopped parsley, and ⅔ cup of fish stock. Cover and simmer very gently for 15 short minutes on the side of the range, shaking the pan frequently. Dress the lobster pieces on a hot, round, deep platter; reduce the cooking liquor slightly and finish with a generous tablespoon of sweet butter. Pour over the lobster pieces, garnish with small triangles of bread fried in butter, interspersed with quartered lemon, and serve with a side dish of plain boiled small potato balls, rolled in butter, then in finely chopped parsley. A side dish of cucumber salad with French dressing may also be served.

LOBSTER À LA NEWBURG

Remove the lobster meat from the shell of enough lobsters, previously cooked in plain boiling salted water, to obtain 2½ lbs. of meat and cut in slices. Melt a generous ¼ cup of butter, add the lobster meat, cook 4 or 5 minutes, stirring gently. Season to taste with salt, Cayenne pepper, and a few grains of nutmeg and cook 2 minutes longer over a very gentle fire, then add 1 cup of heavy cream and stir in very gently and slowly 3 egg yolks, slightly beaten, and continue stirring until the sauce begins to thicken. Finish with 2 generous tablespoons of sherry wine. Dress on a hot platter over pieces of toast, or toast served aside, and garnish with small triangles of bread fried in butter.

LOBSTER PALESTINE

Prepare a mirepoix or braise of a teaspoon of coarsely chopped onion, a very small carrot, finely sliced, a tablespoon of celery, finely sliced, a large sprig of parsley, a bit of bay leaf, 1 clove, 4 or 5 thyme leaves, and salt and pepper to taste and cook 5 minutes in 3 tablespoons of butter, stirring once in a while; then add 3 live lobsters of 2 lbs. each, cut in serving pieces, shell removed. Let simmer 5 minutes, stirring once or twice and pour over a cup of white wine and a cup of fish stock. Place in a ladle 2 generous tablespoons of brandy and light it over the pan, dropping immediately into the mixture; cover tightly and let simmer very gently 10 to 15 minutes. Pound the shells, claws, and trimmings in a mortar and sauté in 5 tablespoons of olive oil with a few thin slices of onion, carrot, celery, and a sprig of parsley all chopped finely, over a hot fire. Moisten with a small quantity of the cooking liquor of the lobster and simmer very gently for 10 minutes; strain through a fine cloth and let stand awhile to allow the oil to float, which remove entirely, and reduce the liquid to half volume. Add to the cooking lobster, boil once or twice. After rectifying the seasoning, dress the lobster on a hot round platter, making a border of boiled rice, finish the sauce with 2 tablespoons of butter and a dash of curry powder dissolved in a little cold fish stock and pour over the lobster. Serve with a side dish of creamed cucumber.

LOBSTER SOUFFLÉ

Proceed exactly as for a cheese soufflé or any other kind of soufflé, substituting lobster for cheese. A side dish of creamed French peas besides that of shoestring potatoes is very suitable with this fine dish.

LOBSTER THERMIDOR

Split from the middle, lengthwise, 3 live lobsters of 2 lbs. each; clean, season with salt and pepper to taste, and broil very slowly under the flame of the broiling oven, basting frequently with melted butter. Remove the meat from the shell and cut in small pieces, slantwise; pour in the shell a tablespoon or two of CREAM SAUCE III, page 37, to which is added about a scant teaspoon of dry English mustard (more or less according to taste); refill the shell with the sliced lobster and cover with the same sauce and dust with a little paprika and glaze rapidly under the flame of the broiling oven. Dress on a hot platter; garnish with fresh parsley or young crisp watercress and quartered lemon and serve with a side dish of cucumber salad with French dressing.

LOBSTER TIMBALE I

Sprinkle lightly buttered timbale molds with lobster coral rubbed through a fine strainer. Line the mold (or individual molds) with FISH FORCEMEAT III (*see* FISH FORCEMEAT AND FISH STUFFING), fill the center with CREAMED LOBSTER, page 299, and cover with Fish Forcemeat. Put in a pan containing hot water, cover the mold or molds with buttered paper, and set in a moderately hot oven (350°) for 20 to 25 minutes. Unmold on a hot round platter; garnish with fresh parsley and large cooked shrimps, dipped in melted anchovy butter, and serve with a side dish of small French fried potatoes and a side dish of your favorite green salad with French dressing.

LOBSTER TIMBALE II

Split 2 live lobsters each weighing 2 lbs.; remove intestinal vein, liver, and stomach, crack the claws with mallet or meat cleaver, and remove all meat, scraping as close as possible to the shell. Force the lobster meat through a meat chopper and add a scant cup of fine soft bread crumbs, ¾ cup of heavy cream, to which is added 3 slightly beaten fresh eggs and season with salt, pepper, and a few grains each of nutmeg and Cayenne pepper, then pour in 2 generous tablespoons of good sherry wine. Fill well-buttered individual small molds with this mixture up to ⅔ full and place in a pan containing hot water up to the height of the mold, being careful not to have any spill on the mixture, and cover with a buttered paper. Cook over the range until firm, keeping the water below the boiling point. Unmold on a hot round platter, making a border of plain boiled spinach, generously buttered, and garnish the space between the molded lobster and spinach with small plain boiled potato balls, rolled in butter, then in finely chopped parsley mixed with a little paprika. Serve with a side dish of HOLLANDAISE SAUCE I, page 40.

PLANKED LIVE LOBSTER

Split 3 live lobsters, weighing 2 lbs. each, clean and season with salt and pepper and a few grains of Cayenne pepper, sprinkle with melted butter, or olive oil, which gives a nutty flavor to the meat, and place on a double broiler to sear, basting frequently; remove immediately and finish cooking in a shallow baking pan placed in a hot oven (400°). Remove to plank and garnish with julienne potatoes (shoestring potatoes), slices of peeled and chilled tomatoes overlapping one another, slices of cucumber also overlapping one another, a bunch of fresh crisp watercress, and quartered lemon. Pour the butter from the baking pan over the lobsters and serve with a side dish of melted clarified butter and a side dish of French fried potatoes.

COLD LOBSTER

Cold lobster makes a good adjunct to a summer luncheon and may be served with any one of the cold FISH SAUCES indicated in this book, using either canned or fresh lobster. When serving cold lobster, care should be taken to have it well chilled. The usual and most popular sauce, however, is mayonnaise, with which many appetizing dishes may be prepared.

Cold lobster is usually served in its shell, the latter being loosened, the claws cracked with a mallet or cleaver, the dish garnished with a crisp cup of lettuce containing mayonnaise, which may be forced through a pastry bag with fancy tube. Hard-boiled quartered eggs are used for garnishing, a few capers may be sprinkled over the mayonnaise; crisp fresh parsley or young watercress makes a good decoration for a dish of cold lobster; slices of well-chilled cucumber may also be used; well-chilled slices of tomatoes or tomato-plums are effective; stuffed olives, slices of red beets, strips of gherkins, or strips of green pepper may also be used as decoration.

It should be borne in mind that it is absolutely unwise to serve lobster in the evening and that pastry or creamed desserts should not be eaten after lobster.

SHRIMPS

Closely allied to the crayfish and prawns, are shrimps, belonging to the caridean family.

Of elongated form, tapering and arched as if hunchback, the whole structure is delicate, almost translucent, the colors are such that the shrimp may escape observation whether resting on a sandy bottom or swimming. The quick darting movements of these little shellfish betray them to one who looks attentively into a pool of water left by the tide. When alarmed, they bury themselves in the sand by a peculiar movement of the fanlike tail fin.

Shrimps are found abundantly in America, off the Atlantic and Pacific seaboards, wherever the bottom is sandy. Their natural color tint is greenish-grey, speckled with brown. Swarming in untold millions, they form a considerable part of the food of the flatfish and other shallow-water species.

The largest and best specimens, called by the epicures "bouquet," come from the region of Lake Pontchartrain, in Louisiana, and are about two inches long. Shrimps are in season from May first to October first and are used mainly for garnishing, salads, hors d'œuvres, and the like, but they may also be prepared in many delicious ways.

CURRIED SHRIMPS

Melt 4 tablespoons of butter and add 3 tablespoons of flour, blend well, and add a teaspoon of curry powder, or more according to taste, dissolved in a little cold water or cold fish stock, preferably; pour on gradually a cup or more of scalded milk, while stirring constantly, to obtain a smooth sauce. Season with salt and a few grains of Cayenne pepper and add 5 generous tablespoons of tomato catsup, a few drops of Worcestershire sauce, and 1½ lbs. of shrimps, freshly cooked, black line removed, and thoroughly shelled. Simmer very gently for 5 minutes and dress on a hot round platter with a border of plain boiled rice. Serve with a side dish of green salad with French dressing.

FRIED SHRIMPS TARTARE SAUCE

Dip 2½ cups of freshly cooked shrimps, thoroughly shelled and black line removed, in BATTER IV (*see* BATTER FOR FRYING FISH) and place in a wire basket. When ready to serve, and not before, plunge in a boiling deep frying fat until golden brown. Drain, dress on a hot platter covered with a napkin, garnish with fried curled parsley between small mounds of shoestring potatoes and quartered lemon and serve with a side dish of TARTARE SAUCE, page 52, and a side dish of creamed small potato balls.

JAMBALAYA CREOLE

(*Shrimps Creole*)

2½ cups cooked shrimps shelled and black line removed	2 cups boiling water
	2 teaspoons of beef extract
1 medium-sized onion finely chopped, a tiny bit of bay leaf, 6 thyme leaves	½ cup of uncooked rice
	Salt, pepper, and a few grains of Cayenne to
1 small clove of garlic	taste
1 pepper pod	½ scant teaspoon sugar
1 tablespoon of flour	2 drops Kitchen Bouquet
¾ cup canned tomatoes	Freshly made toast

Cook the onion in the butter and, when beginning to brown, stir in the flour, seasonings, and tomatoes and let simmer very gently for 10 minutes. Add the shrimps (after removing the black line), the water in which the beef extract has been dissolved (fish stock instead of water will enhance the flavor), and the well-washed, drained rice. Bring to the boiling point, stirring constantly and gently to prevent the rice from scorching and sticking; reduce the heat to very moderate and set the pan into another containing boiling water; cover and let simmer very slowly until the rice is cooked thoroughly, but not sticky, adding a little more water (or fish stock) if necessary when the mixture thickens. Color with Kitchen Bouquet, or any other coloring; rectify the seasonings and dress on a deep, hot round platter. Garnish with small triangles of bread fried in butter and serve with freshly made toast and a side dish of cucumber salad with French dressing.

SHRIMP SPANISH STYLE

Melt 3 tablespoons of butter and add 5 tablespoons of finely chopped green pepper mixed with 3 tablespoons of very finely chopped onions. Cook 3 to 4 minutes, tossing in the pan meanwhile, then add 2½ to 3 cups of freshly cooked shrimps, shelled and black line removed. Cook 3 to 4 minutes over a very hot fire, tossing and stirring meanwhile and constantly, and add 1½ cups of boiled rice, 1 cup of sliced fresh mushrooms cooked in butter, and a small can of tomatoes, juice and pulp. Season with salt, crushed peppercorns, and a few grains of Cayenne pepper to taste; continue cooking over a gentle fire while stirring constantly for 5 minutes. Cover and set aside to simmer very slowly for 10 minutes. Dress on a hot platter, surround with French fried onions, interspersed with slices of lemon dipped in paprika and a small bunch of watercress. Serve piping hot.

SHRIMPS À LA POULETTE

Proceed as indicated for Mussel à la Poulette, page 257, for the sauce, using 2½ cups of freshly cooked shrimps, after shelling and removing the black line. Dress in small ramekins placed on individual plates covered with doilies and garnish each with a sprig of watercress or parsley and a small quarter of lemon. Serve with a side dish of plain boiled small potato balls, rolled in butter, then in finely chopped parsley.

SHRIMPS AU GRATIN

Border 6 scallop shells with mashed potatoes forced through a pastry bag with a small tube; spread on the bottom of each shell a tablespoon of sliced fresh mushrooms, cooked in butter and well drained, and garnish with creamed fresh shrimps heaped on the shell; sprinkle with well-buttered crumbs mixed with equal parts of grated cheese and glaze under the flame of the broiling oven. Dress rapidly on individual plates covered with doilies; garnish each with a sprig of parsley or watercress and a small quarter of lemon and serve with a side dish of small French fried potatoes.

SHRIMPS NEWBURG

This delicious dish may be prepared on the table in a chafing dish.

Cook 2½ cups of cleaned, cooked fresh shrimps in 4 tablespoons of butter for 5 or 6 minutes over a low fire, stirring often; remove the shrimps, set aside, and keep hot. Add to the butter, salt, a few grains of Cayenne pepper, a scant tablespoon of lemon juice, and bring to a boil. Place 1 tablespoon of butter in the chafing dish, add the other butter with the lemon juice, stir in a generous tablespoon of flour; blend well and pour on gradually, while stirring constantly, 1 cup of fresh cream, previously scalded. When thickened, add, off the fire, 3 egg yolks, one by one, stirring meanwhile, the shrimps and 3 tablespoons of good sherry wine. Rectify the seasoning, let simmer very, very gently a few minutes to mellow and serve with a side dish of freshly made dry toast and a side dish of shoestring potatoes.

SHRIMP PATTY PARISIAN STYLE

To 1½ cups of rich CREAM SAUCE III, page 37, add ½ cup of sliced fresh mushrooms cooked in butter and well drained, 2 tablespoons of coarsely chopped red pimento, and 2 tablespoons of chopped green pepper blanched in salt water and well drained. Season highly with salt, crushed peppercorns, and a few grains of Cayenne pepper as well as a few grains of nutmeg. Add then 2½ cups of cooked shrimps, shelled, black line removed, and cut in two, crosswise. Rectify the seasoning and fill individual heated patty shells and dress on individual plates; garnish with a large sprig of watercress and serve with a side dish of diced artichoke bottoms sautéed in butter and mixed with equal parts of small white onions glazed in butter and sugar. A side dish of cucumber salad with French dressing will complete the meal.

FROGS' LEGS

FROGS' LEGS

Among both civilized men and savages, frogs are a culinary dainty. The edible European frog is so much prized in France that it is bred for the market on large preserves, while in our own country frogs are raised for national consumption in Wisconsin, Florida, and New Orleans.

The bullfrog, so named because of its bellowing note, is perhaps our most widely known, and is our most characteristic, frog. It is very large, attaining sometimes a length of eight inches, loves the shores and clean water, and is green-colored with olive and dusky blotches. It is equaled in size by the French species.

The green spring frog inhabits cold springs. It is brown or green olive and white beneath, and may be readily distinguished by the very large eardrums.

In the United States, both the bullfrog and spring frog are sold in the markets. In France and the United States, the hind legs alone are eaten; they are known as "saddles," are very wholesome, are similar in flavor to the flesh of chicken, and may be prepared in many delicious ways.

FRIED FROGS' LEGS

Soak 1 lb. of cleaned frogs' legs in salt water for 15 minutes, drain and sponge well; roll in fine bread crumbs, then in beaten eggs and again in crumbs, well seasoned with salt, pepper, and a few grains each of nutmeg and Cayenne pepper. When ready to serve, and not before, place in a wire basket and shake gently to remove excess of crumbs and plunge rapidly in boiling deep frying fat. Drain, dress on a hot platter covered with a napkin, and garnish with fried parsley and quartered lemon. Serve with a side dish of TARTARE SAUCE, page 52, and a side dish of French fried potatoes. A side dish of cucumber salad is often served with this delicious dish.

VARIATION

You may dip the frogs' legs in BATTER I or II (*see* BATTER FOR FRY-ING FISH) and deep fry, or roll in salted, peppered flour and fry in plenty of butter. You may substitute for Tartare Sauce any other cold sauce you may desire, or serve with a side dish of melted butter. You may use fine cracker crumbs instead of bread crumbs.

FROGS' LEGS POULETTE FRENCH STYLE

Disgorge 1 lb. of frogs' legs in a generous cup and a half of cold milk mixed with 1 cup of well-salted water for 2 hours. Meanwhile, mince a small carrot and 1 small onion and brown slightly in 2 table-spoons of butter over a very low fire. Drain the frogs' legs, sponge, and add to the onion, stirring and tossing in the pan, raise the fire to hot and cook 5 minutes; then sprinkle over the frogs' legs 1 gener-ous tablespoon or more of flour. Stir and moisten with a wineglass of white wine and an equal amount of strained fish stock, season highly with salt, pepper, and a few grains of Cayenne pepper, and add 1 tablespoon of finely chopped parsley. Bring to a boil, remove aside, and let simmer very gently for 15 minutes. Skim; strain the sauce and place the frogs' legs on a deep hot platter; keep hot. Add to the sauce ½ cup of thin cream, boil once or twice, then add, off the fire, 3 egg yolks, slightly beaten, pouring gradually, while stir-ring constantly. Finish with a generous tablespoon of strained lemon juice, a tablespoon of sweet butter, and a tablespoon of very finely chopped parsley. Mix, rectify the seasoning, add the frogs' legs, let stand a few minutes to mellow (do not let boil any more), and dress on a hot round platter or in individual casseroles or ramekins, placed on individual plates covered with doilies. Place on each a large sprig of crisp watercress and serve with a side dish of freshly made toast.

VARIATION

You may serve in heated patty shells or in a large one called "vol-au-vent."

FROGS' LEGS STEW BOURGEOISE

Prepare a golden yellow roux with 3 tablespoons of butter and 3 tablespoons of flour and moisten with 2 cups of fish stock; season highly with salt and pepper, a few grains of nutmeg, and a few grains of Cayenne pepper and add a small bouquet garni, a very tiny bit of garlic, a crushed clove, and 6 thyme leaves. Cover and let simmer gently for 15 minutes. Add 1 lb. of cleaned and disgorged frogs' legs and cook for 20 minutes over a gentle fire; rectify the seasoning. Dress on a hot, deep, round platter, sprinkle with finely chopped parsley, and garnish with slices of lemon dipped in paprika, interspersed with small triangles of bread fried in butter. Serve with a side dish of freshly made toast and a side dish of plain boiled small potato balls, rolled in butter, then in finely chopped parsley.

FROGS' LEGS OMELET

Melt 4 tablespoons of butter and add ½ lb. of frogs' legs, cleaned, disgorged, washed thoroughly in cold water, and well sponged; season to taste with salt and pepper and sauté gently for 15 minutes. Prepare an omelet in the usual way and, just before folding, add the well-drained, cooked frogs' legs. Dress on a hot platter, brush the omelet with melted extract of meat, then with melted butter, and place 1 short minute under the flame of the broiling oven; remove, garnish both ends of the omelet with a tablespoon of cooked frogs' legs set aside for this purpose, and on each side of the omelet place 3 thick slices of broiled green tomato, interspersed with fresh, young, crisp watercress. Serve with a side dish of freshly made French fried potatoes.

FROGS' LEGS EPICURE

Clean, bone, and flake enough crab meat to fill 1 cup, peel and slice enough fresh mushrooms to fill a cup, and clean, disgorge in strong salt water, then wash thoroughly in clear water, sufficient frogs' legs to have 2 cups (about 1 lb.). Sauté the mushrooms separately in 2 generous tablespoons of butter, then sauté the frogs' legs in 3 tablespoons of butter, drain both and mix together; add the crab meat. Cover and let stand aside the range to keep hot, while preparing 1½ cups of WHITE BUTTER SAUCE, page 48. Fold the frogs' leg mixture into the White Butter Sauce and fill 6 ramekins or small individual casseroles, and dress on individual plates covered with doilies. Garnish each with a large sprig of crisp green watercress and serve with a side dish of small sandwiches of brown bread and butter spread with a little MAÎTRE D'HÔTEL BUTTER, page 57, and cut like lady's-fingers, and a side dish of asparagus tips with HOLLANDAISE SAUCE I, page 40.

SNAILS

SNAILS

SNAILS BOURGUIGNONNE

The so-called epicureans who ignore completely the tiny delicate snails, which may be prepared so deliciously, are numerous.

Snails feed solely on soft leaves in the spring, summer, and fall and are among the cleanest of the edible shell creation. During the winter months they hibernate under the ground, after sealing themselves securely in their portable houses, and fast. Besides furnishing the most delicious of food, they are useful for medical purposes, being the base of many syrups and mixtures for internal use in certain bronchial ailments.

Whether taken from the vines of Ohio, the fields of hops of the Middle West, the bushes of Virginia, or imported from Europe, the inexpensive snails are always delicious and deserve to appear on the tables of rich and poor alike.

When the snails are collected from bush or vine, they are kept in a cool cellar for a week and fed on tender green lettuce, growing plump and firm on such fare. They are then thrown into a pail containing salt and vinegar and stirred vigorously with a stick. During this procedure the inedible secretions are cast off, and the snails are washed under running water until the liquid is perfectly clear.

The snails are now plunged into a large kettle of violently boiling salted water, allowed to boil for a good half hour, and then thrown into a large colander to drain. The next operation consists in pulling them out of their shells, which are set aside for later use, and removing the green gall or intestine.

Now comes the most delicate and artistic part of the preparation. In a clean kettle, place the snails and add the traditional bouquet garni of fresh parsley, bay leaves, and thyme, then a large golden onion, sliced, a clove of garlic, and half a wineglass of cognac for every 6 dozen snails. Cover the mixture to the level with cold water, season to taste with salt and white pepper (the latter generously) and set on a gentle fire for 6 to 7 hours, covered tightly.

Meanwhile, wash and dry the shells thoroughly, which have been put aside, and into each shell carefully pour good meat juice without fat and slightly heated, and then return a snail to each shell, closing the opening with a thick coat of beaten butter, profusely mixed with chives, shallots, and parsley very finely chopped, then seasoned with salt and white pepper (you may flavor the butter with a morsel of very finely chopped garlic).

Dress all the little domes in a ring and shelter these highly flavored preparations on a flat baking tin and set in an open oven, until the butter melts and runs, and the aromas penetrate through the limp flesh of the snails.

This real French preparation of the widely defamed snail is a culinary treat which will gladden the heart of you and your guests. Dress the snails ring-shape on a platter without any garnishing.

CREAMED SNAILS ABBEY STYLE

(Old Monk's Recipe)

Cook 6 minutes, or until golden brown, 2 tablespoons of finely chopped onions and add 6 dozen snails cooked as indicated above (but not in their shells), seasoned with salt and pepper to taste, and sprinkle over 2 tablespoons of flour; mix and blend well and moisten with 1½ cups of freshly scalded thick cream. Let simmer for 15 minutes over a low fire and finish off the fire with 4 egg yolks, added one by one, while stirring constantly, and a tablespoon of butter. Rectify the seasoning and dress on a hot platter, sprinkle with finely chopped parsley and serve with a side dish of freshly made toast and a side dish of French fried potatoes.

SNAIL FRITTERS

Cook 6 dozen snails as indicated and, while still hot, sauté in butter, to which add a tablespoon of finely chopped shallot, a bit of garlic and salt and pepper to taste. Dip in BATTER V (*see* BATTER FOR FRYING FISH) and when ready to serve, place in a wire basket and plunge in boiling deep frying fat. Drain; dress on a hot platter covered with a napkin; garnish with fried parsley and serve with a side dish of TARTARE SAUCE, page 52.

NOTE: Snails fried in deep boiling oil have a delicious flavor. Snails may be chopped and prepared as for corn fritters. They may be prepared in cutlet shape or croquette or in any shape according to your fancy. In patty shells, they are delicious, especially when sliced mushrooms have been added, à la Poulette, or Newburg, etc.

TURTLES AND TERRAPINS

TURTLES AND TERRAPINS

The green turtle and its numerous relatives among the edible turtles are the most highly esteemed as food, then come the terrapins, snapping turtles, and other fresh-water turtles.

The green turtle, of turtle-soup fame, which may attain a weight of 350 pounds, is a vegetable-feeding sea turtle which occasionally makes its way as far north as Long Island Sound. Its principal food is eelgrass. The eggs are found buried in the sand along the shores of the islands of the South Atlantic.

The turtles are captured while ashore at night laying the eggs, or more often are taken in nets, and sometimes they are speared when swimming and are transported alive to the northern markets.

The terrapin is a fresh-water turtle and feeds partly on vegetable food, but also devours fish and other aquatic animals. The family of terrapin is represented in the United States by about twenty popular species.

The word "terrapin" has no confined significance, but in America it is more commonly applied to the diamond back terrapin of grey color with black markings, found in salt marshes from New York to Texas, its flesh being high in favor as a table delicacy. In certain areas along the southern coast, these turtles are raised in large numbers in enclosures, or parks, for the markets.

The snapping turtle is a large fresh-water turtle noted for its fierceness, with jaws so large and strong that it is often lifted from the ground by the object bitten. This turtle sometimes exceeds three feet in length, although ordinarily about one-half that size; the shell is too small to permit it to retract the snakelike head and neck or the long tail at the same time, the carapace is covered with pyramidally thickened plates, and the plastron is reduced to a cruciform shape.

The snapping turtle feeds upon fish and all sorts of aquatic organisms. Its flesh, although delicious, is not so widely used as the green turtle or the terrapin, although some gourmets prefer it because of its distinctively agreeable flavor.

HOW TO PREPARE AND COOK TURTLE

In order to soften and dissolve the foreign matter attached to the flesh or the shell, plunge the turtle into a pan containing sufficient water to allow it to swim easily, renew the water several times, and allow the turtle to remain thus for about an hour. Then scrub thoroughly with a brush and immediately plunge into *unsalted* water boiling rapidly, until the skin of the head and feet becomes white and may be easily removed by rubbing with a dry, clean towel.

Cook the turtle in plain *unsalted* water, or it may be steamed; the time will vary according to size, although more than three-quarters of an hour should not be necessary for an ordinary-sized turtle, the cooking point being determined when the feet are soft under pressure of the fingers. Any turtle of ordinary size requiring more than three-quarters of an hour to cook is probably of inferior quality, and should be set aside, as the meat, although acquiring tenderness through the long cooking process, is liable to be stringy and of poor quality.

Once cooked to the required point, the turtle is set aside to cool, then the nails are pulled from the feet, the under shell is cut close to the upper shell and the flesh carefully removed, the feet separated from the body, cut in small pieces, and set aside. The upper shell is emptied and the gall bladder discarded (any small particle of the gall bladder remaining in the meat will impart a bitter flavor to the dish). The sand bag, heart, tail, and intestines are also discarded, as well as the white muscles of the inside.

The eggs are carefully removed and set aside with the feet and liver, and these are immediately sprinkled with salt and coarse black pepper, placed in a kettle with the turtle meat, and covered with cold salted water, a few slices of carrot and onion, a bay leaf and two whole slightly bruised cloves are added. The covered kettle is set on the range for twenty minutes, to boil rapidly, then moved into a moderately hot oven, still covered, and the cooking process continued for another twenty or twenty-five minutes.

If the turtle thus cooked is not to be used immediately it is packed into an earthenware or porcelain jar holding approximately two pounds (meat and bones), tightly covered and kept cool until wanted.

TERRAPIN BALTIMORE

1 terrapin	1½ tablespoons of butter
¾ cup of white stock	Salt and coarse black pepper to taste
1½ tablespoons sherry wine	
A few grains of Cayenne pepper	2 egg yolks
	Toast

Add the wine to the stock, then the terrapin with the bones cut in small pieces. Set on a very moderate fire and cook slowly until the liquor is reduced to half volume. Then add the liver, cut in small pieces, butter, salt, pepper, and Cayenne pepper and lastly the egg yolks, well beaten, stirring meanwhile. Do not cook any longer. Turn into a deep, hot, service platter and serve at once without any garnishing, other than a side dish of freshly made dry toast.

TERRAPIN MARYLAND

Proceed as indicated for TERRAPIN BALTIMORE, above, adding 1 tablespoon each of butter and flour kneaded, ½ cup of scalded thick cream, 2 additional egg yolks, well beaten, and a generous teaspoon of strained lemon juice. Then, just before serving, add the sherry wine; pour in deep, hot, service platter and garnish with small triangles of bread fried in butter.

TERRAPIN WASHINGTON

1 terrapin	Salt and pepper to taste and a few grains of Cayenne pepper
1½ tablespoons of butter	
1 cup of thick cream	
1½ tablespoons flour	2 eggs of the terrapin
½ cup finely chopped mushrooms	2 generous tablespoons of good sherry wine
1 hard-boiled egg chopped coarsely	2 egg yolks
	Freshly made toast

Blend the butter and flour over a moderately hot fire until smooth, add the thick cream, previously scalded, gradually, while stirring constantly, then the terrapin meat and bones cut in small pieces, liver also cut in small pieces, eggs of the terrapin, hard-boiled eggs, and mushrooms. Season to taste with salt, black pepper, and a few grains of Cayenne pepper. Let simmer very gently; do not boil. Just before serving, add the slightly beaten egg yolks, gradually, while stirring, and lastly the sherry wine. Dress on a hot, round, deep platter and garnish with crescents of puff paste golden browned in a hot oven and then dipped in melted butter.